Praise for *Fact Forward*

"Dan Gaylin's *Fact Forward* resonates deeply with USAFacts' mission of empowering Americans with the facts. It shows how we can build a society where facts aren't just available but truly empower citizens to make informed decisions. This is exactly the kind of resource we need to help citizens and leaders alike ground their choices in evidence rather than rhetoric."

—**Poppy MacDonald**
President, USAFacts

"When trust in institutions and in information itself is in decline, 'good' data is essential for social progress and individual well-being. Dan Gaylin's *Fact Forward* offers an accessible roadmap for building the 'data-savvy' skills needed for smart decisions by everyday people and the institutions and organizations that affect their lives."

—**Julia Stasch**
Immediate Past President
John D. and Catherine T.
MacArthur Foundation

"Having led research institutions and educational organizations, I've seen how data can illuminate or obscure critical social realities. Dan Gaylin's *Fact Forward* shows us how to understand and use data responsibly – not just to advance knowledge but to create better outcomes across society. This is precisely the kind of guidance we need to transform data literacy from an academic skill into an essential life skill for everyone."

—**Raynard Kington**
MD, PhD, Head of School, Philips
Academy; President Emeritus, Grinnell College

FACT
FORWARD

DAN GAYLIN

FACT FORWARD

The Perils of Bad Information and the Promise of a Data-Savvy Society

WILEY

Published by John Wiley & Sons, Inc., Hoboken, New Jersey.
Published simultaneously in Canada.

For general information on our other products and services or for technical support, please contact our Customer Care Department within the United States at (800) 762-2974, outside the United States at (317) 572-3993 or fax (317) 572-4002.

Wiley also publishes its books in a variety of electronic formats. Some content that appears in print may not be available in electronic formats. For more information about Wiley products, visit our web site at www.wiley.com.

Library of Congress Cataloging-in-Publication Data is available:

ISBN: 9781394219896 (cloth)
ISBN: 9781394219902 (ePub)
ISBN: 9781394219919 (ePDF)

Cover Design: Wiley
Cover Image: Courtesy of NORC
Author Photo: © John Zich

SKY10098288_021225

Contents

About the Cover

THE *FACT FORWARD* cover image is a data visualization that NORC created to illustrate the displacement of people due to Superstorm Sandy. It is one of several NORC explorations of how different methods of visualizing social media data could help track population movements during and after natural disasters. Each arc represents an individual Twitter account. The beginning of each arc represents the account holder's primary location two days before Superstorm Sandy, as measured by the zip codes where most of their tweets originated. The end of each arc represents the account holder's primary location two days after the storm.[1]

To see the original artwork, visit fact-forward.norc.org/coverart.

Preface

FACT FORWARD IS my first book. But really, it is not just my book. Rather, it is a broad rendering of the ethos of researchers everywhere who care about using data effectively and responsibly. To be fact forward, a person needs to develop a basic understanding of how to use data that I refer to as data savvy. The central theme of *Fact Forward* is that having data-savvy skills is no longer solely for researchers. With data now woven into the fabric of our daily activities, it is incumbent on all of us to become responsible and effective users of data. In the pages that follow I offer a road map for doing that.

This book is grounded in the fundamental values of the research institutes I have been a part of for most of my professional career and the lessons I have learned from the dedicated researchers and colleagues who mentored me. In particular, the chapters ahead describe how we think at NORC at the University of Chicago, the 84-year-old organization that I have had the honor of leading for more than a decade. NORC is an objective, nonpartisan research organization known for delivering scientifically rigorous, trustworthy data and analysis to decision-makers across society: individuals, families, communities, journalists, business leaders, people in government, policymakers, and legislators.

The decisions all of us make – at least the important ones – have the goal of producing the best outcomes possible for the people, principles, and ideas that we care about. That means we all have a common interest to ensure that we base our key decisions on the most reliable and trustworthy data available.

But how can you evaluate the data you encounter? If, for the moment, we call reliable and trustworthy data "good" data, how do we tell the difference between good data and bad data? What skills do all of us need to understand and identify these differences? What, specifically, are the obligations and responsibilities all of us have, as we produce, analyze, use, or share information? And at a deeper level, how do we determine what the *best* available data are to inform the particular decision we are trying to make? These are the central questions *Fact Forward* explores. And more than just exploring them, it offers insights along the way about how to do this, and the data-savvy knowledge and skills we need to develop as individuals and as a society to be more effective in this arena.

In an increasingly data-driven world, it is ever more imperative for all of us to become data savvy. Not so long ago, we thought of data analysts as a very specialized group of people with very particular roles. Today, one way or another, each of us is a data analyst – and a lot more. We all generate data, assess and interpret data, and share and discuss data. We do these things knowingly and (unfortunately) unknowingly as well. With the vast proliferation of digital technology, a simple mobile device becomes a mechanism for doing all these things. And in our day-to-day interactions with media, businesses, government, and one another, each of us is constantly bombarded with rapidly changing and newly emerging types of data.

What's more, with the spread of data analytics and data science, many (if not most) organizational actors are creating and pushing data to their audiences and stakeholders as a core part of what they do. Sometimes these data are reliable and trustworthy. Sometimes they are not. And sometimes they are designed to actively manipulate or mislead their audiences. It's fair to say that the concept of *caveat emptor* (Latin for let the buyer beware), originally applied to the marketplace of goods and services, now is equally relevant to the world of data, but with an added level of responsibility: We need to be aware of the risks both as consumers of data and as producers of data.

This is the key rationale for why we must all, as individuals and as a society, develop data-savvy skills. A world filled with data is now an essential aspect of our existence. Piles of data are all around us. They're growing and evolving. They're there for the taking and the giving. They're there for all of us to use, and for all of us to misuse. We must all become fact forward – for our own sake and for the greater good.

1

The Importance of Being Data Savvy

ONE OF THE central causes of the Global Financial Crisis of 2008 and the Great Recession that followed was bad data. The available information on key financial instruments at the heart of the crisis was faulty. Even so, investors – from individual homeowners to our most storied financial institutions – bet billions of dollars on that information. The root cause of one of the worst economic meltdowns in history was a combination of poor-quality information, lack of transparency on its origins and limitations, and wishful thinking (and in some cases outright fraud) on the part of the people and organizations generating and analyzing and sharing the data.

The result was bankruptcies, crashing markets, thousands of jobs lost, hundreds of billions of dollars in government bailouts, a disaster that took years to recover from, and lasting damage to the public's trust in financial and governmental institutions.[1]

This book is the story of the central role of data in the way citizens, consumers, companies, institutions, and governments perceive and act in the world – and how we can all improve our skills and interactions within that data ecosystem. Limitations in our ability to use data effectively, together with inaccurate data or data of poor quality, lead to widespread misunderstanding, uncertainty, and deception: problems in which we all play a part that undermine the common workings of the society.

Why This Matters

We'll get back to the details of the data failures that created the Global Financial Crisis shortly. But first, let me explain why I care about this and why you should, too.

I have the privilege of serving as president and chief executive officer of NORC, one of the largest independent research organizations in the world. NORC is an objective, nonpartisan, global research institute that conducts hundreds of millions of dollars in research every year for governments, nonprofits, and businesses in the United States and many other nations. My background includes 35 years of conducting research using a wide range of data at some of the world's leading research institutes, and in private consulting, and also serving as a senior health policy advisor at the US Department of Health and Human Services.

I am committed not just to promoting and supporting honest, unbiased, and transparent research but also to helping everyone understand how data are generated[2] and how to use and interpret data to inform their most important decisions.

Today, many forces combine to create a vast sea of information of varying quality, leading to uncertainty across all aspects of society. These forces include the creation of flawed or biased data, a lack of transparency about data sources, and the distortion of data to manipulate and mislead people. This book provides a framework for understanding all forms of data and their limitations, and what I hope will become common expectations about appropriate use of data. The idea is to live in a fact-forward world in which we consistently advance facts as the basis for making critical decisions. While this may sound elusive, I believe that the promise of a fact-forward world is before us. To get there, all of us as individuals and as a society must prioritize the development of better data skills, in how we create, access, use, and share data. The broad development of these skills across these multiple dimensions is what I refer to throughout the book as becoming "data savvy."

While it has been more than 15 years since the Global Financial Crisis, the data challenges it reveals are just as relevant today as they were in the 2000s. Moreover, we are now sufficiently far removed from these events to be able to look back at them and assess what went wrong and why. Four data problems led directly to this crisis: failures of data integrity, failures of data transparency, failures of data neutrality, and failures of data literacy. These problems remain highly relevant today, which means that we continue to be very much at risk for additional global disasters based on information failure.

The Role of Bad Data in the 2008 Global Financial Crisis

It was easy to get a mortgage in the 2000s.[3] Consumers with limited incomes, poor credit, or inadequate down payments could still qualify for low-documentation or no-documentation mortgages. Mortgage brokers who made money on loan volume assured borrowers that they had the economic means to take on excessive mortgage debt. And mortgage bankers, incentivized to originate loans, were willing to lend money to underqualified borrowers. Many of these loans were adjustable-rate mortgages with "teaser" interest rates that stayed low for the first two years but increased rapidly thereafter.

According to a paper by the economist Thomas Herndon, 70% of the eventual losses in the mortgage markets were caused by defaults on these low-documentation and no-documentation loans.[4] But on their own, these loan defaults would never have brought down global financial markets.

At the center of the crisis was a stack of financial instruments known as CDOs and CDSs. *Collateralized debt obligations* (CDOs) were bonds based on hundreds or thousands of mortgages, while *credit default swaps* (CDSs) were insurance on the value of those bonds.

The task of accurately measuring the risk in these instruments fell to the independent bond-rating agencies: Standard & Poor's (S&P), Moody's, and Fitch. An agency like S&P might rate a CDO bond backed by the highest-quality homeowners and mortgages AA, indicating an investment grade bond with a very low risk of default, while a bond backed by lower-quality mortgages might be graded BBB – still investment grade, but with a higher risk of default. The ratings agencies also assigned the highest possible ratings to most of the CDSs, indicating perhaps a 1-in-1,000 risk that their buyers would ever need to pay off the insurance.

The allure of low-risk, high-reward investments is enormous. The investment-grade ratings on CDOs and CDSs encouraged financial institutions throughout Wall Street to buy billions of dollars of them.

As long as home values continued to increase, homeowners were able either to refinance with a new mortgage or to sell their highly mortgaged houses at a profit before their teaser rates expired. Financial firms profited from the bonds and derivatives based on those homes. This in turn further fueled home values and attracted still more questionable borrowers into low-documentation loans to cash in on appreciating prices.

That, of course, is what a bubble looks like. And in 2008 – slowly, and then catastrophically – everything collapsed.

Home buyers began to default on their loans – especially as those two-year low-interest lockup periods began to expire, and their payments ballooned. The CDOs based on those mortgages became worthless. This triggered billions of dollars in insurance payments for the owners of the CDSs. The largest blue-chip investment firms on Wall Street – including AIG, Lehman Brothers, Bear Stearns, and Merrill Lynch – found themselves with massive, completely unanticipated losses. The resulting implosion in financial markets froze monetary liquidity and led to the Great Recession. Despite a $700 billion government bailout for Wall Street, the recession put almost 9 million Americans out of work.

The global financial crisis was caused by the triple whammy of the risky loans, which were then bundled into CDOs and CDSs, and were then rated as low risk by the ratings agencies. Despite the excellent ratings for these investments, they were all built on adjustable-rate mortgages doomed to eventually tumble, creating a highly correlated set of risks that blindsided all the major financial institutions at once. Each step was riddled with limited or bad data. This was the central cause of the crisis.

The Financial Disaster Reveals the Four Types of Data Failure

Now let's ask a crucially important question: *Why* were the ratings agencies creating the faulty ratings that led to the global financial crisis, even though these agencies' key purpose is to accurately assess risk?

The answer to that question illuminates the four main types of data failure that threaten every part of our global society that depends on data and, as I'll show, that includes virtually everything that government, business, and consumers do. Consider the four failures that led to the overoptimistic bond ratings that brought on the crisis:

- **A failure of data integrity.**[5] Data integrity means that data are based on solid information interpreted in statistically valid ways. But the ratings agencies were not actually assessing risks of default; they were instead looking at broad general characteristics of loan pools, such as the median credit scores of borrowers. Unfortunately, such measures could conceal vast numbers of risky mortgages. As one former Goldman Sachs bond trader explained to the author Michael Lewis, "The ratings agencies didn't really have their own CDO model."[6]
- **A failure of data transparency.** Anyone using data to make decisions must be able to understand where the data came from and how they were analyzed. But for the ratings agencies to maintain their proprietary advantage and keep the creators of securities from gaming their ratings, they needed to keep their methods secret. As a result, there was no way for financial institutions to question or verify a given security's AA rating. The mortgage brokers originated lots of loans with very little transparency as well.
- **A failure of data neutrality.** Data neutrality demands analysis based only on the actual data, not the prejudices of those analyzing it. But regrettably, people collecting and analyzing data may, consciously or unconsciously, seek data and analyses that confirm their beliefs or prior knowledge. Then everyone working with data is subject to confirmation bias: that is, finding what they *hope* to be true. The ratings agencies were predisposed to

see the CDOs and CDSs as good financial instruments. The conventional wisdom was that, on average, housing prices would continue to rise. Given competition among the agencies and the huge market power of the large Wall Street investment banks, the ratings agencies were essentially expected by the banks to produce desirable ratings. Given the complexity of the CDOs and CDSs, it was difficult for a ratings agency to model the risks effectively. And the Wall Street banks invested significant effort to shape the data to meet those expectations, skewing the resulting ratings to the bond traders' advantage and thus hiding risk from investors.

- **A failure of data literacy.** None of these data failures would matter if the ultimate consumers of the data were aware of and accounted for the flaws. But failures of interpretation pervaded the financial crisis. The homeowners ignored the risks that their adjustable rates might rise and that they couldn't refinance if home prices fell. The large financial institutions took the investment-grade ratings on CDOs and CDSs as gospel, failing to spot the huge, nationwide risk from a bursting home price bubble. These investors failed to notice that they were cross-insuring each other's investments, which added systemic risk to these instruments. Data literacy demands a skeptical attitude toward data and the skills and willingness to assess the uncertainty of the data on which you are basing your most important decisions. Borrowers and investors failed both of these tests.

What Does It Mean to Be Data Savvy and Why Is It Important?

Whether people realize it or not, data underlie every decision they make: in companies, in government, and as consumers.

Your doctor uses data to determine which treatments to recommend. Your boss uses data to determine where you stand among other employees and whether you deserve a raise. Your town uses data to determine how much to tax your house and how much to invest in schools for your kids. Data are at the center of government decisions about how to set interest rates, how to invest tax revenues, how to investigate crime, how to price unemployment insurance, and where to build new roads and highways. Political campaigns intensively assess data to determine what positions to take, what speeches to give, what actions to publicize, and what messages to send. Companies use data to determine what products to build, what features to add, where to invest resources, how much to pay staff, what products are popular, how consumer tastes are shifting, what marketing campaigns are working, and how aggressively and where to compete. Data are quite simply the backdrop and driver for every decision, everywhere.

Ideally, we would all adopt a fact-forward attitude about data. That is, we'd attempt to make sure the data on which we based decisions are of the highest possible quality and relevance. But to become fact forward, every smart decision-maker – that is, all of us – must be data savvy.

But what does it mean to be data savvy?

A data-savvy decision-maker asks questions about the context of data before acting on it. With what level of integrity were the data created? How transparently were they assembled, analyzed, and shared? Were the creators, consumers, and disseminators of the data acting in a neutral and bias-free way? Have we applied data literacy in our interpretation of the data?

To be data savvy is to understand that all data are created in context, and to interpret, consume, and share data with that context in mind. This applies whether you are a data creator, a data disseminator, or a data consumer. In each of these roles, we each have essential responsibilities to ensure that data are used to inform and not to mislead.

Because data underlie so many important personal, corporate, and governmental decisions, it's essential for all decision-makers to be as data savvy as possible. Unless we can recognize data challenges – and unless we as a society can create an environment that maximizes data quality and data literacy – we are going to make questionable decisions based on poorly informed ideas about the world. That's harmful and potentially catastrophic.

Why does that matter? Let's look at a few additional examples of how data failures have led people astray.

Google Flu Trends Made Remarkable Predictions, Until It Didn't

Are more data necessarily better for making predictions? Consider the case of Google Flu Trends.

In 2008, Google researchers attempted to take advantage of data derived from human behavior. Prior to these efforts, the best way to measure the spread of flu variants was based on data from the US Centers for Disease Control and Prevention (CDC), compiled regionally using reporting from doctors who tested patients reporting flu symptoms. But the Google researchers recognized that the first thing people do when they think they may have the flu is not to go to the doctor, but to do a web search on flu symptoms. Track those searches, they reasoned, and you'll be able to model flu outbreaks well ahead of the CDC reporting.

Sure enough, the Google Flu Trends tracker was able to identify flu outbreaks several days *before* the CDC reporting. The tracker was also able to make predictions that were eerily close to where and when influenza ended up spreading.[7]

But as any sports gambling operator will tell you, making a few accurate predictions doesn't mean you've beaten the system.

The Google Flu Trends algorithm needed adjustments in 2009, as it significantly underestimated influenza infections, possibly because the model was poorly matched to the virulence of the newly emerged H1N1 (swine flu) strain. But more problematic was the model's massive over-prediction – by more than 100% – of the peak of the flu season in 2013 (see Figure 1-1).

Another challenge was created by improvements in Google's search tool, which now suggested related terms for browser users to search. While this improved Google's generic search function, it distorted the Google Flu Trends model, which was based on manual, unprompted searches. And, at least originally, according to the researchers, "Google's efforts . . . were remarkably opaque in terms of methods and data—making it dangerous to rely on Google Flu Trends for any decision making."[8]

Google Flu Trends is no longer available, perhaps due to the compounding of these errors. The model it created had data integrity problems due to changes in search features. While it was running, it lacked the transparency that would allow researchers to analyze flaws

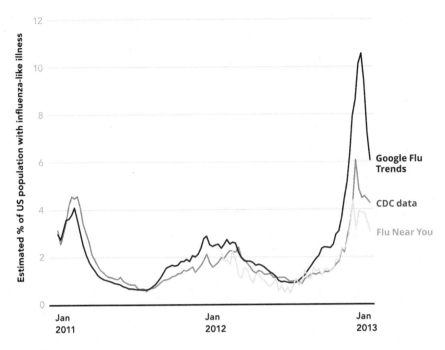

Figure 1-1: The Google Flu model's initial success in predicting actual flu cases was overshadowed by its substantial overprediction in 2013.

Source: Adapted from original graphic in "When Google got flu wrong" by Declan Butler, February 13, 2013, in the journal *Nature*. Original data sources: Google Flu Trends; CDC; Flu Near You. Adapted by permission.

in its methods.[9] The excitement around the successful early predictions may have undermined its researchers' neutrality. And perhaps more data literacy on the part of consumers and journalists would have put a check on the unbridled enthusiasm surrounding the Google flu model described in news stories in CNN, the *New York Times*,[10] the *Wall Street Journal*, and other sources.

Donald Trump's Victory in the 2016 US Presidential Election Flummoxed Pollsters and Pundits

Leading up to the 2016 presidential election, the polls were clear. Hillary Rodham Clinton was likely to coast to an easy victory. Donald Trump, who'd never held a political office before, had very little chance to win.

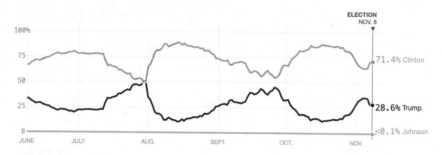

Figure 1-2: Candidates' estimated chances of winning in the 2016 US presidential election changed rapidly at several key points in time, including very close to election day.

Source: FiveThirtyEight. Used by permission.

As with Google Flu Trends, the challenge here was certainly not a lack of data. Polling organizations conducted many hundreds of polls in the months leading up to the election, both in the nation at large and in battleground states like Pennsylvania, Michigan, and Wisconsin. On the eve of the election, a RealClearPolitics average of 10 solid national polls projected a popular vote lead of about 3% for Clinton over Trump, a prediction that turned out to be within a single percentage point of the final result.[11]

Based on these polls, election watchers built models that combined national and state polls, weighted them based on poll quality and recency, and projected a percentage likelihood of who would win the election. The *New York Times* gave Clinton an 85% chance of winning.[12] The model at FiveThirtyEight, which had given Clinton an 87% chance of winning on October 19, shifted toward Trump as the election drew near and new polls came in. On election eve, it was predicting Clinton's chances of victory at 71% (see Figure 1-2).[13]

Clinton's widely expected victory, of course, never happened. Were the data at fault?

Several factors influenced the challenges with the predictions. There were polling errors in key battleground states including Pennsylvania, Wisconsin, and Michigan, all of which the polls predicted would narrowly vote for Clinton. But it's important to understand the meaning of the term "error" here. Pre-election polls, since they reach only a small subset of voters, will inevitably generate different results from what actually happens at the ballot box. The difference between the poll results and the election results is called "polling error."

What happened in 2016 that upended the prediction was *systematic* polling error – that is, a set of errors that were all skewed in the same direction. One cause is that low-education voters were under-represented in many of the state-level polling samples, although they made up a significant share of Trump voters, especially in the three key post-industrial Midwest states. The pollsters did not weight their results to correct for this deficiency. This oversight was largely the result of reusing the status quo approach, even in the face of an election that was proving to be quite different.

In recent elections prior to 2016, many pollsters didn't include education in their weighting, and they still generated accurate results. In those elections, voters with the lowest levels of formal education and voters with the highest levels of formal education both tended to vote for the Democratic candidate, especially in the Rust Belt states. When those pre-2016 polls over-represented high-education voters and under-represented low-education voters, it didn't impact the vote choice results because both groups were supporting the Democratic candidate at similar levels. Perhaps leaning too heavily on an approach that had always worked in the past, many pollsters didn't realize the importance of incorporating education into their survey weighting to correct for these changing voting patterns. Even though the broad national polls were accurate, because of the way US presidential elections work, wrong predictions in three close states led to incorrect predictions for the winner of the race.

Polls can capture only a snapshot at the time the data are being collected. Few polls were fielded in the final days of the election and were therefore unable to capture the effect of events that happen too close to Election Day. Later estimates from a committee of pollsters suggest that 13% of voters in key swing states didn't make up their minds until the final week before the election, and these voters overwhelmingly supported Trump at the ballot box.[14] One late-breaking event was the release of a statement by FBI chief James Comey on the eve of the election regarding the investigation into Clinton's mishandling of emails. By the time Comey released the statement, all pre-election polling had already been completed.

I believe a failure of data neutrality may have had something to do with the predictions as well. Most experienced politics-watchers were used to predicting elections with politicians who behaved in predictable ways, like John McCain, Mitt Romney, and Barack Obama. The back and forth between conventional Democrats and Republicans was their favored turf; predicting the impact of a completely unconventional politician like Donald Trump was outside of their experience. This may have led to mainstream media coverage that predicted a continuation of politics as usual, which is likely what would have happened had Hillary Clinton won the election.

A final challenge here has to do with data literacy, that is, with how people interpreted the predictions of election-tracking pundits. In the mind of the average reader, an 85% chance of a candidate winning immediately registers as, "He or she will win." We make decisions like this in our lives all the time. If the weather forecaster predicts a 15% chance of rain, you probably leave the raincoat at home. On the other hand, if you were about to step into an intersection to cross the street and knew you had a 15% chance of getting hit by a car, you'd probably stay on the curb. Homeowners buy home insurance, not because they think there's a good chance their house will burn down, but because in the unlikely event that it does, they don't want to be completely ruined. Everyone knows a 15% chance is not zero, but they behave in many cases as if it is.

The Artificial Intelligence Tool ChatGPT Swallows Huge Amounts of Data – And Hallucinates

In the 2020s we started to become aware, as a society, of one of the most far-reaching, and potentially disruptive, technologies created by masses of data: artificial intelligence (AI). ChatGPT, the generative AI chatbot tool created by OpenAI, is trained on, basically, the entire readable portion of the World Wide Web, tens of trillions of gigabytes of content. If quantity of data predicted quality of output, you would expect ChatGPT to be nearly perfect, since it "knows" nearly everything readable online.

ChatGPT is indeed a powerful tool. It's excellent at summarizing the contents of a document. It's good at producing first drafts of text based on online research. Because it communicates in plain English, it's easy to use. And it's particularly good at generative tasks, as its name suggests, using the vast amount of information it has assimilated to produce new content. So, for example, ChatGPT can virtually instantaneously write a convincing speech that a politician might deliver extolling the virtues of green technology (or, alternatively, fossil fuels). It can even write that speech in the style of an ancient Roman orator or as a country music ballad! And unlike ordinary web searches on sites like Google, you can have a conversation with it, adjusting your prompts to explain the shortcomings of what it came up with and how to generate better output on the second or third try. In this sense, it feels more like working with a research assistant than interacting with a computer.

This very quality, though, contributes to one of the main problems with generative AI tools: The text they produce is so convincing that it *seems* accurate, even when it's not.

ChatGPT routinely gets facts wrong, a phenomenon often described as "hallucinations." For example, when Jon Christian, editor of *Futurism*, asked ChatGPT to write a short biography for him, this is what it generated[15]:

> Jon Christian is a journalist who covers technology and science. He has written for a number of publications, including The Outline, Motherboard, and Wired, among others. His work often focuses on topics such as artificial intelligence, robotics, and the impact of technology on society.
>
> Christian has been recognized for his writing, receiving awards such as the National Magazine Award and the Society of Professional Journalists' Sigma Delta Chi award. He has also been a finalist for the Livingston Award for Young Journalists.
>
> In addition to his work as a journalist, Christian has also taught courses on science writing at Columbia University's Graduate School of Journalism.

Most of that, though, is wrong. Christian has not won any of those awards, and he doesn't teach at Columbia.

This is not an isolated case. In Georgia, a radio host named Mark Walters sued OpenAI for spreading false information about him, because its output implied that, as chief financial officer (CFO) and treasurer of an organization called the Second Amendment Foundation (SAF), he "misappropriated funds for personal expenses without authorization or reimbursement, manipulated financial records and bank statements to conceal his activities, and failed to provide accurate and timely financial reports and disclosures to the SAF's leadership."[16] In fact, Walters was never accused of any of these misdeeds and never even held the CFO or treasurer positions as Chat-GPT claims.

If you spend some time interacting with ChatGPT or similar AI chatbots on a subject on which you are knowledgeable (which I encourage you to do), you will readily get to a point where the AI is providing incorrect answers, even though it appears certain that what it is telling you is accurate.

Why is ChatGPT getting so much wrong?

ChatGPT is based on a deep learning neural network model that ingests large amounts of data and then uses patterns from that data to generate plausible text. It's very good at generating coherent collections of sentences, because it has been trained on trillions of gigabytes of such text. But it has no actual intelligence. Sometimes patterns lead it to generate things that aren't true. Apparently, people like Jon Christian tend to teach at journalism schools. Apparently, if you mindlessly consume the text of enough lawsuits, you spit out text about people embezzling who were never even accused of any wrongdoing.

The challenge of the hallucinations goes further. Unless a person using these systems notices the problem, they may depend on the spurious data. Such data can then get published online and further exacerbate the spread of false information.

Generative AI systems like ChatGPT, at least in the state in which they exist as I write this, are practically the poster boy for data failures. They are built on masses of data without any discrimination about the relative accuracy of the different data sources.[17] Because neural networks, unlike traditional computer code, operate on a *gestalt* of all of the information they ingest, there's no transparency to how the AI reaches any given conclusion – it's not very easy to interrogate the model about the sources of its conclusions, or the uncertainty that surrounds them (although developers are trying to improve this). As Alex Reisner wrote in the *Atlantic*, "Few people outside of companies such as Meta and OpenAI know the full extent of the texts these programs have been trained on."[18]

AI also inherently suffers from a neutrality problem, because it automatically inherits all the prejudices of the data it's trained on. And the very plausibility of ChatGPT's highly articulate and readable output undermines data literacy: Looking at a piece of AI-generated text, there's no way to know whether it's accurate or completely invented. And of course, there are always errors due to the limits of the information that the model has been trained on – we have no way of knowing what might be left out.

Because AI will have such an important role in data analysis and our understanding of truth and facts in the future, I've dedicated a whole chapter, Chapter 10, to it.

Understanding Roles in Data Proliferation

I've stated that data underlie most decisions people make. But where do the data come from, how do they spread, and how do they get to the people who need to make the decisions?

Any understanding of data and its value and failures must acknowledge the ecosystem through which masses of data flow. Just as products in the real-world economy are built through supply chains – raw materials to component parts to finished products to retail outlets – the data ecosystem has its own supply chain. There are three main roles in the ecosystem:

- **Data producer.** Many organizations gather raw data. For example, Google collected data for Google Flu Trends, and polling organizations collected data from samples of voters about the 2016 election. In fact, we are all producing data every day with every purchase we make, the clicks we register with our online behavior, and information gathered and uploaded from our mobile devices. But raw data alone aren't particularly useful.

Someone has to analyze the data to turn them into a form that's helpful in making decisions. The general term for individuals who use technical skills and business knowledge to analyze and derive insights from data is "data scientist." This includes, for example, data analysts in companies who gather up data from sales and marketing and use the data to suggest ways to improve products or their positioning. In government, a slew of statisticians, data scientists, and subject-matter experts analyze raw data about, say, unemployment or prices, and generate analysis of labor trends and inflation.

- **Data disseminator.** For data to have influence, someone has to make others aware of the analysis. News media fulfill this function – for example, when the *Wall Street Journal* publishes data from a poll, or a popular publication makes readers aware of the results of a medical study. Decades ago, data disseminators were generally in some position of authority in media or data analysis firms. But these days, everyone on social media has the potential to spread information to others, outside of normal media channels. If you see an article about voter attitudes about gun regulation or nuclear energy and then share it with others on Facebook or Instagram, you're a data disseminator. Given the potential that numbers, charts, and videos have to "go viral," data sharing is now an essential part of the data ecosystem.

- **Data consumer.** This description fits anyone who uses data – in other words, all of us. If you're checking reviews of car models at *Consumer Reports*, you're a data consumer. You're also a data consumer if you review the latest trends and articles on virus variants to decide whether to get an updated vaccination. Or you might review inflation data to help decide which politicians to vote for. There are, of course, data consumers throughout all decision-making organizations. A CEO who decides whether to green-light a new product and how to price it is a data consumer, as is a Federal Reserve Bank official reviewing economic data to decide whether to raise or lower interest rates.

The supply chains for real-word products are relatively nice and neat, moving in one direction from producer to consumer. But that's not how the data ecosystem works. In the world of data any of us can, at any moment, play any role: We all produce data, we all analyze data, and we all tend to disseminate data, as well. The average person may not be doing this with the formality and sophistication of a data professional, and that is a big part of the problem.

Looking back at the four data challenges I described, you can now see that all these roles may run afoul of any of the data challenges. For example, a data producer who uses samples that are too small can run afoul of data integrity problems, and if those samples are biased in directions that support their preconceived ideas, they can suffer data neutrality issues. A news organization that only publishes news supporting what its readers or advertisers want to hear and cherry-picks studies to support its viewpoint is a data disseminator with a neutrality problem. As data spread throughout the ecosystem, people often share them without access to the underlying methodology, creating data transparency issues. And of course, all of us who read and share data, perhaps without fully understanding where they come from, are at risk of errors based on limits of our data literacy.

I'll describe more about data problems throughout the ecosystem in Chapter 2.

The Spread of Faulty Data Is Destructive to Society

I've described how central data are to all decision-making. Our collective decisions about everything from products to buy to how to vote to whom to marry are essential to the society we live in. For this reason, issues with data quality and data proliferation are powerful influences.

Perhaps the best way to visualize this is to think about the body politic as an actual body, like the ones that each of us has. Just as our bodies run on the food we eat, our society runs on the data it consumes.

Consider what happens to your body if there are problems with the food you eat.

Food products that are raised or manufactured without sufficient attention to quality are unhealthy and may even be dangerous. Just as tainted food can make us sick, data created with poor data integrity can cause society to make poor decisions.

Food that's produced without transparency is also subject to issues. Food labels can tell you whether a product contains dairy or nuts and which order at a fast-food restaurant has the greatest number of calories. Without transparency, you can't make good decisions about what foods to eat. And without data transparency, people can't effectively evaluate the quality of the data on which they base their decisions.

Food is subject to biases and neutrality issues, just like data. Many of us were pleased to learn that a daily glass of red wine was part of a healthy Mediterranean diet – a result that matched up to wine lovers' prejudices.[19] (More recent research has revealed that it may be healthier to avoid consuming any alcohol at all.[20])

And, of course, none of us can make wise food choices without developing a more sophisticated knowledge of nutrition. Food literacy, like data literacy, is essential to making good decisions.

Food decisions are made more complicated by the complex ecosystem that brings our food to us, including farms, food manufacturers, grocery retailers, and restaurants. At every stage of the supply chain, problems with integrity, transparency, neutrality, and literacy can undermine our ability to feed our families in the healthiest way possible.

These factors may seem obvious, since all of us eat food. But we don't usually think of data proliferation and consumption in the way we do food consumption, since we just take the data surrounding us for granted. If you've ever read a food label carefully or decided that the fast-food french fries weren't worth it, you took at least some interest in the food choices you made. Now it's time for each of us to develop at least as sophisticated an approach to the data diet we all consume.

The Solution to Data Failures

In the rest of this book, I'll address not just the problems with data proliferation but the solutions we can embrace as a society, as data producers, as media members, and as data consumers. It is my goal to educate all members of the data ecosystem on ways that we can improve our data diet and society's understanding and use of the data we are all surrounded with.

Here's what's in store.

In Chapter 2, we'll explore the data ecosystem in greater depth and how we can each participate to improve our collective efforts toward better data quality and understanding.

Chapter 3 is an overview of the breadth of the data universe – all the types of sources of data, as well as the basic methods analysts use to draw conclusions from it. The aim is to ground everyone in the data basics from a layperson's perspective.

Chapters 4–7 explore the four imperatives for improving societal data quality, imperatives that match up to the four data failures I've described in this chapter.

Chapter 4 explains all the dimensions of data integrity. This includes making sure data are representative of the populations they purport to describe, designing research and questions that are fit for purpose, identifying and limiting data bias, and ensuring sufficient size samples to draw useful conclusions.

Chapter 5 explores all elements of data and algorithmic transparency: ensuring that for any data set or analysis, there is clear documentation of data sources and analysis methods.

Chapter 6 dives into the thorny problem of data neutrality. We already suffer from data designs that include intentionally biased samples and methods. But a more insidious issue is how to guard against inadvertent bias from honest researchers wrestling with many unsuspected forms of confirmation bias.

Chapter 7 is crucial for all data consumers, since it explains all aspects of data literacy. I recommend processes for educating the public, both in schools and in broader society, about the limitations of data they will encounter. I include the key questions all data consumers must ask when confronted with data on which decisions will be made.

Chapter 8 describes how standards have contributed to the spread of useful data and explores how data privacy regulations are essential to the fair use of data without harming the people it pertains to.

Chapter 9 reveals an overarching plan to advance a data-savvy society: a public data infrastructure program. A standardized data infrastructure could significantly improve the quality of the data we create, the ways we analyze it, and, most important, the way we access it. Using my organization's experience with the creation of a social science data explorer product, I explain how we as a nation could invest in tools and standards that would promulgate better and more advanced data practices for operators throughout the ecosystem.

Chapter 10 examines one of the fastest-growing and most promising, if problematic, trend in data analysis: artificial intelligence. AI has the promise to rapidly improve the speed and power of data analysis and to generate new insights inaccessible in any other way. It also has an unparalleled potential to generate false, misleading, and distorted conclusions. I'll show how, despite the current risks, developments in AI may actually generate tools to advance a fact-forward world.

Finally, in the last chapter, I'll describe what a fact-forward future with improved data quality might mean for improvements in how we as a society make decisions and understand each other. This is a world I am passionately dedicated to helping create. My hope is that after reading this book, you will be, too.

2

Understanding the Data Ecosystem

YOU MAY HAVE gotten the impression from the previous chapter that data failures are endemic and data cannot be trusted. But if you examine how data travel from their point of origin to your brain, you see that the truth is far more complex – and more interesting. All data and statistics flow through a three-part ecosystem encompassing data producers, data disseminators, and data consumers. When the ecosystem functions well, it becomes a fact-forward force that surfaces new insights, provides appropriate context for statistics, and allows both consumers and people in power to make better decisions.

There may be no better illustration of the power of data spreading through the ecosystem than the way that statistics transformed the public's understanding of the health dangers of smoking, eventually leading to significant shifts in public policy and major changes in our collective behavior.

Lung cancer was once extremely rare; as of 1900, only 140 cases had ever been described in medical literature.[1] But as both smoking and lung cancer became more common in the 1930s and 1940s, some medical researchers began to suspect that there was a connection. Most notably, in 1954, lung cancer researchers Richard Doll and A. Bradford

Hill conducted an extensive study of lung cancer patients, concluding that heavy smokers were 40 times as likely to die of lung cancer.

Some of the most dramatic cancer studies attracted the attention of media. *LIFE* magazine published a multipage spread about the scientists Evarts Graham and Adele Croninger, who were able to generate tumors by painting cigarette tars onto the shaved backs of mice. Graham, quoted in *TIME*, stated that their experiment, "shows conclusively that there is something in cigarette smoke which can produce cancer.... Our experiments have proved it beyond any doubt."[2]

Despite the pains that the cancer researchers had taken to avoid bias, account for confounding variables, and assemble unassailable amounts of data, the tobacco industry challenged the results with its own scientists and studies.

In 1953, the CEOs of the six largest tobacco manufacturers devised a plan to create white papers, ads, and press releases to refute the cancer evidence, conducting public relations outreach to science writers and journalists. As *TIME* later reported, "The tobacco industry's main medical spokesman, Dr. Clarence Cook Little, is an 80-year-old retired biologist who headed the predecessor of the American Cancer Society in the 1930s. As chief of the industry's Council for Tobacco Research since 1954, he has steadfastly maintained that evidence linking smoking and disease consists largely of statistical associations, which cannot 'prove' a causal relationship."[3]

The published research supported by the tobacco industry was anything but fact forward, with an agenda based not on open scientific inquiry but on the goals of a public relations campaign on behalf of the cigarette industry.[4] It was an unprecedented effort to weaponize science for commercial gain, but despite the tobacco industry's failure to actually study links between smoking and human disease, it effectively muddied the water both for journalists and for a public that included many smokers.

A turning point occurred in 1964 with US Surgeon General Luther Terry's publication of a report titled *Smoking and Health: Report of the Advisory Committee to the Surgeon General of the Public Health Service*. Researchers commissioned by Terry reviewed 7,000 scientific articles, concluding that smoking led to a 70% increase in the mortality rate as compared with the baseline for non-smokers.[5]

The surgeon general's report turned suspicions about cancer into settled fact. It catalyzed responses from Congress and many state and local lawmakers. Congress banned TV and radio cigarette ads in 1971. In 1984, lawmakers required all cigarette packages to include the surgeon general's warning. By 1997, a settlement with the tobacco industry ended outdoor billboards in 46 states and prohibited cartoon characters like Joe Camel that appealed to young people. President Clinton banned smoking in federal government buildings in 1997, and now 27 states have required smoking bans in many workplaces as well as restaurants and bars.

Smoking is one of the few phenomena in which it is possible to demonstrate a correlation between media coverage and public attitudes. A 2001 study by researchers John P. Pierce and Elizabeth A. Gilpin tracked trends in articles from major magazines and attitudes about smoking and health from 1950 to the early 1980s. The study revealed patterns in people quitting smoking as news coverage swelled, including a spike to more than 70 articles in 1964 around the publication of the surgeon general's report. The steady drumbeat of coverage changed public opinion; by the early 1980s, more than 90% of people believed that smoking caused cancer.[6] It also likely helped boost the market share of low-tar cigarette brands from 9% in 1974 to 45% in 1980. More recently, anti-smoking ad campaigns have further changed behavior. A 2009 study found that smokers were exposed to an average of more than 200 anti-smoking ads over a two-year period and that the greater number of such ads they were exposed to, the more likely they were to have quit smoking at the end of the study.[7]

An Evolving Data Ecosystem Shapes Our Understanding of Statistics

The shift in attitudes and behaviors around smoking demonstrates the fundamental role of the data ecosystem in decision-making. Insights from data become accepted truths, which then spur action. The data that medical researchers collected in the middle of the twentieth century led quite directly to media coverage, government action, and, eventually, changes in behavior as tobacco users quit smoking and young people became far less likely to start.

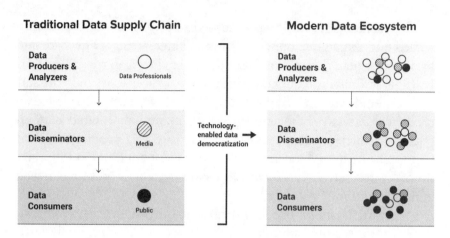

Figure 2-1: Data democratization expands roles in the ecosystem.
Source: NORC.

The data ecosystem used to follow a relatively straightforward chain of influence. Experts, including scientists and researchers in government, academia, research companies, and corporations, identified and created needed data and analyzed them according to an accepted set of statistical techniques to generate insights. News organizations functioned as data disseminators, with journalists and newscasters reporting results and explaining their significance. Both ordinary consumers and decision-makers in government and business generally trusted and consumed the data shared by the news media and, as the word got around, changed their behavior.

Originally, the key actors stuck to their traditional roles. Although this led to some good outcomes, such as trust in science, and (in some cases) changes in human behavior, it also had its limits. Because the creation, analysis, and dissemination of data was the domain of experts, the consumer generally had to take on faith what the experts said was correct. Furthermore, the consumer was only exposed to results that the media chose to broadcast. The results were further limited by what researchers chose to research, which depended on what government grants or other funding they could obtain. Because of the limited diversity of both the research sources and the media outlets, some bias was inevitable.

The advent of digital technology has completely upended this traditional (and often rigid) data supply chain (see Figure 2-1). In a lot of respects, this shake-up is a good thing. It creates a situation where just about anyone, at any time – and sometimes simultaneously – can play the role of data creator, analyzer, disseminator, and consumer. This fundamental shift, "data democratization," reflects how digital, Internet, and mobile technologies put the power of data creation, analysis, and sharing in the hands of anybody with a computer or smartphone.[8] Data democratization is reshaping the social construct of expertise, knowledge, and accepted truth. Let's consider each of the roles in the data ecosystem in the context of data democratization.

Start with data producers and analyzers. Prior to data democratization, the process of collecting data was almost entirely the domain of scientific experts. Collecting data or identifying existing sources of data was beyond the knowledge, technical capabilities, and resource constraints of the general public. Today, with digital tools, just about anyone can collect data. A teenager with a smartphone and a TikTok following can conduct a poll of their followers and summarize the results. Anybody, with statistical training or without, can field a survey with inexpensive tools like SurveyMonkey or Qualtrics and analyze the results with free tools like Google Sheets.[9] And corporations with access to masses of digital data – say, a trillion Google searches, or everyone who clicked on and bought things at an online store like Wayfair – are constantly gathering data in real time as a byproduct of e-commerce.

There is both an upside and a downside to this extraordinary expansion of data producers. On the one hand, many more types of organizations and people are producing a lot more data, and the interests of a lot more people are potentially being served by these data. Furthermore, with more actors producing data, there is an accompanying increase in societal appreciation of data and their usefulness. And the data analyses produced by this broader group of actors have the potential to inform society on a much wider range of topics and with a more diverse range of perspectives. On the other hand, the proliferation of data and data producers introduces a great deal of uncertainty about the quality, validity, and reliability of the data, the rigor of the analyses, and whether they are a suitable basis for making important decisions.

Just as with data producers, the number of data disseminators has exploded, thanks to information technology and social media. Organizations that consider themselves news media have multiplied: Harvard researcher Heidi Legg counted 3,000 sites that call themselves newsrooms of one type or another.[10] Perhaps more significantly, anyone with a mobile device can now disseminate data and data analyses to thousands of people through their social media accounts.

The upside here is again one of data democratization. Instead of being the province of an exclusive group of experts, virtually anyone can disseminate information very broadly; if it's cleverly packaged, for example, as a meme, it may quickly spread to an audience of millions. This produces a much greater familiarity and fluency with data among the general public, and in theory increases the availability of knowledge in society. But the potential downsides are substantial as well. There are thousands and thousands of sources of information and little oversight over what content they display. Many are explicitly biased in one direction or another; some are maintained by entities (PR firms, political actors, nation states) for the purpose of promoting an agenda.[11] Even traditional media sites like Forbes now host hundreds of "contributors" who are not trained as journalists and have few standards on what they can publish.

This explosion in news sources has been accompanied by an erosion of trust in media. According to the NORC's General Social Survey, which has been tracking consumer attitudes for decades, in 1973, only 14% of respondents said they had "hardly any confidence" in the press. By 2022, that number had swelled to 54%.[12] And in 2023, 40% of people agreed with the statement that news media are hurting democracy more than they are protecting it.[13]

Meanwhile, social media networks like Facebook and TikTok make it easy for any individual to post content that can then spread unchecked based only on its popularity, not its accuracy. The law – specifically Section 230 of the Communications Decency Act of 1996 – explicitly protects social networks from being sued for false or defamatory information spread by their users.[14] As a result, bad information can spread or become viral with few guardrails.

Members of the general public used to be the passive recipients of information. As a consumer, you learned things from the data and analyses made available to you by traditional media, results that were limited by choices made by data producers and disseminators higher up the data supply chain. You had little ability to analyze the data further or seek out additional data on related topics to expand your understanding of what you were reading in the newspaper or watching on TV. And your ability to spread information was pretty much limited to discussions with your family at the dinner table or with your neighbor across the backyard fence.

Now, thanks to the proliferation of data and the explosion of data disseminators, the consumer has access to a virtually unlimited amount of data on every topic imaginable. With the internet and various online tools, you can actively seek out data on topics that interest you, and you can perform your own analyses of data. And with social media, every data consumer now literally holds a digital bullhorn in the palm of their hand.

This newly active role of the data consumer is a very powerful one. And as with the other elements of the data ecosystem, this empowerment comes with upsides and downsides. The general public now has the ability to inform themselves in a much more proactive way and to share what they have learned very widely. But there are fundamental downsides. The sheer volume of data we are bombarded with every day is overwhelming. And the skills with which people interpret and share information are highly variable.

We are all steeped in this chaotic ecosystem of data producers, data disseminators, and data consumers. And consumers are, increasingly, overwhelmed by this firehose of data. According to a national survey conducted by NORC in 2016, while 81% of Americans believe it is now easier than ever to find useful information, 16% say they are often overwhelmed by the quantity of information, and another 62% say that the quantity can sometimes be too much (see Figure 2-2).[15]

This overabundance of data makes it almost impossible to stay abreast of things and determine what information to prioritize. And without appropriate context and understanding, the newly powerful data consumer can misinterpret, misunderstand, misrepresent, misinform, and even mislead. These challenges may arise from the problems or limitations of the data they are sharing (and a lack of awareness of

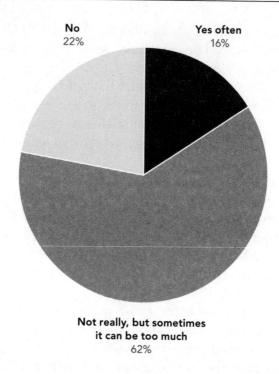

Figure 2-2: Most Americans are overwhelmed at times by the amount of information that comes to them. Survey question: "Do you ever feel overwhelmed by how much information comes to you? Would you say ...?"

Source: NORC 75th Anniversary survey of 1,007 US adults via AmeriSpeak panel, January 2016.

those), from incorrect or flawed conclusions based on the data they are analyzing, or because they are actively promoting a certain way of viewing the data they share. We examine these pitfalls – and potential solutions to them – throughout the remainder of this book.

A key aspect of understanding these opportunities and risks is that for much of the 20th century and prior to that, the traditional roles in the data ecosystem were tightly defined. But with data democratization, those roles have become blurred: Anyone can collect data, anyone can analyze data, anyone can disseminate data, and everyone consumes a vastly larger amount of data every day. And given this blurring in roles, we need new tools and approaches – both as individuals and as a society – to help ensure that we can perform these roles responsibly and in ways that maximize the upsides and minimize the downsides of data democratization.

Data Consumers Are Generally Thoughtful About the Data Ecosystem

If consumers were oblivious to the sources and level of accuracy of the information they consumed and shared, there'd be little hope for a fact-forward society. But in fact, most data consumers are quite aware of how the ecosystem can reveal both useful facts and bad information.

My colleagues at NORC and researchers at the American Press Institute have been investigating how people navigate the information ecosystem in a program called the Media Insight Project. Surveying 2,727 consumers in 2019, they found that while 64% say they actively seek out news and information, a surprising 35% just sort of bump into it as they do other things or participate in social media.[16] Even so, these consumers mostly believe they are open to learning the truth: 71% agreed that, "The more facts people have, the more likely it is they will get to the truth," and 74% thought, "For most things, knowing what is true is a matter of gathering evidence and proof."

And most people remain aware of the danger of bad information. In an AP-NORC poll of 1,002 adults conducted in 2023, 71% said that the spread of information was a major problem, and 65% expected stories they encountered on social media to be mostly inaccurate.[17]

How do data consumers navigate this minefield of potentially false information? They depend on cues, not only from the news source, but on who shared the information. In 2016, the Media Insight Project researchers tested this with an experiment that showed 1,454 consumers a Facebook-style news feed, but varied the original reporting source and who apparently shared it. People who saw an article

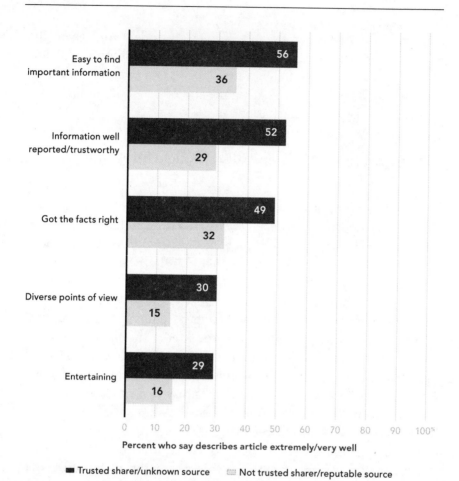

Figure 2-3: People trust social media more if it comes from a trusted sharer, even when the original source is unknown. Survey question: "How well does each of the following statements describe the article shared in this social media post?" Chart shows: extremely/very well.

Source: Media Insight Project survey of 1,454 US adults via AmeriSpeak panel, November–December 2016.

shared by someone they trusted were inclined to believe it, even if it appeared to come from an unknown source (see Figure 2-3).[18]

In a follow-up analysis, my colleagues and I further investigated how people share data in the ecosystem by conducting the NORC Data-Savvy Survey, a June 2024 survey of 1,071 adults about their attitudes about information on social media.[19] We found that 64% regularly or

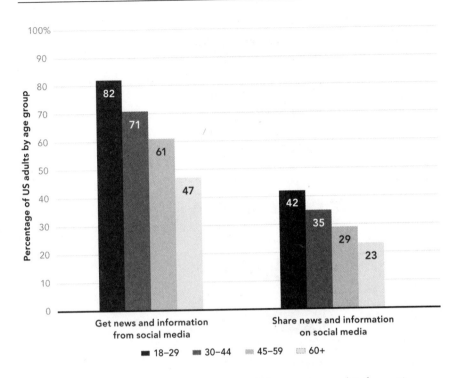

Figure 2-4: Older Americans acquire and share news and information less on social media. Survey question: "How often do you do any of the following?" Chart shows: regularly/occasionally.

Source: NORC Data-Savvy Survey of 1,071 US adults via AmeriSpeak panel, June 2024.

occasionally get news on social media, and 31% share it either regularly or occasionally. As you might expect, this is highly variable by age. Among those 60 or older, 23% share news on social media, while among those 18 – 29, 42% do (see Figure 2-4). Whether they share information or not depends on many factors, including whether it came from a trusted news organization, whether they've personally checked the information, or whether it was trusted by a person or organization they trusted (see Figure 2-5). Of course, it is also the case that trusted news sources for some people will be highly biased ones. But our research indicates that most people are still interested in the facts, even if they are increasingly willing to believe that their favorite (often biased) sources provide them with the truth.

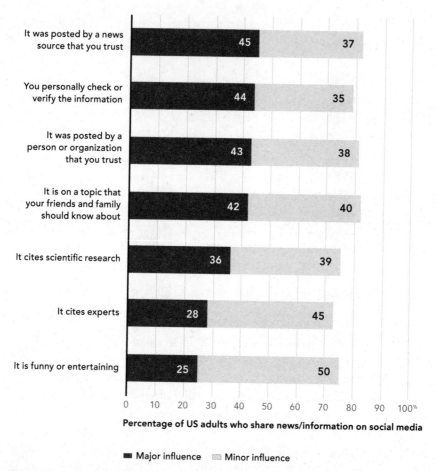

Figure 2-5: Factors that influence whether people share information on social media. Survey question: "How much do the following factors influence your decision about whether or not to share news and information on social media?"

Source: NORC Data-Savvy Survey of 1,071 US adults via AmeriSpeak panel, June 2024.

Building a Fact-Forward Society in a World of Data Democratization

Today's data ecosystem easily spreads information. And it is just as likely – or perhaps more likely – to spread the most sensational or partisan statistics as those that are most trustworthy. Data democratization, while on its face a very benign force, can contribute to undermining a fact-forward society.

This creates responsibilities for all ecosystem participants, including you. If you create data, you must follow principles to avoid bias and be as transparent as possible in documenting your methods, described in detail in Chapters 4–6. If you are a data consumer, you must develop skills based in data literacy, a goal described in Chapter 7. And anyone who acts as a data disseminator – whether in media or as an ordinary consumer – must take pains to avoid spreading misleading data and statistics.

Let's explore some examples of pitfalls that actors in each of the main data ecosystem roles face and consider them in the context of growing data democratization.

Data Producer Pitfall: The Apparent Legitimacy of a Number

A favorite joke among data scientists is "87.3% of statistics are made up on the spot." While there are certainly numerous examples of people (often politicians) simply making up numbers, there are also more nuanced ways in which data of questionable value can take on apparent legitimacy. And as data and analyses proliferate, even trusted disseminators can conclude that limited or questionable data are broadly useful.

The popular *New Yorker* writer Malcolm Gladwell pulled back the curtain on one such set of statistics: the *US News & World Report* rankings of universities.[20] *US News* synthesizes the rankings based on a weighted average of variables including undergraduate academic reputation, graduation rates, student selectivity, and alumni giving.

Many of the variables included in the *US News* college rankings have an ill-defined relationship to any measure of academic quality. For example, the academic reputation score that makes up the largest proportion of each rating comes from a survey of university and college presidents, provosts, and deans of admission, plus some high-school guidance counselors, grading all the schools in their category on a five-point scale. As Gladwell points out, there's no reason to expect these survey respondents to have insights into the hundreds of schools they're being asked to rate. Many respondents are assigning reputation scores based on what they've heard, which may very well be strongly correlated with previous *US News* rankings, making the whole thing an exercise in self-reinforcing circular reasoning.

Clearly, the *US News* rankings are rating *something* – there is an actual formula and there are actual surveys – but the output doesn't necessarily correlate with students' academic success. And yet millions of college students and their families are likely making decisions on where to apply and where to attend based in part on these rankings.

While most people know not to take statistics used in advertising at face value, it's important to note that advertisers use clever techniques to give limited data apparent legitimacy. In ads in the United Kingdom, Colgate toothpaste stated that more than 80% of dentists recommend it. The obvious conclusion for a reader seeing that number on a billboard or in a magazine ad was that Colgate was preferred by most dentists. But in fact, Colgate's survey had allowed the dentists surveyed to put check marks next to multiple brands, so it would have been more accurate to say, "For 80% of dentists, Colgate is one of the brands they recommend." The UK's Advertising Standards Authority deemed the statistic "misleading" and required the brand to stop using the claim in advertising.

Consider both examples as we think about an increasingly broad base of data producers. With data democratization, we have seen an enormous proliferation of rating systems on virtually every aspect of life: travel, consumer goods, entertainment, healthcare. I am not suggesting that these rating systems are worthless, but in many instances, there is a total lack of clarity around the question of what is being measured, how well it is being measured, and thus, whether the results are likely to be useful to you. With data democratization, if data producers want to convince you of something (as advertisers do) they tend to use apparently legitimate numbers, while omitting important limitations of what the data actually say.

Data Disseminator Pitfall: Oversimplifying or Omitting Context

Statistics created by diligent researchers typically come with a complex context or explanation. These details are often omitted in popular news articles, so reporters may simplify their descriptions of the statistics. These context-free numbers then spread widely through media articles and sharing on social media.

Take the question of whether eating processed meats will increase your risk for breast cancer. In 2018, 10 cancer researchers published a meta-analysis – an overview of other studies examining the relationship between diet and cancer risk – in the *International Journal of Cancer*.[21] The journal article's conclusion was that the "highest category" of processed meat consumption – a description that varied across the other studies the researchers reviewed – was "associated with" an 9% increase of breast cancer risk.

This dramatic result generated notable reporting. A small, sober item in the *New York Times* accurately reported, "high consumption of processed meat (about 25 to 30 grams a day, on average) was associated with a 9 percent increased risk for breast cancer" but "[t]he authors acknowledge that these are observational studies that do not draw conclusions about cause and effect, and that none could control for all possible risk factors."[22] But CNN wrote "Regularly consuming the foods was linked with a 9% higher risk of breast cancer,"[23] and the headline in *People* magazine was "Eating Processed Meats Linked to a Greater Risk of Breast Cancer."[24]

There are two problems with all these headlines. First, the studies do not show that eating salami, for example, *causes* cancer, which is why responsible journalists write only about "links" and "association." Even so, a Google search on "processed meat" and "breast cancer" yields 172,000 hits. And many of those citing the research to drive site traffic to websites use dramatic headlines and content that oversimplify the results; Medical News Today, in an article with no byline, flatly claims, "Just two sausages per week may raise breast cancer risk."[25]

The second problem with these headlines is that readers may not understand what a 9% increased risk actually means. According to the American Cancer Society, the chances of a woman getting breast cancer at some point in her life are 13%.[26] Does the 9% increase push this to 22%? That would be alarming, but it would also be a misinterpretation. Nine percent of 13% is about 1%. So the actual increase in risk is from 13% to 14%, not to 22%. That's still not great news, but it is a very different conclusion.

In some cases, the press offices of researchers themselves are responsible for stripping away the crucial context. A *British Medical Journal* study examined 462 press releases and compared their content to the papers they were promoting.[27] The researchers found that one in three press releases contained "either exaggerated claims of causation (when the study itself only suggested correlation), unwarranted implications about animal studies for people, or unfounded health advice." And once the press releases had conflated correlation with causation or overpromised results of animal studies, the resulting news articles were overwhelmingly likely to uncritically repeat the error.

Consider these examples in the new world of data democratization. Even when data producers are careful with how they report their results, it is very easy for data disseminators to leave out details and important context that would help a data consumer to properly interpret what they are reading. The result is that the data disseminator often fails to inform the people who consume the data, and in fact may misinform them.

Data Consumer Pitfall: Thinking of Statistics as Standalone or Static

Every number generated from data is part of a story. As more data emerge, that story may evolve over time or be viewed from different perspectives. The data ecosystem can help provide that evolving context, but only if data producers, disseminators, and consumers recognize that a single number is not the end of the story.

Perhaps the best example of this is research on sexual orientation. One of the first researchers to attempt an answer to this question was Alfred Kinsey, who conducted interviews with 5,300 men over a 15-year period and described the results in the 1948 book *Sexual Behavior in the Human Male*. Kinsey found that 37% of men had had at least one homosexual experience and 10% were overwhelmingly or exclusively homosexual.[28] This 10% figure was widely cited in media for decades after Kinsey's book came out, because it was the only statistic available. But Kinsey's sample was far from a random sample of American males. His interviewees were three times more likely to be college students than the US average.[29] They were concentrated in northeastern and upper midwestern states. A disproportionate number of his inter-viewees were prison inmates, and he may have recruited some partici-pants from organizations and magazines that were more open to homosexuality.[30]

Since Kinsey's report was published, the topic of homosexuality has become the subject of far more discussion. That openness made it possible to conduct more representative surveys. At the same time, shifts in attitudes have also revealed that the topic of sexual-ity is more complex than just "gay" or "not gay." Using recent CDC data, UCLA's Williams Institute published a report in 2023 that concludes that 5.5% of the US population identified as gay, lesbian, bisexual, or transgender.[31] This incidence is higher than the results they found in an earlier study (2017), which showed that 3.9% identified as LGBT.

Nevertheless, the public thinks the percentage is much higher: Gallup reported in 2019 that the average US adult believes about 24% of men are gay.[32] A likely cause is the prevalence of gay topics in media and entertainment; the LGBTQ advocacy group GLAAD found that 8.8% of regular characters in primetime TV series were gay, and politicians frequently take highly visible positions on issues of sexual orientation and gender. At the same time, NORC's Gen-eral Social Survey, which we've conducted for many years, shows that acceptance of homosexuality has increased dramatically over time: In 2002, 55% of the US population thought sex between two people of the same sex was always wrong, while in 2022, such disap-proval had decreased by nearly half to 28%. And of course, increased acceptance makes it more likely that people will identify as LGBT. So the seemingly simple question of the prevalence of gay people in the US is actually quite complex, and our understanding of it is changing over time.

When viewing this example from the perspective of data democra-tization, the key thing to keep in mind is that as we are all bombarded with so much information every day, playing the role of a data-savvy consumer becomes ever more important but ever more difficult. It is just too easy to take a statistic and consider it as "the" result we need, as opposed to considering the broader information stream of which it is a part.

To Understand Any Data, You Must Be Aware of Its Data Ecosystem Context

The main lesson from these examples of statistics being reported, spreading, and influencing the world is this: A number is never just a number. A data-savvy observer – regardless of whether they are participating in the data ecosystem as producer, disseminator, or consumer – considers not just a statistic, but its context. Where did the data originate? How were data analyzed? How were statistics publicized? How did the data fit with other data that came before, and how might our perspective change based on data that follows? Do the data confirm or conflict with our prejudices? Who is spreading the number, and why? Unless you consider factors like these, your understanding of any insight derived from data is missing a crucial perspective.

A key purpose of this book is to advance fact-forward attitudes by creating as much insight and clarity as possible among all participants of the data ecosystem. This means we must all be aware, not just of the principles that apply to proper data analysis, but of our own roles in the ecosystem.

For data producers – academics, research companies, and anyone else who collects and analyzes data (which, of course, increasingly is all of us) – this means understanding and rigorously adopting the principles described in the first chapter: data integrity, data transparency, and data neutrality. We need to create and share data with proven statistical principles around samples, bias, and statistical significance, as discussed in detail in Chapters 4–6. But beyond that, data producers must be aware of the broader ecosystem in which they participate. In their interactions with public relations professionals at their own organization as well as with journalists, they must be as clear as possible about the limitations of their own research. It also makes sense to follow up; if a published article misinterprets or exaggerates conclusions from a piece of research, it is the responsibility of the researchers and their PR colleagues to clarify and correct those conclusions. This is an unaccustomed role for many data producers, but to limit distortions, they must accept responsibility, not just for analyzing data, but for helping others, including journalists and lay people, to understand the context of their analyses.

For data disseminators, there must be an emphasis on clarity and context in presenting data. Responsibly conducted research includes detail about sample sizes, confounding variables, and limitations of conclusions; journalists must scrupulously include such details in their explanations. Even as the quest for clicks encourages stories that glorify new, unproven cancer cures or radical shifts in public attitudes, journalists – and anyone who wants to share data with integrity – must maintain their commitment to presenting statistics with appropriate context. And this means that one cannot simply quote another data source without looking carefully at the context and provenance of the data. Journalists must also take seriously their responsibility *not* to publicize results of questionable validity.

In a world awash in social media where each of us has a mobile device, we are all data disseminators. Each of us must be wary of context- and source-free numbers begging to be shared. The more you want to believe a number, the more you should do a little research into where it came from. And if you see friends sharing misleading statistics, as a social media participant, you have the power to restore the missing context in the form of a constructive and empirically grounded comment.

For data consumers – which includes all of us – data and statistics matter because they inform our decisions. Based on what we read, we may change our diets, the products we buy, the way we vote, the way we raise our families, and the way we embrace or reject the choices of others. Data-savvy consumers make better decisions because they understand not just the data they consume, but the limitations of statistics derived from those data. In the new ecosystem, this enables them to responsibly participate in the roles of data producers or data disseminators, as well. A data-savvy attitude keeps us honest and safe in a world awash in numbers shared endlessly throughout the increasingly chaotic data ecosystem.

3

The Breadth of the Data Universe

THE TREND OF data democratization means more of us are interacting with, attempting to understand, and generating a broad and varied collection of data on a daily basis. This creates new demands on us to understand the significance of those data. That starts with the common language in which quantitative information is usually presented, which people typically refer to as "statistics."

For those not trained in statistics or data science, it's easy to get confused by the various statistics and accompanying jargon that are constantly thrown at us. If you feel any of that confusion, this chapter is for you. The chapter provides an overview of the different ways in which quantitative information is analyzed, assessed, and presented. If you are already well-versed in statistical concepts, feel free to skip this chapter and move on to the next.

An Illustrative Example: Unemployment Statistics

For the month of October 2023, the US Bureau of Labor Statistics (BLS) reported that the unemployment rate in the United States was 3.9%.[1] But if you recall the lessons of Chapter 1, it's not enough to just read a statistic and accept it. To understand a number, it pays to take a little effort to understand where it came from.[2]

To start, you might ask, 3.9% of what? In this case, the base for this number is the US labor force, which BLS defines as US residents (specifically, civilians age 16 or older who are not in institutions such as prisons) who are either working or looking for work. Among those, a person counts as unemployed if they were actively looking for work, didn't work, and weren't on temporary leave from a job.

So how does the government figure out who's looking for a job?

As with many statistics you read, that number comes from a survey of a sample of the population. Every month, the government surveys 60,000 households (covering about 110,000 total individuals) and asks whether people in those households are working or are looking for work, along with how much they were paid and other employment information. Even with a survey this large, random variability in who the survey reaches can affect the result. This means the 3.9% unemployment statistic is not actually a single number; it's part of a range – a "confidence interval" – that reflects the uncertainty that comes from sampling a subset of households (because contacting everyone in America every month would be prohibitively expensive and impossible to actually do). It would be more accurate to say that, due to sampling error, the unemployment rate has a 90% chance of being between 3.8% and 4.0%. Even that doesn't account for sources of uncertainty beyond the size of the sample, like failing to reach the kind of people who refuse to answer surveys, people misunderstanding the questions, or even dealing with respondents who might lie about their employment status (such as thieves, drug dealers, and workers paid under the table), but generally it is considered a very close approximation to the "real" number.

Perhaps you're more interested in whether unemployment is going up or down. The 3.9% unemployment rate that the Bureau of Labor Statistics reported for October 2023 was slightly higher than the previous month's 3.8%.[3] In the same month, the BLS reported that new unemployment insurance claims had *decreased* by 3,000 to 217,000, which would imply a reduction in unemployment. And a separate survey that the BLS conducts – of employers – suggested that employers *added* 150,000 jobs in the month.

How can these all be true at the same time? For one thing, these different statistics aren't measuring exactly the same thing. Moreover, all those measurements include potential sources of error. We're looking at three separate data sources here: a survey of consumers, a survey of employers, and a compilation of claims from state unemployment departments. They measure different aspects of the employment situation in the United States with different methods.

The nature of data is that every statistic has potential sources of error and uncertainty. As a rule, it's not feasible (both logistically and cost-wise) to collect data on the entire universe of a population you are trying to study. The US Census Bureau, which is constitutionally required to count everyone in the United States every 10 years, always undercounts the population, even though they have some of the best technology and methods, highly capable staff, and an enormous budget (just under $14 billion in the last round). If the Census weren't required by the Constitution, it is unclear whether we would even attempt it at that frequency.

Instead, people who make decisions based on these data – like the bankers at the Federal Reserve, for example, in the case of employment statistics – compile statistics from multiple sources and attempt to understand the big picture, recognizing that uncertainty is always a factor.

Tying into the discussion of uncertainty in data is the concept and promise of "big data." In today's digital world, computers and electronic processes generate huge amounts of data, hundreds of millions of records or more, that can be used to analyze subjects of interest (for example, consumer financial transactions). Theoretically, these data sets are so large that some of the traditional sources of uncertainty in survey data go away. However, the reality is more complicated. While big data sets do offer an enormous amount of information, they have other forms of uncertainty; often they do not cover the entire population of interest, or the administrative process that generates the data ends up creating data that don't correctly measure what you are trying to analyze.

The point is that *all* data have strengths and weaknesses, and all data have some uncertainty. Similarly, data types are often complementary – the strengths of one type of data may be the weaknesses of another. It is often helpful to use multiple kinds of data to produce useful analyses. *A key aspect of being data savvy is understanding this essential uncertainty in data to become an informed data consumer.*

Ubiquitous Data

The modern digital world creates a massive torrent of data. We – and the machines we have created – generate tens of billions of terabytes every year, filling a rapidly growing collection of data centers world-wide.[4] The data collection includes all the clicks on social media, all the data about the human genomes of millions of individuals, all the digital photographs taken by satellites, and the thousands of online surveys conducted by researchers and marketers – and unimaginably much more.

This mass of data creates endless opportunities for informing important decisions of all types, whether it's legislators trying to create a good policy, businesspeople trying to manage their businesses effectively, government officials trying to run and evaluate programs, or households trying to make the best decisions for their families. Analyzing all these data gives us the potential to gain all sorts of insights into how the world works.

Most pools of data, of course, aren't in a place where people can draw conclusions from them. Here's an illustrative overview of the range of many of the data sources available to analyze, along with some features and limitations of each type to keep in mind:

- **Survey data.** If you want to know how much consumers spend on their pets, how voters' views on abortion affect the way they vote, or how buyers would react to an electric car with a 500-mile range – or any of thousands of other questions – often the most appropriate tool is a survey. In 2022, just one of the many survey tools, SurveyMonkey, enabled researchers to ask respondents 20 million questions every day.[5] But just because there are lots of questions being asked doesn't mean they are *good* questions, nor does it mean that the group of people who are answering the questions are the intended group. Just as with any other means for collecting data, surveys can be of higher and lower quality. A well-crafted survey is designed to reach a representative sample of a target population (pet owners, likely voters, or car buyers, for example) with questions that are easily understood and pertinent to the decisions at hand. Survey research can be subject to limitations that arise from small, unrepresentative, or biased samples. And respondents' misinterpretation of questions or potential to lie about things they'd rather not share can muddy the results, too. (For more details on limitations of samples and bias, see Chapter 4.)

- **Administrative records.** Administrative data are data generated by the operations of governments or other institutions. For example, the FBI assembles data about crime from law enforcement agencies, and the CDC gathers disease data from reports from doctors and hospitals. In addition to surveys, the government uses data from tax filings and other regulatory documents to estimate spending and investment and to project the gross domestic product and economic growth. There are similar data streams for home sales, car registrations, company formation, and so on. These data sets are often large (they contain many millions of "records" or "observations") and have lots of different data items (they contain many thousands of "variables"). Statisticians analyzing them must manage the massive data sets as well as addressing cases of biased, missing, or inaccurate reporting. And agencies that collect administrative data sets can sometimes focus too much on quantity of data at the expense of deeper or higher quality data collection to reveal details that would be helpful for making decisions.

- **Data collected by companies.** Companies collect and analyze data of all kinds for all sorts of reasons. Proprietary research companies like Nielsen and Circana collect data on who watches which TV programs and how many of each book are sold at retail.[6] Companies that act as a middleman or facilitator in a market can collect data about those markets; for example, credit card companies can track a substantial portion of retail purchases. Companies like Google can report trends in what people are searching for online. Companies also collect proprietary corporate data about their own customer transactions and interactions and may choose to publicize some of those data. In all these cases, there may be gaps and biases in the data sets that mean they're not 100% representative of the markets and quantities that analysts are modeling.

- **Sensor data.** Digital devices now generate masses of data that can be fodder for later analysis. The comprehensive data collection from weather sensors managed by The Weather Channel was so valuable that IBM bought the company. Personal devices like Fitbits and smart watches generate data about people's behavior, while today's cars also generate tons of data about how people drive and how well their vehicles function. Many municipal transit authorities, including Greater Boston's MBTA, make data available on the real-time location of buses and trains. The challenge in any of these cases is getting representative access to data sets controlled by others and assembling the raw data into a form that's useful.

- **Web traffic data.** Every click and tap generated by people using computers, browsers, mobile devices, and apps feeds into log files maintained by the sites and apps people are visiting. As a result, companies maintaining websites and apps have broad collections of information that they can analyze to determine how factors like advertising, email marketing, and social media outreach are influencing their commercial results. While those data sets are locked up within the companies that collect them, other companies aggregate samples of such information across the whole web; for example, Similarweb uses tracking from volunteers to map global volume of traffic to websites with its Alexa service. Whenever you read about web traffic data, be aware that any publicly available information may reflect biases based on which statistics the companies choose to publicize.

- **Data from experiments.** Researchers worldwide conduct thousands of experiments intended to generate data and answer questions. For example, before a drug like Humira is approved as safe and effective for use to treat rheumatoid arthritis, the drug's manufacturers must collect data from studies in both animals and, later, humans, to show that the drug has a positive impact on the disease condition and to monitor any potentially dangerous side effects. To try to ensure that the results they are observing are attributable to the drug (or more generally, the "treatment" or "intervention"), experimental design requires at least two matched groups, one that receives the treatment (the experimental group) and one that receives a placebo (the control group). To avoid biases generated by the optimism of the research subjects and researchers, such studies are often "double-blind": neither the subjects nor the researchers know who is getting the treatment and who is in the control group receiving an inactive placebo. And it isn't only scientists who conduct experiments; marketers may test market products, or test changes in their online tactics, collecting data to see which strategies are effective and profitable. As carefully as researchers attempt to control the conditions in experiments, the results are subject to uncertainty from sampling error due to size or bias of samples, as well as from the influence of unsuspected or unmeasured additional variables. And results that look promising under controlled lab conditions may not work as effectively in the real world.

- **Public financial data.** Stock and bond markets generate masses of information every day including prices, trading volumes, and public reporting of financial results like revenue and profit. Financial analysts can attempt to find patterns in these data, often with the aid of sophisticated analytic models. The problem here isn't so much one of data quality or access but simply the fact that there are massive amounts of private financial data and transactions representing a substantial portion of overall financial and economic activity that the publicly available data do not capture.

- **Data from the open web, including public records.** Large language models such as ChatGPT are built by consuming and seeking patterns in masses of web information. If you ask ChatGPT to describe what makes Taylor Swift popular, its answer is a summary of common themes drawn from hundreds or thousands of articles. AI-based drawing tools such as Midjourney work similarly, operating based on patterns in billions of graphics. Because AI tools have no actual insights into the data they are consuming, their output is often inaccurate – either because of biases in the source materials or because of inaccurate perceptions of patterns in the underlying data.

- **Qualitative data.** Not all data are hard facts and numbers. Qualitative research can also generate insights. For example, ethnographic researchers may observe consumers in their everyday activities (with permission, of course) to learn more about how they use products and how they make decisions. Researchers seeking insights into how people think may bring small groups of people together for focus groups where they can discuss their attitudes and thought processes. Companies like C Space manage small, proprietary online social communities for the purpose of generating insights about everything from how people manage their health to how they make financial decisions. The best feature of qualitative data methods is the way that they allow researchers to go deeper and ask more questions in search of actionable insights. Their weakness, of course, is that they reach only very small groups of people, and the often subjective conclusions that researchers reach may not generalize the whole population they are supposed to represent.

No list like this can be exhaustive because there are always more sources of data becoming available for analysis – and even in this list, many of the data types overlap. Still, this list illustrates the enormous breadth and depth of the data universe. Human ingenuity combined with digital data generation (including, increasingly, AI) is constantly creating new forms of data to analyze. The data that can be used to understand key societal topics (the economy, healthcare, education, crime) are a complex web of interrelated, and often complementary, types where surveys, administrative data, qualitative data, private and public data, and novel data sources are all used to inform our understanding of a topic.

Analyzing Data Enables Smart Decisions

Data sets by themselves aren't sufficient for making decisions. We need to analyze those data to turn them into useful insights.

But remember, statistical facts, unlike observed facts, come with uncertainty. If you watched a hockey game in which the Chicago Blackhawks beat the Washington Capitals 4-2, you can be certain that the Blackhawks scored exactly four goals. But if Gallup reports that 3%

of Americans say ice hockey is their favorite sport, that 3% is accompanied by some uncertainty based on limitations in the survey that percentage comes from.[7]

Here's a simple experiment to demonstrate the concepts of confidence and uncertainty in statistics. Imagine that you have a coin. It may be a normal coin with equal probability of heads or tails, or it may be a "cheater's coin," weighted so that heads always comes up. You flip the coin five times, and it comes up heads five times. How confident are you that it is a biased coin?

The probability that a normal coin would land heads five times in a row is $\frac{1}{2} \times \frac{1}{2} \times \frac{1}{2} \times \frac{1}{2} \times \frac{1}{2}$, which means there is about a 3% chance (or more precisely, 3.125%) that an unweighted coin might generate the same unusual result. With those low odds, you might guess the streak of five heads means that the coin is weighted, but you can't be certain. Part of the reason you can't be certain is that five coin tosses is a pretty small sample size on which to base your judgment. If you flipped the coin 10 times and got heads each time, you still couldn't be absolutely sure, but you'd be a lot more confident in asserting that the coin is weighted.

Confidence and uncertainty like this accompany every statistical result based on samples. Every number comes with some degree of uncertainty, reflecting the expected difference between that number and the true value the sample is approximating. And we are able to characterize this uncertainty by discussing our level of confidence in the result. The confidence level expresses the probability that the result is due to random chance.

Beyond random variation, there is also likely to be some error in the very way something is measured. In science, we strive to have both precision and accuracy in our measurements. Precision is the consistency with which something is measured, meaning it produces the same result repeatedly under similar conditions. Accuracy is the degree to which the measure represents the phenomenon it designed to measure.

Let's illustrate these concepts with an example. Imagine a study designed to understand the amount of leisure time residents of a city spend outdoors. Conducting a representative survey of city residents and asking them a range of questions designed to inventory their time spent outdoors over the past weekend would likely be a more accurate measure than tracking sales of athletic shoes or bicycles. However, the survey may have precision problems if we don't define what we mean by "leisure time," because respondents will each use their own particular idea about what leisure time is. Another way to make the survey more precise would be to ensure we administer the survey on a Sunday night or Monday morning, since people's ability to recall their time spent outdoors will degrade over time. Even with a representative survey and a good definition of leisure time, there is still an underlying flaw (systematic bias) in the study: We only asked people about their weekend, and many residents of a city work on weekends and have other days of the week off.

Just because most statistical results come with uncertainty and other limitations doesn't mean that they aren't extremely useful. It just means that, as a data-savvy consumer, you should keep the uncertainty and data limitations in mind whenever you're interpreting them.

Let's look at some types of statistics and how the concept of confidence shapes our understanding of those statistics.

Prevalence Percentages and Point Estimates

Sampling and surveys are effective at answering questions about how common a belief is in the population, also known as prevalence. For example, a 2022 report from the Associated Press and NORC reported that 44% of US adults think "a great deal" or "a lot" of progress has been made in achieving equal access to a good education for African Americans.[8] How accurate is that number?

The report includes the information that the "margin of sampling error" is plus or minus 3.7 percentage points at the 95% confidence level. Sampling error is one of the sources of error that may impact survey estimates and it reflects the fact that, purely at random, the poll might have reached a sample of people whose confidence about African Americans' access to education is either lower or higher than the actual population. As you think about typical findings from the survey, the margin of error number is a reminder that true value for the population is quite likely within plus or minus 3.7 percentage points of what the survey found. In this case, the 44% of adults who believe a great deal or a lot of progress has been made in achieving equal access to education for African Americans might be as low as 40%, or as high as 48%.

But the margin of error changes when you look at subsamples. In the poll, a far smaller 27% of Black Americans felt progress had been made on education. The margin of sampling error for a point estimate of 27% for this subgroup of Black adults is 6.4 percentage points, larger than the 3.7 percentage points cited earlier. So, for Black adults, the actual prevalence of this opinion is likely to be somewhere between 21% and 33%.

Of course, percentages are not the only type of point estimate you can get from surveys. For example, according to the 2022 National Survey of Fishing, Hunting, and Wildlife-Associated Recreation, which NORC conducted for the US Fish & Wildlife Service, the average American angler spends $2,490 per year on fishing.[9] This survey reached more than 40,000 people. Just as with percentages, when a point estimate is an average value of some measure, the researchers should report a margin of error or a confidence interval. Based on the number of respondents, the report on this survey reports a 95% confidence interval of $2,395–$2,584, indicating that if these respondents are representative of the population of men and women who fish, the average annual spending for anglers has a 95% likelihood of being between those two values.

Averages, Medians, and Percentiles

Every estimate of a number like annual spending on fishing reflects a distribution of values. The average of $2,490 clearly comes from a range of answers: Some people may be spending only $100, while others may be spending $3,000 or more.

While some reports of this kind will cite the average, also called the mean, others will cite the median. What's the difference?

To compute the median, the researchers sort all the answers in order from lowest to highest and then report the answer that is exactly in the middle of that listing. For a collection of observations, the median is the number such that half of the observations are higher, and the other half lower.

The reason that statisticians sometimes use medians rather than averages is because it minimizes the impact of extreme values on understanding what is "typical" for the result in question. Take, for example, home prices. According to the St. Louis branch of the Federal Reserve, the median sale price of a home in the United States in the third quarter of 2023 was $435,400 – half of the houses sold for more than that, and half for less.[10] Why not just use an average? Well, as you might imagine, there are huge mansions that may have sold for many millions of dollars. One home in Palm Beach, Florida, sold for $170 million.[11] A few extreme values like that Palm Beach mansion would distort any reported average, without accurately reflecting the trend in less extreme house sales. A median, on the other hand, won't be unduly affected by extreme values, which makes it a much better measure for comparison purposes.

Medians are useful for income comparisons for the same reason. In January 2023, the BLS reported that median weekly earnings for full-time and salaried workers were $1,176 for men and $975 for women.[12] Salaries are a good example of a skewed (asymmetrical) distribution, with lots of workers clustered at the bottom at the minimum wage and a few executives, celebrities, and professional athletes at the extreme high end with salaries in the millions or tens of millions. The median allows for a fair comparison unaffected by the magnitude of the extreme salaries.

Percentiles are a more general version of the concept behind the median. The median of a set of incomes is the 50th percentile, since 50% of the values are higher than it and 50% lower. You can also look at, say, the 10th percentile, the income number with 10% of the population below it and 90% above it, or the 90th percentile, with 90% of the population below it and 10% above it. These values are useful, for example, for assessing income inequality. In November 2023, the *Wall Street Journal* reported that hourly earnings at the 10th percentile, adjusted for inflation, had risen by 8.1% between January 2020 and June 2023, while those at the 90th percentile decreased by 1.5%.[13] This indicates that due to labor shortages, employers were having to pay people more at the bottom of the income scale, and that highly compensated workers were getting a little less – a slight reduction in income inequality. Percentiles, like medians, provide a more complete understanding of a data distribution without the distortion of extreme high or low values.

Statistically Significant Differences Between Groups

Single measures (also called point estimates) may be insufficient to support decisions. Sometimes the real decision power comes from comparisons. Are people under 30 more likely to vote for gun control than people over 60? Are the value of job offers to Black people lower than offers to similarly qualified white people?

To answer these types of questions, you need to know whether a point estimate is different across the two groups. And simply seeing two different point estimates and concluding they are different is inappropriate. Why? Once again because you need to consider the uncertainty inherent in the point estimates. This is where the concept of *statistical significance* enters the picture. It poses the question: What is the probability that the difference we are seeing is a real difference as opposed to one that might happen randomly due to the uncertainty in our measurement? If that probability is low, the researcher can have a high confidence that the measured difference reflects an actual difference between the groups.

Medical studies are particularly useful for explaining the concept of statistical significance. For example, let's look at the medical evidence for the injectable drug semaglutide – currently marketed under the names Ozempic and Wegovy – as a weight-loss treatment. Researchers including Thomas A. Wadden conducted a clinical trial with 611 adults who were overweight or obese.[14] Over a course of 68 weeks, all the participants received behavioral therapy, but only two-thirds received semaglutide injections; the others received a placebo injection without the drug in it. Those on the drug treatment averaged a 16.0% weight reduction. Those who got the placebo averaged a weight loss of 5.7%.

Is this difference of 10.3 percentage points due to the drug's effect, or is it potentially just random chance? The study reports a 95% confidence interval for the difference, specifically a range of between 8.6 and 12.0 percentage points. In other words, the theoretical true result of the difference in weight loss between the two groups has a 95% chance of being in the range of 8.6–12.0 percentage points. The study also says that there is only a one-in-one-thousand chance ("$p < 0.001$") that the group getting the drug and those not receiving it are actually not different, and the measured difference was just due to random chance. These findings give us a great deal of confidence in the concept that the medication has the desired effect.

As always, there are limitations. Is this possibly an effect of some other variable that's different between the two groups? The researchers made sure that the groups were similar in age, gender split, and race, so probably not. Does this apply to people with diabetes? No, they screened out participants with diabetes, so that would require another study. Would the effect be the same without the behavioral counseling? Since everyone in the study received the counseling, you'd need a different study to answer that. Will the weight loss persist beyond the end of the drug treatment? Again, the study doesn't answer that.

Even so, this study strongly suggests that this medication has an impact on weight loss for overweight, otherwise healthy people. As a data-savvy reader, you can use studies like this to help you and your doctors to make decisions with an awareness of both the results and the limitations of those results.

It's important to keep in mind that some differences are *not* statistically significant. For example, William C. Hiss of Bates College compared college students who submitted SAT or ACT scores when they applied to college with those who did not.[15] Students whose applications did not include scores had a mean grade point average of 2.83, while those who did submit scores averaged 2.88. The difference, 0.05 grade points, was not statistically significant. In other words, the difference in scores could easily have happened by chance. In this case, the sample size was certainly large, with 123,000 total students, 30% of whom had been admitted without submitting test scores. There were wide variations in grade point average among both groups of students, so the differences in any student's GPA were easily explained by many factors other than whether the students had submitted test scores when they applied to college.

Correlation: A Measure of Relationships Between Variables

Another common question that statistics attempt to answer is: Do two quantitative measures track with one another? The term for this is correlation. For example, it is generally the case that, other things being equal, people with more years of schooling have higher incomes. In other words, the two variables, years of schooling and income, are correlated. But how would you measure that relationship, and how would you measure confidence that it's not just happening by chance?

A great example of correlation comes from the well-researched area of exercise and health. Nine researchers from the Harvard School of Public Health and other institutions studied the amount of physical activity and the mortality (likelihood of dying) for 116,221 adults in two studies of nurses and other health professionals.[16] Based on this study, people who reported doing moderate exercise at least 150 minutes per week reduced their risk of dying by 20% (see Figure 3-1). Those who said they exercised at least 200 minutes per week reduced their risk of dying by an additional 3%.

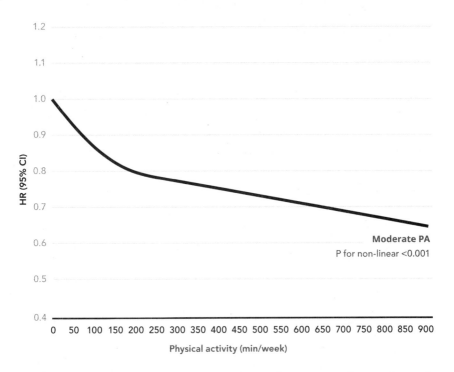

Figure 3-1: There is a significant correlation between moderate physical activity and reduced mortality from all causes. Note: Hazard ratio (HR) is a measure of the relative risk of mortality.

Source: "Long-Term Leisure-Time Physical Activity Intensity and All-Cause and Cause-Specific Mortality: A Prospective Cohort of US Adults" by Dong Hoon Lee et al., July 25, 2022 in the journal *Circulation*. Used by permission.

Here's how to understand this clear correlation. It doesn't necessarily mean that if you start exercising, you'll live longer. There is of course, no way to predict when you'll die; you could start running three times a week and die from an accident a month later. But the large number of adults in the study makes it clear that this association is extremely unlikely to be the result of random chance; people who exercise more *are significantly more likely* to live longer. We have all heard the phrase *correlation is not causation*. When you read that two variables are correlated, be skeptical about whether one is causing the other, or some third factor is influencing both. In the case of the correlation between exercise and reduced mortality, the researchers used advanced statistical techniques to control for other variables that might muddy the data, such as smoking, sufficient amounts of sleep, body mass index (obesity), and healthy eating. Although they still haven't proven that exercise causes the mortality reduction, they have at least shown that other key factors are not responsible for what they have observed.

Consider a tongue-in-cheek study that was published by Franz H. Messerli in the *New England Journal of Medicine*.[17] The author obtained data on consumption of chocolate per person in 23 countries and compared it to the number of Nobel Prize laureates per 10 million population (see Figure 3-2). The two quantities were highly correlated, and a test of significance showed a less than 1 in 10,000 chance that the correlation was random (in statistical terms, $p < 0.0001$). Switzerland, Denmark, Austria, Norway, and the United Kingdom were among the nations with both high chocolate consumption and disproportionate numbers of Nobel Prizes. (Sweden, clearly an outlier, had plenty of Nobel Prizes despite only average consumption of chocolate.)

The author suggests reasoning for how eating chocolate improves cognitive function and could therefore generate Nobel Prizes, but it's not meant to be taken seriously. And it's quite unlikely that winning Nobel Prizes causes whole nations to consume large quantities of chocolate. It's far more likely that a third factor (such as the relative affluence or cultural differences in the nations at the upper-right corner of the chart) is causing both chocolate consumption and Nobel Prizes to go up.

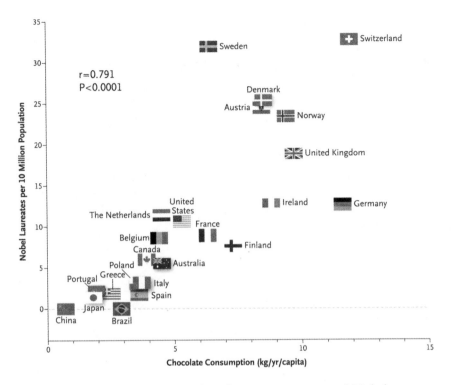

Figure 3-2: The correlation of chocolate consumption and Nobel laureates per capita may be interesting, but it is not particularly meaningful.

Source: "Chocolate Consumption, Cognitive Function, and Nobel Laureates" by Franz H. Messerli, October 18, 2012, in the *New England Journal of Medicine*. Used by permission.

Trends Over Time Provide Context

So far, we've looked at statistics at a fixed point in time. But data sets that include the same questions or measure the same quantities over time can reveal fascinating trends. Analyzing trends over time is called longitudinal analysis. Many large survey organizations, including the one I lead, NORC at the University of Chicago, as well as the Pew Research Center, Gallup, Gartner, Forrester, and many federal agencies, publish longitudinal data that decision-makers can use to gain insights.

Let's look at one large-scale survey, the General Social Survey (GSS), which has surveyed the US adult population nearly every other year since 1972. NORC conducts the GSS with funding from the National Science Foundation. The GSS's questions about religion reveal a clear decline in attendance at religious services: The number of people who say they never attend religious services has increased steadily from 10% in 1972 to 34% in 2022, while the number who attend every week or more has decreased from 34% to 18% (see Figure 3-3).[18] There are small fluctuations between years, some of which may be due to sampling error. (The GSS helpfully provides measures of sampling error for each data point, which tend to be between 0.5 and 2.0 percentage points.)

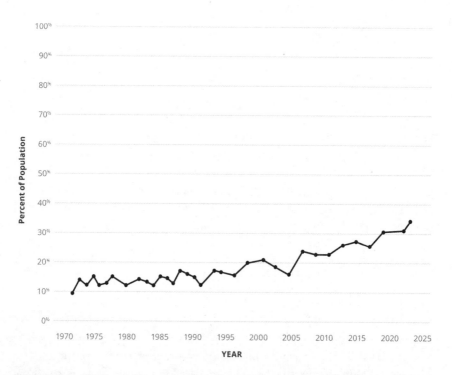

Figure 3-3: The number of US adults who never attend religious services is rising. Survey question: "How often do you attend religious services?" Chart shows: never.

Source: GSS Data Explorer.

The GSS also shows a steady increase in acceptance of gay marriage. In 1988, only 11% of respondents agreed that marriage between people of the same sex should be legal. By 2022, 67% favored it.

Of course, not all trends are steady; fluctuations can be particularly interesting. Consider a study of Americans' life expectancy over time by Angus Deaton and Anne Case of Princeton University.[19] You would likely guess that with medical advances over the years life expectancy would be steadily increasing (ignoring the pandemic, of course). And that is certainly true for Americans with a bachelor's degree. But for those without a degree, life expectancy has steadily *decreased* by about half a year since 2010 (see Figure 3-4). Drug overdoses, suicide, and alcoholic liver disease – or as the study's authors describe them, "deaths of despair" – account for much of the decline.

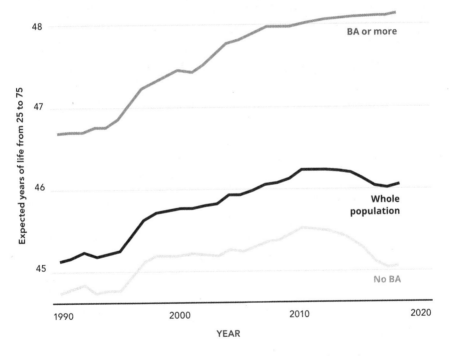

Figure 3-4: Life expectancy recently declined for people without a college degree.

Source: "Life expectancy in adulthood is falling for those without a BA degree, but as educational gaps have widened, racial gaps have narrowed," by Anne Case and Angus Deaton, December 29, 2020, in the journal *Proceedings of the National Academy of Sciences* (PNAS). Used by permission.

The most valuable quality of trends in data analysis is context. A statistic like the inflation rate, the proportion of people smoking, life expectancy, or the number of people likely to vote for a given candidate is far more meaningful if you know how it's changed over time. When reviewing trend data, be mindful of changes in how the data were collected. An online survey in 2023 isn't necessarily comparable to a telephone survey in 1985 (due to differences in who had access to telephones in 1985 and who is online in 2023, as well as overall changes in the population), and a presidential election poll of likely voters in October of an election year isn't equivalent to a poll of all adults conducted in the previous month (since voters' preferences become more definite closer to the election). Trends can also be influenced by other factors that aren't necessarily visible, such as changes in economic conditions. And as with any statistic, sample size matters. Specifically, if a poll of 200 voters today shows a three-percentage-point jump in a candidate's support compared to a similar poll last week, that shift is likely to be within the margin of sampling error and could fail to reflect any actual change in the electorate's intentions.

Modeling Multiple Factors to Make Predictions

If the purpose of data and analysis is to help make decisions, why not try to replicate real-world conditions where many variables are operating at the same time? Data scientists do this by creating models that aim to assemble data on a whole range of factors to understand their total impact on an outcome of interest. A modeler analyzes data, often from multiple sources, to build a model to predict an outcome based on those data. Models are ubiquitous in business, government, and science, but because a model assembles data points that each have associated error and uncertainty, the results of the model have uncertainty too.

Models are effective when a system's response to variables is well-studied and understood. As you read in Chapter 2, the link between cancer and smoking became clearer and more easily measured in the last half of the twentieth century. In the first part of this century, it became possible to model how different policy and media strategies might impact a reduction in smoking. That's what researchers including the University of Baltimore's David Levy did in 2004.[20] The strategies the researchers studied included increases in cigarette taxes; bans on smoking in workplaces, restaurants, and schools; anti-smoking media advertising; mandating insurance coverage of quitting programs; and better enforcement of age restrictions on cigarette purchases. The researchers used data from various studies to assess the impact each factor might have on reduction of smoking rates, examining factors like who starts smoking and at what age, how effective smoking cessation programs are, and death rates for smokers. Based on their model, they predicted that even if policymakers implemented all these strategies, they would fail to reach the hoped-for goal of reducing the smoking rate to 12% by 2010; their model suggested a 2010 smoking rate of 18.4%.

Subsequent surveys by the CDC estimate an actual smoking rate of 19.3% of adults in 2010.[21] So the model did a reasonably good job in predicting the actual result; however, as is typical with models like this, the prediction was not perfect because all models contain uncertainty. There was also uncertainty in the CDC estimate. But these strategies did combine, possibly with the help of other factors like more effective smoking treatments and social pressure, to continue to reduce the smoking rate. By 2021, CDC was reporting a smoking rate of only 14.5%.[22] By that point, another factor had influenced the data: 4.5% of adults were smoking e-cigarettes ("vaping"). Unanticipated changes like vaping often confound models because they introduce influence from variables the model didn't include.

Economists in the Federal Reserve use models to predict the effect of interest rates on inflation and unemployment while controlling for other variables. Financial analysts use them to predict stock prices from financial data. Elections analysts at organizations like the *New York Times* and FiveThirtyEight use them to predict election outcomes from poll results and historical voting patterns. All these models are sophisticated, but none of them is likely to be completely accurate; if confounding and unanticipated variables like vaping in the smoking study or unexpected scandalous revelations about candidates arise, the models will be off.

But as the statistician George Box has stated, "All models are wrong; [but] some are useful."[23] The purpose of a model is not to make completely accurate predictions, but to enable decision-makers to understand the relationships among variables and how they influence outcomes. It's important to remember this whenever you read a prediction based on statistical data. Models may represent the best possible prediction about outcomes, but the more uncertainty there is in the relationships among variables and in the data fed into the model – and the more unexpected events occur – the less dependable the model's predictions become. For example, everyone loves to complain about forecasts from weather models. They tend to be quite accurate for predicting temperatures, but less accurate for predicting snowfall amounts, because there is much more uncertainty in the interactions of key inputs into the model.

Predictive Analytics: Making Choices Based on Predicted Outcomes

Predictive analytics is the application of these models into the actual work that organizations are doing. With predictive analytics, an organization can turn data into a tool for identifying opportunity and integrate it directly into processes like customer service, maintenance, or marketing.

The most famous example of predictive analytics is the way that the Oakland A's general manager Billy Beane used it to revolutionize the way his team identified and coached baseball players. As dramatically related in the book *Moneyball* by Michael Lewis and the movie based on that book, starring Brad Pitt and Jonah Hill, Beane and his protégé Paul DePodesta crunched data to prove that a player's on-base percentage, more than any other statistic, determined that player's contribution to the team's chance to win. They used this knowledge to identify undervalued players like Kevin Youkilis (the "Greek God of Walks") who could help the team win with a far lower payroll than other teams. In the year that the A's adopted predictive analytics in the form of Moneyball, they won their division, including a run of 20 consecutive wins.

Predictive analytics has broad applications. For example, airlines use sensor data from aircraft engines to predict when they are likely to need extra maintenance to prevent future failures.[24] Airbnb used predictive analytics to determine which messages and interactions were most likely to get individual potential customers to commit to a rental, a strategy that Airbnb's head of data science, Riley Newman, credited for contributing to the company's explosive growth.[25] NORC, together with the producers of the musical *Hamilton*, even used predictive analytics based on survey questions and administrative ticket sales data to predict the likely successful durations of tours in specific cities.[26]

Predictive analytics is also a key element of AI-based chatbots. When you ask a chatbot a question, a model based on predictive analytics looks at the textual elements in your question and makes a prediction about what type of answer you may be looking for.[27]

Because the future is inherently uncertain, predictive analytics can't always give the right answer. A baseball player may get injured or lose focus; an aircraft engine might fail due to problems sensors can't identify; a chatbot might guess wrong about what information you were looking for. But predictive analytics increases the *effectiveness* of predictions. The basic premise is, based on all the data we've collected and all the outcomes we've tracked, this is what's most likely to happen. Collected over hundreds or thousands of baseball players, aircraft engines, or customer service requests, this can help define strategies that maximize the chances of success.

Common Principles Amid the Diversity of Data Types and Analysis

As you've seen from this broad survey of the universe of data and statistics, there is enormous variety in the ways that data can be generated and analyzed. Given the rapid growth of digital technology and tools, you can certainly expect that variety to increase.

Even when surrounded by all this variety, data-savvy individuals can still be smart about the actual meaning of those statistics. Start with the fundamental principle that no analysis is completely definitive and no answer completely precise. All data sources have limitations. All forms of analysis have uncertainty. There is always a level of confidence and a level of expected error associated with any statistical analysis.

Becoming comfortable with that fuzziness is a big part of what it means to be data savvy. You can still make decisions based on the numbers you read. You must just acknowledge the limitations of those numbers and avoid treating them as if they're just as precise as the balance in your bank account.

The rest of this book gets into a broader discussion of what it means to be data savvy and how we can create a data-savvy society. But this all starts with understanding the statistics you read and their limitations. For now, keep four principles in mind:

- **Consider the source.** Data and statistics circulate in an ecosystem of producers, disseminators, and consumers. To understand possible sources of bias, inaccuracy, and misinterpretation, try to identify the original sources of data, not just the most recent place you are reading or hearing about them. Chapter 2 described this.
- **Identify potential biases.** Bias emerges from both biased data sets and biased analysis techniques. For more detail on sources of bias, see Chapter 4. The dangers of data advocacy are covered in Chapter 6.
- **Value transparency.** Trustworthy analysis requires documenting the work in such a way that readers can verify both the source of the original data and the analysis techniques. You should also put more faith in analyses that use established and well-documented techniques and include measures of potential uncertainty, such as confidence intervals and margins of error. For more detail on the value of transparency, see Chapter 5.
- **Account for error.** The key question is, how large is that error likely to be, and are the conclusions being drawn still valid considering the size of the error? Is there any other potential explanation for the conclusion, such as random variation or unsuspected variables?

4

The Challenge of Data Integrity

A FAVORITE DEBATE among writers of all kinds is this: Should there be one space after a period, or two?

Writers who learned in the era of the typewriter had the two-space method drilled into them. Those who grew up with word processors generally embraced a single space. The battle between the two methods continued, bereft of actual data ... or at least it did, until *The Atlantic's* James Hamblin published an article in 2018 titled, "The Scientific Case for Two Spaces After a Period."[1] Thousands of writers and editors forwarded links to the article in emails and social media, with comments like, "See, I was right!" or, "Oh, no, the Philistines are taking over."

But was the evidence credible? As Hamblin wrote, quoting the researcher Rebecca L. Johnson who had conducted the original study:

> "Increased spacing has been shown to help facilitate processing in a number of other reading studies," Johnson explained to me by email, using two spaces after each period. "Removing the spaces between words altogether drastically hurts our ability to read fluently, and increasing the amount of space between words helps us process the text."

Whenever you read a purported fact like this based on a study, it pays to approach it skeptically. The first step is to review the actual study on which the conclusions are based. The *Atlantic* article links you to a research paper by Johnson, Becky Bui, and Lindsay L. Schmidt in the scientific journal *Attention, Perception, & Psychophysics*. The title of the research paper is "Are Two Spaces Better Than One? The Effect of Spacing Following Periods and Commas During Reading."[2] Already, there's a little cause for skepticism: The confident title of the *Atlantic* article has now been replaced with a question.

A quick perusal of the study reveals:

- The researchers conducted the study on 60 students at Skidmore College.
- All the study participants were native speakers of English with either normal vision or glasses to correct to normal vision.
- The study's authors divided the participants into two groups: 39 "one-spacers" who typically typed with a single space after a period, and 21 "two-spacers" who doubled their spaces.
- The experimental subjects were monitored with their heads fixed in an eye-tracking machine, looking at a screen as they read passages with either one or two spaces after each period.
- The test passages were displayed in a fixed-width font called "Courier New," similar to type from a typewriter, and very different from the typical variable-width type used in any book or online article. The passage shown also included four times the usual amount of space between successive lines of type.
- The study found no statistically significant differences in reading comprehension based on the number of post-period spaces.
- The number of spaces after a period also made no difference in reading speed for the subjects who normally type with one space. But among the "two-spacers," reading speed was 3% faster if the passage being read had two spaces after a period.

Now that you know the details, would you still say there is "a scientific case" for two spaces after a period? Or would you say our understanding of the purported benefits of two spaces is more limited?

Perhaps it would be more accurate to say, "Based on one study, there is a very slight but statistically significant increase in reading speed for passages with two spaces after a period, at least inasmuch as we can tell from experiments with 21 college students with normal vision who normally type with two spaces, monitored with their heads fixed in a machine, reading type shown in a font and format completely different from the type people normally read every day." Of course, that's not a very engaging headline for a news article.

Does this study apply to older people who use reading glasses? People for whom English is not their first language? People reading text on paper? People reading on a mobile phone? People who move their heads as they read?

There's no way to know. We are left to draw conclusions from a very small, homogeneous sample of 21 students in unnatural reading conditions. It's hard to generalize from that to all people reading in all situations.

Should you use two spaces after a period? Maybe. But I sure wouldn't use this study as proof that it's a better way to write.

Data Must Be Fit for Purpose

In everyday life, we know the value of using the right tool for the job at hand. If you try to loosen a hex nut with pliers, it might very well work, but it might also destroy the nut and mess up the whole project you're working on. Professionals would use a wrench – but even amateurs can appreciate when a wrench is the right tool and a set of pliers is not.

The same thinking applies to data and its analysis. Researchers, statisticians, and data scientists go about their work using tools that, as far as possible, are "fit for purpose." This means that the set of data they are collecting, the methods they are using to collect it, and the methods that they are using to analyze it are appropriate for the decisions the data are supposed to inform.

Among other qualities, data collections that are fit for purpose must be relevant to the decisions being made; the resulting analyses must use statistical methods appropriate for the particular type of data and generate a result precise enough to be actionable. For example, recalling the statistics and research methods described in Chapter 3, temperature averages are probably not the best way to understand extreme weather, and focus groups are not the best way to determine if a drug is safe and effective.

In the spaces-after-a-period study, there are serious problems with using the reported statistics to make any decisions about how text should be rendered. The research conditions aren't clearly relevant to the problems of general readers and the set of people studied can't fairly be generalized to the whole population of people who read.

As you might imagine, the whole question of "fitness for purpose" is a complex challenge that researchers and statistical professionals wrestle with all the time. And you might wonder if a lay person is able to apply it. But like the amateur mechanic who still knows not to use a pliers when a wrench is appropriate, you can still be a data-savvy consumer, applying a little analytical and skeptical thinking to the results you read about to see if, at least to a first approximation, they're fit for the purpose they're being applied to.

This is where you analyze the integrity of the data you're dealing with, whether as a producer, a consumer, or a disseminator of those data. That analysis breaks down into three basic questions about the methods used to select the sample and collect the data:

- **Are the data and analysis asking the right questions?** For example, in the study about two spaces after a period, the researchers used text in a fixed-width font with lots of room between lines and study participants with their heads fixed in place. This doesn't answer the question of how general readers read text in normal conditions.
- **Is the data set large enough to draw meaningful conclusions?** Results from a poll of voters in a state won't be credible unless there are enough people surveyed to make a reasonably precise estimate of the proportion voting for each candidate. Small samples come with large potential sampling errors and margins of error, making the results far less credible or useful. Similarly, it's hard to draw conclusions about readers from a sample of only 60 students – and harder still if the conclusion applies only to the 21 students who use two spaces after a period when they type.
- **Is the data set representative of the underlying population you are interested in?** Since it's usually not possible to find a data set that includes everyone in a population, most data sets consist of a smaller number of people – that is, a sample – and then

generalize from them to the full population. But since each observation in that sample may represent many hundreds or thousands of observations from the complete set, the sample needs to be representative of all the possible subgroups in the population – including people of all ages, genders, and attitudes, for example. Samples can also include biases – people who answer surveys may be more politically active than the general population, for example. Even very large data sets (including enormous data sets termed "big data") that seem, by their very size, to provide a solid foundation for basing conclusions under-sample key groups, introducing biases that skew the resulting conclusions. In fact, as discussed earlier, there is a tendency in the business world to assume that an enormous data set is inherently better than a smaller one. But if the enormous data set has under-representation of key subgroups, a carefully constructed, smaller sample might be more useful. In the reading study, there are multiple problems: We have the small sample size (60 students), and it's very unrepresentative – a group of college students with normal vision is not representative of the millions of people who read, many of whom may be older or less educated with poorer vision than the students.

The rest of this chapter explains these concepts in more detail so you can use them to be data savvy about the statistics you encounter.

Matching Research Questions and Methods

Why do researchers sometimes ask the wrong questions? It's not usually a case of lack of skill on the part of the researcher. Instead, it boils down to this: The answers we seek are often prohibitively expensive, or practically unmanageable to get with research.

Will a political candidate capture the public's imagination? You can ask people about what they know about the candidate, and about what they want in a candidate, but you can't predict what events might eventually develop – or scandals might be revealed – that could affect people's views.

Will a drug effectively treat a specific disease condition? While it's possible to test a drug under controlled conditions, in the real world it might turn out to have long-term effects or interactions with other drugs or conditions that are impossible to detect in a research study, or it simply may not be as effective as it was in controlled experimental conditions.

Nevertheless, despite these limitations, high-quality, effective research studies can offer us useful insights for key decisions we need to make, contributing to a fact-forward society. Let's look at some examples where researchers used effective – and ineffective – methods to support important decisions.

The Gillette company, for example, used an innovative research method – monitoring social media posts – to identify an unmet need in the market.[3] Every razor the company had ever produced and marketed was designed for people to shave themselves. But some comments on social media demonstrated a gap in the market: people who needed to shave others. Caregivers complained that existing razors were clumsy and inadequate for the job.

Gillette principal design engineer Matt Hodgson decided to check out the problem himself, attempting to shave a colleague in the office and finding it maddeningly difficult. He also visited a local nursing home to watch caregivers struggling to shave residents with existing razors – a classic example of ethnographic research, where researchers observe people in their natural settings. Caregivers typically shaved men who were sitting down or in bed, at angles that Gillette's razors weren't designed for, and without access to running water to rinse off the razor.

These insights led to the design of the Gillette TREO razor, a product designed for shaving others with a water-based gel in the handle. Distributing free samples to nursing homes enabled Gillette to test the design and verify its effectiveness. The TREO succeeded and is now available for sale in commercial outlets.

Gillette's research approach combined social media monitoring, ethnographic research, and user testing. These are appropriate tools for developing a new product for a new type of customer because you can't easily identify new markets by asking existing customers what they want.

In fact, asking existing customers what they want can often lead to expensive errors.

For example, in the mid-1980s, the Coca-Cola company, facing intense competition from Pepsi, considered changing its nearly century-old formula. Having conceived a sweeter product that seemed better suited to changing tastes, Coke embarked on a massive testing program.[4] Nearly 200,000 people were tested with small samples of the existing Coca-Cola, Pepsi, and a new, sweeter cola formulation. The majority preferred the new product. To avoid prejudices from brand preconceptions, these were blind tests: None of the test subjects knew which formula was which.

All this data gave the management at Coca-Cola the confidence to roll out a new formulation for Coca-Cola. CEO Roberto Goizueta told investors that the launch of New Coke was "the surest move ever made."[5] But in the end it was a multibillion-dollar failure. After fielding 8,000 calls a day from irate consumers, Coke pulled the new product from the market and retreated to the original "Coca-Cola Classic" formulation.

What went wrong? For one thing, Coke underestimated the sentimental attachment to the original brand and taste, a factor impossible to measure in a blind taste test. And for another, the much sweeter flavor of New Coke, while attractive a few sips at a time, became overpowering when consumed in larger quantities that are more typical of the average Coke drinker.[6] Coca-Cola's researchers asked a good question – "Which flavor do you like best?" – but were unable to ask the right question: "Would you be happy drinking glass after glass of this beverage everywhere that you drink Coca-Cola right now?" (This is of course a stylized version of the right question. It would take some careful thought and cognitive testing to figure out how to ask the question in a way that would produce meaningful, quantifiable research data.)

Another research failure changed the way America dieted for decades. By the 1950s, nutritional research had clearly established that weight loss and weight gain was a consequence of the net consumption of calories in the diet, minus energy burned by exercise and other activities. It made logical sense that fewer calories meant more weight loss.[7] Fatty foods, being calorie-rich, were bad. Clinical trials demonstrated that a low-fat diet led to weight loss, at least during the brief period during which dieters were monitored.[8] The diet industry jumped on board, and the food companies rolled out low-fat everything, from crackers to salad dressing. According to Harvard Medical School Professor David Ludwig, "Despite concerns for the lack of high-quality scientific evidence, the government and all the major professional nutrition associations had by the 1990s recommended that everyone beyond infancy eat a high-carbohydrate/low-fat diet. Americans were told to substitute all fats with a variety of carbohydrates, including six to 11 servings of grain products daily, as exemplified by the original Food Guide Pyramid."

Modern nutritional research has called these conclusions into question. Diets high in simple carbohydrates like sugar and white flour are associated with higher risk for diabetes and cardiovascular diseases.[9] Just as important, diets that work for days or weeks often don't work for months or years. Nearly everyone who restricts calories on a diet gains the weight back, plus more, in the long term.[10] To the extent that there is a solution for those hoping to lose weight without medication or surgery, it comes from paying attention to *satiety*: foods that are filling and signal to the body that it's time to stop eating. Among the most satisfying foods in this context are many of the very fats that were demonized by a previous generation of dietary experts.

If data can fool the CEO of Coca-Cola and generations of medical professionals, is it really possible for everyday individuals to be to be data savvy about the statistics they read and the conclusions they draw? Yes, it is. In all these cases, the decision-makers had blind spots about the limitations of the research they were interpreting. Coke's taste tests didn't answer the question, "What soft drink does America want?" They only answered the question, "Which drink do people think tastes better in small sips?" And the dietetic research answered the question, "Do calorie restrictions and less fat lead to people losing weight for a few months?" and not, "Is a low-fat diet a sustainable path to weight loss in the long term?"

If your job is to design research, make sure you understand which questions you're answering and which ones you're not. And data-savvy consumers should keep in mind the limitations of the research they're consuming. What meaning do the statistics you're reading have for your specific purpose, what might they be missing, and where are they potentially misleading? This fact-forward attitude is especially important for those who disseminate research, whether that's a journalist writing an article attempting to explain the significance of a study or statistic, or a consumer sharing information on a social media site or a text message.

To Trust Research, You Need an Adequate Sample Size

In everyday life, we are tempted to generalize based on our personal experiences. If you met a woman from Italy and she was an incredible cook, maybe you'd think "Ah, Italians are good cooks." But this is what is known as "anecdotal evidence," that is, an interesting story you heard that fits some hypothesis. Anecdotal evidence might just be a fluke – perhaps your Italian friend just happened to have a talent for flavor.

How many observations or bits of data are sufficient? Generally, more observations are better (for example, more people in a survey, or more subjects in a medical study). Some of the most valuable and predictive data sets contain millions of pieces of data. The Framingham Heart Study, for example, was a large-scale study intended to determine the effects of various behaviors on heart health. It began in 1948 with 5,209 participants. What makes this data set so vast and predictive is not just the number of participants, but the careful tracking of all their health and behaviors that took place over decades, including several subsequent generations ("cohorts") of participants. The study definitively showed that high blood pressure was associated with heart disease and stroke, and later revealed the association of blood cholesterol with heart disease.[11] These findings transformed health recommendations for millions of Americans.

Most researchers, of course, don't have the resources or budget to conduct a study over decades with many thousands of participants. So instead, they must make a trade-off between cost and predictive power. A poll of 100 people is obviously less dependable than a poll of 1,000. The statistical concept that quantifies this is the "margin of sampling error."

In the previous chapter, we described how the poll that reported that 44% of respondents felt a great deal or a lot of progress had been made in achieving equal access to a good education for African Americans had a margin of sampling error at the 95% confidence level of 3.7 percentage points. This number is derived from a statistical calculation based on the sample size of 1,289 adults.[12] Because the survey reached a smaller group of Black people, 301 respondents, the sampling error for statistics on the opinions of Black adults was about plus or minus 7.2 percentage points. (A well-reported poll like this will generally provide access to details on the methodology, including more detailed confidence measures for subgroup analysis.)

Small samples can be highly misleading. Take this hypothetical sports example. One team, the Albatrosses, has won exactly 50% of its games, but that includes a four-game winning streak leading up to today. Their opponent, the Bullfrogs, also has a 50-50 record, including a four-game losing streak before the upcoming game. What is the likelihood that the Albatrosses will beat the Bullfrogs today?

Some might guess that the recent streaks would continue: The Albatrosses would win, and the Bullfrogs would lose. Or you could take the opposite position, adopting the idea of "regression to the mean," that is, the Albatrosses would go back to losing and the Bullfrogs to winning. Both guesses are based on the last four games, a tiny sample, and as a result both are a poor way to make predictions. In fact, all other things being equal, if the records of the two teams are indicative of their level of skills, the best estimate is that each team would have a 50–50 chance of winning. (Obviously, you might change your estimate based on which players are playing or injured, which team is the home team, or other factors, but ignoring those factors, the previous winning percentages would still predict a 50% chance of either team winning.)

Depending on small samples can be risky. A study by the physician Andrew Wakefield, published in *The Lancet*, looked at 12 English children with autism or other developmental problems.[13] All the children developed autism within one month of receiving the measles, mumps, and rubella (MMR) vaccine. That seemed to suggest that the vaccine *caused* the autism, which created quite a stir.

But let's look closer at this small sample. At the time the paper was written in 1998, about 90% of the children in England received the MMR vaccine.[14] Because of the timing of typical autism diagnoses and childhood vaccinations, a child diagnosed with autism was highly likely to have had a recent MMR vaccination – just like all the other hundreds of thousands of nonautistic children of the same age. Subsequent studies by Brent Taylor and others in 1999 looked at a far larger sample, 498 children diagnosed with autism or a similar disorder, found that the proportion who had been vaccinated was the same as other children, that the diagnosis of autism happened at the same age in vaccinated and unvaccinated children, and that symptoms of autism weren't notably likely to develop after having a vaccination.[15] Another study looked at over 500,000 Danish children, 82% of which had received the MMR vaccine, and found no additional risk of autism in the vaccinated children as compared to unvaccinated children.[16] Obviously, the larger studies are far more dependable than a study of 12 children among millions of other vaccinated, non-autistic children.

The Lancet has since retracted Wakefield's study, and the United Kingdom has revoked his license to practice medicine. Even so, millions of people today fear the risks from childhood vaccines based on a movement that started with a study of only 12 children.

Before we leave the topic of sample size, let's dispel the idea that small samples are always bad, and large ones always good.

Researchers routinely conduct focus groups with only a dozen or so participants to get insights into emotions and reasoning of potential buyers or voters. Even with small samples, such exercises can often provide insights into how people think about the world, insights that would never be available from survey questions. Similarly, the designers of the TREO razor for Gillette identified a need from just a few social media comments. But researchers should never extrapolate the behavior of a few people to the general population. These small-sample activities can *suggest* a potential need in the populace, but responsible researchers then follow up with more extensive research with larger samples to find out if that need is common, or just a fluke.

As a data-savvy consumer of research or news articles, you should always be suspicious of reports of a few people doing something as the start of a trend. The same applies if a few of your friends start, say, using air fryers or voting libertarian. These sorts of reports are "anecdotal evidence," but hardly proof that some trend is sweeping the nation. There's always a chance of statistically significant effect even with a small sample – remember the chocolate-eating Nobel Prize winners in the previous chapter – but it's unwise to go making decisions based on those effects.[17]

Conversely, beware of reports of small differences in large samples. These differences may be real, but it is often the case that they are of limited practical value. As James G. Combs, a researcher on the topic of management studies wrote, "Increasing our ability to claim smaller effects as statistically significant does not, however, change their theoretical or managerial relevance."[18]

For example, let's say I have a very large data set with hundreds of thousands of observations of people's taste preferences, along with some of their physical characteristics. The data show that people with brown hair, on average, enjoy dessert more than people with blond hair. Now the first thing to say here is, so what? Do we really think there is something interesting about this finding? Most likely there isn't. Perhaps we might be interested if it were a really large difference, but we'd probably be at a loss to say why this difference exists and it's not clear what use we can make of the information. This goes back to the idea – discussed earlier in this chapter – of asking good questions. But now consider that with a very large sample, even small differences can be detected and considered to be "real." Imagine if the finding is that people with brown hair prefer dessert by one-tenth of a point on a five-point scale compared to people with blonde hair. The sample is large enough that we can assert that this difference is statistically significant. But at this point not only do we have a question that's not very useful (taste difference by hair color), but we have a difference that is so small that – from a practical standpoint – the difference is meaningless. And let's be clear, I'm not suggesting that small differences are always unimportant. For example, a tiny miscalibration in engineering (say in the tolerances of a piece of manufacturing equipment) can lead to unacceptable results (a bunch of ruined products). Therefore, as we assess the meaningfulness of a question, we have to consider context. In the case of taste differences by hair color, it's hard to imagine any basis for considering the small observed difference to be anything worthwhile.

In part because of the pressure to publish something statistically significant, these sorts of issues are far from rare in the scientific literature. For example, a widely cited five-year study of more than 22,000 people found that taking low-dose aspirin reduced the risk of myocardial infarction – that is, heart attacks.[19] In part because of the large sample, the effect was statistically significant – that is, unlikely to have occurred by chance. But the reduction in risk was less than 1%, and in subsequent studies, the effect was even smaller – and taking even baby aspirin increases the risk of bleeding. As a result, authorities now recommend against taking aspirin as a preventative for those who've never had a heart attack, even for people aged 60 and over, since the small, but real, positive effect isn't worth the additional risk.

Only a Representative, Unbiased Sample Can Support a Fair Statistical Analysis

As I've described, a sample allows you to draw conclusions about the world without testing every individual in it. For that method to be effective, each member of the sample must represent a member of the population. If the population is residents of Missouri, of which there are about 6 million, but you only have the resources to contact 600, then every person you contact represents 10,000 Missourians. That is only effective if the mix of people in the sample matches the mix of people in the state.

To ensure a representative sample, people who conduct surveys must match the characteristics of the sample to the population as a whole. According to the US Census, which is the best reference for comparison since it counts nearly everybody, 18% of the population of Missouri is over 65.[20] Slightly more than 50% are female. About 12% are Black or African American and 5% are Hispanic or Latino/Latina. Of those over 16, 63% are working. Half make $68,920 a year or more, and 12% live below the poverty line.

As you might imagine, it's challenging to get a sample of a few hundred or even a few thousand people to match those statistics exactly. To get around this, researchers use weighting. For example, if your survey reaches 5% fewer Black respondents than the proportion in the general population, you can weight the responses from those respondents 5% more heavily. But weighting can't make up for a highly nonrepresentative sample. If there are only 36 Black Missourians in your sample and a representative sample would include 72, you can count each Black person's responses double – but that's going to make the results less dependably representative, just as too small an overall sample might.

And it's not just demographics you need to balance. In December 2021, NORC, together with the Associated Press, conducted research into the voters who believe in "Replacement Theory," the idea that some interest groups are trying to replace native-born Americans with immigrants to achieve their electoral goals.[21]

What we found was instructive. Around one in three Americans – 32% – are concerned that, to make political gains, some interest groups are encouraging immigrants to be brought to the United States. This is a central tenet of Replacement Theory. Nearly a quarter – 24% – think immigrants come to the US to change the American way of life, and 22% feel these immigrants want to influence elections. And roughly four in five Americans believe immigrants come to the US to get access to government assistance.

As it turned out, while Republicans are more likely than Democrats to be concerned about immigration, it's actually a specific subgroup – those whose answers to questions indicate a propensity to engage in conspiratorial thinking – who are most anxious about the motives of immigrants. These conspiratorial thinkers are nearly three times as likely to believe that wars, recessions, and the outcome of elections are controlled by small groups working against the public's interest (see Figure 4-1). Conspiratorial thinkers – regardless of other factors, such as race – are more likely to think that they're getting discriminated against.

We learned that these conspiratorial thinkers are harder to recruit to participate in surveys. But to generate accurate data on immigration attitudes and policy in this country, we need to think about representation beyond just balancing on demographics, and we need to ensure that our samples are representative of people who hold these beliefs as well.

Representation is crucial in all data sets, not just data sets about people, and not just surveys. Here's an intriguing example. The city of Boston set out in 2012 to collect data on potholes. It encouraged drivers to use a mobile app called Street Bump that could identify irregularities in street surfaces: Smartphones could detect when a car was in

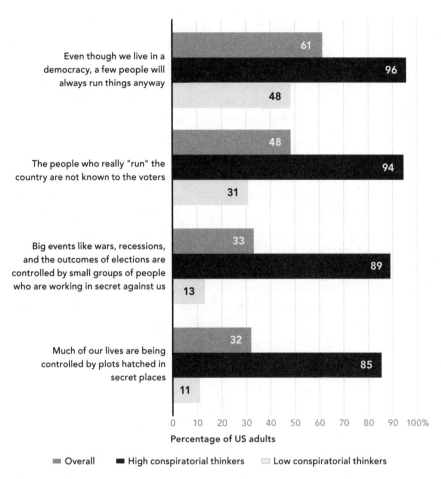

Figure 4-1: Conspiratorial thinkers are characterized by certain core beliefs. Survey question: "Do you agree or disagree with the following statements?" Chart shows: strongly/somewhat agree.

Source: "IMMIGRATION ATTITUDES AND CONSPIRATORIAL THINKERS: A Study Issued on the 10th Anniversary of The Associated Press-NORC Center for Public Affairs Research," May 2022 based on an AP-NORC survey of 4,173 US adults via AmeriSpeak TrueNorth, December 2021.

motion, when it moved irregularly because of potholes and other flaws in the road, and where such bumps were, based on the mobile phones' GPS capabilities.[22] The system detected 813 bumps, with about 60 readings per bump. Researchers were able to set the tolerances of the system such that 50% of the bumps detected were actionable (that is, the public works department would normally fix them), and only 20% were "false alarms."

But the system had a blind spot. At the time of its deployment, lower-income and older consumers were less likely to have smartphones. As a result, the system overreported potholes in affluent parts of the city where more smartphone owners were driving and underreported them in poor neighborhoods.[23] The huge collection of data collected by Street Bump may have been "big data," but it wasn't representative of all the potholes in Boston.

Failures of representation typically come down to leaving people out – just as Street Bump left out the potholes in poor neighborhoods. If you survey people and don't speak to Spanish speakers, the data won't be representative. If you look at a database of credit card charges that includes only American Express transactions, you'll be missing a huge segment of the population, because American Express only offers credit cards to those with very good credit ratings. Ask who is left out, and you'll be identifying where the data aren't representative.

Bias is the term we use to describe systematic differences between the data researchers collect and the actual state of the world. Bias shifts data and research in a specific direction away from the truth.

There are many potential sources of bias in data. Selection bias occurs when researchers choose a sample that's significantly different from the population – for example, if they sourced survey participants from zip codes with above-average incomes, their data would reflect that bias. Sampling bias occurs when your sampling method attracts a skewed clientele; a telephone survey of people that reached only people on landlines, for example, would generate an older-than-average sample.

An important source of bias in surveys is nonresponse bias – which simply means that people who answer surveys may be different in important ways from those who don't. It's a tough problem, because, of course, you can't survey people who don't take surveys and ask them what's different about them. But we do know when certain key groups are under-represented in the respondent pool, and sample weighting can be a partial solution in these cases.

Sometimes poorly designed studies have baked-in selection bias. A key trend in survey research is the increased use of opt-in surveys, which are part of a larger group of so-called "nonprobability" surveys. A lot of online surveys (particularly social media surveys) lack carefully specified sample designs that would make them representative of the underlying population. Rather, they are just samples of people who saw the survey online and opted to participate. These surveys can be quite useful for understanding that particular group of respondents, but they are often used carelessly based on researchers' claims that the results are representative of a more general population than the survey actually includes. Often the surveys are corrected using basic weights to reflect the proportions of various subgroups in the underlying population, but that doesn't address the non-representativeness (known as coverage bias) of the surveys.

One solution is to use probability surveys to calibrate non-probability surveys, so they are representative of the general population. This also can be very cost-effective since one of the main reasons non-probability samples are so popular is that they are inexpensive to conduct. The key point here is that non-probability samples can be quite useful if the data analysts understand their limitations and take the extra analytic steps required to make them interpretable. Unfortunately, too often, basic results from non-probability samples are presented as if they are equivalent to those from probability samples and are then disseminated widely, exacerbating the problem of unreliable and misleading statistics.

Bias in data can generate bad decisions, even when the decisions are based on very large samples. For instance, the Nurses' Health Study, which included 48,470 women who had gone through menopause, suggested that hormone replacement therapy could reduce the rate of serious coronary heart disease by half.[24] But the sample, which was made of nurses, had health habits that were better than average postmenopausal women. Additional research that corrected for the self-selection bias in the Nurses' Health Study cast serious doubt on the recommendation for hormone therapy.[25]

Biased data – and the algorithms based on them – can have serious real-world consequences. A study by UC Berkeley researcher Ziad Obermeyer and four others found that in one algorithm widely used in healthcare, Black patients and white patients were assigned the same level of risk, even though the Black patients tended to be sicker.[26]

As a result, the number of Black patients identified as appropriate for a higher level of care was half what it should have been. That matters because algorithms like the ones these researchers studied are used to make care decisions for 200 million patients.

The bias here arises because the algorithm uses healthcare spending data to predict healthcare use, but Black patients as a group have less access to care, so the healthcare system spends less money on them. As a result, using health spending as a proxy for the need for care perpetuates the problem, assigning a lower need for care to Black patients.

Think closely about this and you see that the challenge is not biased data, but biased *interpretation* of the data. This is typical of many algorithmic biases, in which seemingly balanced data analysis methods fuel skewed recommendations.

A similar challenge arose from a recruiting tool that Amazon used. Amazon's machine learning tool worked based off a data set of résumés of software developers it had hired in the past, and subsequently looked for and recommended candidates whose résumés had similar characteristics. Unfortunately, like the past hires, the newly recommended candidates were overwhelmingly men.[27] The algorithm reflected a pattern in which candidates whose résumés included the word "women" – as in "women's chess club captain" – weren't the type of candidates Amazon had hired in the past. Like most machine learning algorithms, which tend to be opaque, this one proved hard to unskew, and Amazon scrapped it. When the underlying data is biased, the machine learning based on it will almost certainly perpetuate that bias.

Ideally, where there is bias, researchers should attempt to compensate for it. That's what happened in the child protection agency in Allegheny County, Pennsylvania.[28] Researchers from Carnegie Mellon, USC, and the Auckland University of Technology examined the use of "predictive risk modeling," a common algorithm that social services workers use to screen calls to determine if a child is at risk. But, as the researchers described, this meant that some racial and ethnic groups and people with lower incomes were at a disadvantage simply because the government kept more data on them, thus boosting their risk scores in a biased way.

The Allegheny County workers attempted to correct for this by developing a call-screening tool that reflects the likelihood that the child will be removed from the home and placed in the social welfare system with two years, based on several factors in the call. This, combined with the call workers' judgment, enabled the creation of a system that was freer from bias than the original predictive risk modeling and more likely to refer children based on factors that would indicate actual dangerous home situations.

The Data-Savvy Consumer

The idea here is not to turn everyone into a data scientist, but to illuminate the limitations of the data you encounter.

Statistics carry the weight of credibility: We believe numbers. But the relationship between numbers and the truth often is not straightforward. When you read a statistic, you should consider whether the research that generated it was fit for the purpose of answering the questions that are important to you and other decision-makers. Are the questions that the research used the right questions to inform this decision? Was the sample large enough to generate credible results, or is it more anecdotal? Are there any groups left out of the data, causing those data to be unrepresentative or biased relative to the population in question? These questions pertain directly to the integrity of the data. All research has limitations; by asking these questions, you can be data savvy about what those limitations are. And that might help you to decide whether a study really should change how many spaces you should type after a period, whether you should reduce fat in your diet, or whether you should bet on the Albatrosses to beat the Bullfrogs in the game today.

To really understand these data integrity problems, of course, you need transparency into how the research was conducted. That's the topic of the next chapter.

5

Data and Algorithmic Transparency

CAN WE TRUST technology companies to be transparent in how they deal with our data? Big tech companies like Microsoft, Apple, Google, and Meta Platforms have all been criticized for lack of transparency. That lack of transparency caused huge and expensive problems. But there are signs that, at least in some ways, they've made improvements.

Consider, for example, the Facebook/Cambridge Analytica scandal that broke in 2018. There's plenty of evidence that poor judgment or ethical lapses at Facebook led to the abuse of data. But when you dig into what happened, you realize that this was fundamentally a violation of *trust* – and that the root of the problem was a lack of *transparency*.

Facebook's problem began in 2014 when Aleksandr Kogan, a data scientist at the University of Cambridge in the United Kingdom, developed an app called This Is Your Digital Life to collect data on Facebook users for the company Cambridge Analytica.[1] As is common in academic research, Kogan's contract with Cambridge Analytica specified that he would obtain informed consent from any Facebook members participating in the research. Several hundred thousand people participating in the study were told that their data would "only be used for research purposes" and would remain "anonymous and safe."[2]

But Cambridge Analytica violated Facebook's rules for academic research. Using the friend-to-friend networking links inherent in the social network, it expanded the data collection beyond the original sample of users who had consented to share their information to include private information and profiles of more than 50 million Facebook users, without those users' knowledge or consent.[3] It then sold its services to the political campaigns of Republican presidential candidates. Those services went far beyond research. They created digital profiles of Facebook users that enabled the campaigns to place personalized ads targeted to those users – for example, showing people in safe Republican states ads featuring triumphant scenes of the Republican candidate, while showing people in swing states ads to create fear of the Democratic candidate Hillary Clinton.[4]

When this information came to light in 2018, the backlash against Facebook was severe. In an AP-NORC poll, 42% of Facebook users said they were using social media platform less often.[5] Amid slowing growth, the market value of Facebook plummeted by $119 billion.[6] In full-page newspaper ads, Facebook CEO Mark Zuckerberg apologized, stating, "We have a responsibility to protect your information. If we can't, we don't deserve it."[7] Facebook's parent Meta Platforms eventually paid $725 million to settle a class-action lawsuit regarding its undisclosed data sharing with Cambridge Analytica.[8]

What did Meta do wrong here? Its willingness to work with academic researchers was not the problem. Neither was its openness to ad targeting, an activity that most Facebook users are quite familiar with. The violation was the abuse of the research and the breach of trust with those who took the original survey. The targeting of the friends and network connections of the original sample made that betrayal far worse.

The researchers had violated transparency – a core value of legitimate researchers, and a fundamental principle that enables the public to trust those researchers. Imagine if Cambridge Analytica and Aleksandr Kogan had honestly told the original survey-takers, "We're going to use your information and that of your friends, not just for academic purposes, but so that political campaigns can gain intelligence about all of you and target ads at you." Very few people (if anyone) would participate under those terms. Cambridge Analytica concealed their true intent to the research subjects, thereby gaining access to all this data under false pretenses. Facebook failed in its responsibility to ensure that companies accessing user data were operating with transparency.

How has Meta Platforms, which also owns Instagram, changed its approach? In 2020, researchers, including my organization NORC, worked with Meta on a series of research projects called the "2020 Facebook and Instagram Election Study (FIES)," revealing fascinating insights about how social media influences people's attitudes. For example, the study showed that among US participants, conservatives saw far more false news stories than liberals did – but that removing their exposure to content shared from other people's feeds had no significant impact on their political views.[9]

As described in the journal *Science*, "Meta collaborated with 17 outside scientists who were not paid by the company, were free to decide what analyses to run, and were given final say over the content of the research papers. But to protect the privacy of Facebook and Instagram users, the outside researchers were not allowed to handle the raw data."

By blocking researchers' access to the profiles, Meta made certain that it wasn't possible to exploit the academic access for commercial gain, as Cambridge Analytica had. And by allowing researchers to determine the experimental design, Meta insulated itself from charges that it was biasing the research by choosing topics.

The researchers themselves followed academic transparency rules. For example, in the study of liberals' and conservatives' exposure to news in line with their beliefs, the researchers described their analysis plan in detail and made their data set (stripped of all data that would identify individual users) publicly available so others could use it to verify or extend their analyses.[10]

Even so, other researchers have called for even more transparency. Social scientist Joe Bak-Coleman at the Columbia School of Journalism criticized the research because it relied "entirely on the company in question [Meta] to process the raw data into what is eventually analyzed." Researchers remain dependent on the companies for access and data to study the full effects of social media – a considerable concern at a time when many of these companies are rolling back transparency.[11]

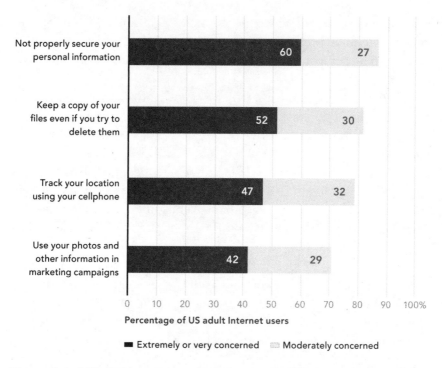

Figure 5-1: US adults are concerned about some data practices at online companies. Survey question: "Thinking about your data, such as email, photos, and other files that you put on the internet, how concerned are you that companies that provide these services would ..."

Source: AP-NORC survey of 1,047 adult internet users via AmeriSpeak panel, April 2018.

The cavalier way that Facebook treated its users' information in 2016 likely affected the public's perspective. An April 2018 poll by AP and NORC revealed that 60% of online consumers were extremely or very concerned that digital companies weren't properly securing their information (see Figure 5-1).[12]

In case you're wondering if other companies are still secretly collecting and sharing data, it happens all the time. As the *New York Times* discovered in 2024, your car's manufacturer may be tracking your vehicle and selling data about your driving practices to your car insurance company.[13] Senator Ed Markey has begun an investigation of whether this is an unfair and deceptive practice.

Why Transparency Matters

Transparency sounds simple. But as the story of what happened at Meta reveals, it isn't. Transparency is a core aspect of scientific integrity that makes research and researchers more trustworthy and their results more credible and verifiable, an essential element of a fact-forward society. However, it's not always clear what level of transparency is appropriate to both clarify research methods and protect research participants' privacy rights.

Data experts often refer to the "provenance" of a data set, which is a term that comes from the art world. For a painting to have value, we need to know how it was produced, who produced it, how they went about producing it, and when and where they produced it. An artwork's provenance includes the context it provides. If we know that Van Gogh painted his sunflowers in the south of France in 1888 or 1889, we can understand the milieu from which his work emerged and judge its authenticity. Being able to trace the painting's ownership back to the original purchaser also helps assure us that the painting is not a fake. Having experts certify that the painting is authentic also helps assure us of its value.

It is similar with data and research conclusions. Without provenance, their value to inform us is greatly diminished. With the context and insights that transparency provides on the provenance of the data, we can judge whether a data set or analysis is valuable to us.

Let's go back to first principles. Anyone consuming data and research *should* want to know where they came from and how they were produced. The emphasis on the word "should" is important: One of the main reasons why bad data and research are so easily created and shared is that people are not always data savvy enough to question the provenance of the data, and this needs to change if we are to become a fact-forward society. (I talk more about how this future can come to pass in Chapter 7, on fostering data literacy.)

If you know who funded the research, how it was conducted, and how the data were analyzed, this enables you to decide how to use the research results effectively (or whether to use them at all) to make informed decisions. But according to the NORC Data-Savvy Survey that was described in Chapter 2, while 70% of adults say that transparency of the research design has an impact on their trust in the research, only 54% say that knowing which organization conducted the research has an impact, and 44% say the same about the organization that funded it (see Figure 5-2).

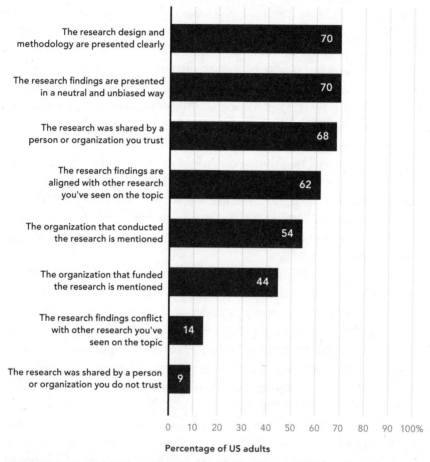

Figure 5-2: Many factors influence people's trust in research. Survey question: "Think about times when you read, watch, or hear about a research study on a topic of interest. How much does each of the following factors impact your trust in the research?" Chart shows: Increases your trust a lot/a little.

Source: NORC Data-Savvy Survey of 1,071 US adults via AmeriSpeak panel, June 2024.

Researchers are more fastidious. They know that transparency confers benefits on data producers, allowing colleagues – regardless of whether they accept or disagree with the conclusions of the original researcher – to examine the data, perform their own independent analyses, and attempt to duplicate or disprove the conclusions. Transparency also allows data consumers to understand the limitations of the research conclusions. For example, if I told you that a poll of 1,000 people, conducted by randomly calling landline telephones, found that 60% were voting for candidate X, you would be wise to question whether the sample was sufficiently representative of likely voters. Why? Because we know that people who use landlines these days are increasingly rare and are more likely to be elderly and to be white than the general US population. A poll that recruited 1,000 people with Internet ads might have different biases, since it will include people who opted in and are likely to be younger and more active online. Then there's the question of the purpose of the poll and who conducted it. It makes sense to consider an election survey conducted by independent researchers in a different light than a poll conducted by an organization aligned with one of the political parties. Without transparency on who conducted the research and why and how they conducted it, it is hard to know how reliable and trustworthy the information is.

Increasingly, researchers and research associations are requiring one another use transparency best practices in their work and establishing standard approaches for doing so, as described later in this chapter. But for us to have a fact-forward world, we need data-savvy data consumers and data disseminators who similarly demand transparency from data producers and practice data transparency as they use and share data.

Let's expand on this thinking a bit. Transparency needs to become standard practice for members of the media. A responsible journalist writing about research, polls, or other data will describe limitations of the research based on transparent statements about how it was conducted. Journalists may point out flaws in research, including biased funding sources. A statistic cited along with its provenance is far more informative than the same statistic stripped of context. And a social media influencer who shares a data journalist's work should not carelessly (or purposefully) strip out information about transparency when sharing the journalist's work. Finally, the people reading the article, whether in the original media source or on social media, should expect and demand transparency and use it when evaluating the quality and usefulness of the article.

Transparency in Research Studies and the Reproducibility Crisis

If one researcher finds a result, it's interesting. If a bunch of others conducting similar research can confirm the result, it's far more believable. This is "reproducibility," a central element of the scientific process. But research results can be reproduced only if the original researchers make their methods and analyses available to others. This is a key reason why transparency is essential in all sciences, including physical sciences, life sciences, and social sciences.

The transparency principles for science are explicit. For example, the guidelines of the Center for Open Science specify that data, analytical methods, and research materials should be posted to a trusted repository.[14] Journals are supposed to allow access to the study methods while the science is going on, including access to planned analysis. Journals also provide guidelines for how to cite research and encourage the submission of replication studies, in which other researchers attempt the same experiments to see if the results are comparable.

Reproducibility is a particular problem in the social sciences, where many experiments have generated results that could not be confirmed. As a result, Brian Nosek, a psychology professor at the University of Virginia, began the Many Labs project in 2012, an attempt to reproduce results from common experiments. As Nosek explained, "Replication is a core concept of science, and yet it's not very often practiced."[15] Many Labs, now known as the Reproducibility Project, has branched out to include cancer research as well.[16] Due to lack of transparency in the original research designs, 67% of the experiments could not be replicated without some modifications. These efforts have strengthened the call for transparency in published research, to ensure results used to design medical therapies for cancer patients could be confirmed.

Transparency enables researchers to effectively vet each other's work. For example, the prominent behavioral economist Dan Ariely and coauthors published research showing that subjects who signed an honesty pledge before filling out a survey for an insurance company gave more honest answers than those who signed at the end, after answering all the questions.[17] However, other researchers pored over the data and found patterns indicating a high likelihood that the data had been faked.[18] Ariely claimed that the data came directly from the insurance company that conducted the experiment for him. Given the problems, the journal that had published the research retracted it. Only the transparency of publicly available data made it possible to challenge Ariely's misleading results.

Contrast this to what happened with South Korean researcher Woo Suk Hwang's research on embryonic stem cells and human cloning, originally published in the journal *Science* in 2004. An investigation that took years was required to establish that much of the data was fabricated, after which the paper was retracted.[19]

While data fabrication is rare, it happens often enough that there's a whole website dedicated to journals retracting fraudulent or questionable results.[20] Five researchers accused of serial fraud have more than 100 retractions listed. Without transparency in science, there would be no way to identify and remove these erroneously published results.

Transparency Is a Continuum

Transparency isn't just a yes-or-no proposition. It's a continuum.

The most transparent researchers are basically conducting their research in public. They not only describe all their methods for data collection and analysis, they make their data sets available (while protecting research participants' identity), reveal who funded their research, describe its limitations, and reveal any conflicts of interest or apparent conflicts of interest that might influence their approach to the work. A completely transparent researcher is basically saying, "Hey, I have nothing to hide."

Some other researchers might still describe their methods clearly but decline to share their data and algorithms. Because they don't have the resources to publicize their data and methods, or because some may be proprietary, they cannot be fully transparent.

At the lower end of the scale, researchers might provide a sentence or a bullet point or two on their methods, without providing details.

Worse still might be a research study in which the researchers purposefully say very little, and cherry-pick what they do say about their methods in order to obfuscate significant limitations of the study.

And perhaps the worst case is when researchers know that the study is highly flawed but provide no insights on their methods or limitations. Related and often accompanying this behavior is storytelling by the "researcher" that is stating "facts" that are unsupported by the study, or conclusions that the study may actually show, but only because it was designed – from the start, and in a fully biased way – to show a particular set of results. The lack of transparency allows the researcher to get away with this, because the data consumer has no ability to suss it out. This might happen when either the people doing the study have a personal interest in telling that story (say, to make a name for themselves) or they work for an organization that has a vested interest in a certain set of results. Regardless of the reason, this behavior undermines trust and confidence in all types of research.

As you read the examples that follow, ask yourself these questions:

- Did the researchers carefully follow general principles of transparency?
- Were they attempting to be as clear as they could?
- Are there fundamental aspects of the data's provenance that are incomplete or missing?
- Did they discuss the study's limitations?
- Did they discuss their potential conflicts of interest?
- Did they conceal key elements of what they did, or otherwise try to intentionally mislead their audience?
- Did they provide references to other studies finding similar results (to address the replicability question)?

I'll describe how to apply these principles in several different domains: public data, public opinion polls, company financial reports, and algorithms. Of course, this doesn't cover every type of research, but these examples are sufficiently broad that you should be able to generalize from them to most research studies you may be trying to evaluate.

Transparency in Public Data

Government agencies and other public entities are continually releasing data about key aspects of our society. We all depend on those data, whether it's measures of air and water quality, on-time statistics about flights, measures of inflation, crime rates, or anything else. But for us to trust those data, we need to know how they're computed.

The US government is very transparent when it comes to statistics that it reports. It has to be, since everyone from the Federal Reserve and members of Congress to big companies and voters make decisions based on those reports.

Let's look at crime, for example. A 2023 Gallup poll found that 77% of Americans believe crime rates are worsening.[21] But the FBI's Uniform Crime Reporting (UCR) system's annual report about crime in 2022, released in October 2023, found that violent crime had declined slightly from 2021, by 1.7%, with murder dropping by 6.1%.[22] Can we trust the FBI reporting?

The FBI's transparent methodology reveals key details. Across the US, there are 18,884 eligible law enforcement agencies. The violent crime rate comes from the FBI's accumulation of data from 15,724 law enforcement agencies whose jurisdictions cover 93.5% of the US population.[23]

A second measure of crime comes from the US Department of Justice (DOJ), which conducts a survey of a large, nationally representative sample of more than 200,000 people aged 12 and older.[24] This survey, the National Crime Victimization Survey (NCVS), estimates that 23.5 people per thousand were victims of violent crime in 2022, an increase from the previous year (16.5 per 1,000), and similar to rates from before the pandemic. To be clear, over the past 30 years, according to this survey, violent crime has fallen by more than two-thirds.[25]

Transparency allows readers and journalists to assess these two seemingly contradictory results (see Figure 5-3), each of which has strengths and weaknesses. The FBI reports track only reported crime,

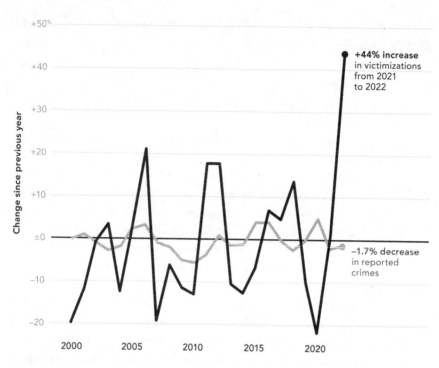

Figure 5-3: Estimates from the Department of Justice National Crime Victimization Survey are more volatile year over year compared to FBI Uniform Crime Reporting Program statistics.

Source: Adapted from Li, W. & Lartey, J, June 27, 2024, "Crime Rates and the 2024 Election: What You Need to Know," The Marshall Project; data from Uniform Crime Reporting program and National Crime Victimization Survey.

and only with the law enforcement agencies that participate; they cannot track unreported crimes. On the other hand, the DOJ survey is subject to potential biases due to sampling error, or to subjects reporting victimization that doesn't match exact legal definitions of violent crimes. Estimates from the survey tend to be more volatile year-over-year compared to the agency reported statistics from the FBI. Furthermore, the NCVS can't measure murder, because people who are killed aren't able to complete a survey. Indeed, the DOJ survey asks victims whether they reported the violent crime they experienced and the data reveal that in 2022, less than half (42%), of violent victimizations were reported to police. And while the survey still shows an increase in violent crime, when you restrict the analysis only to those crimes reported to police, the survey data and FBI are more closely aligned.[26,27]

Knowledgeable experts are quick to point out the advantages of having two different approaches to measuring crime and the deeper insights we get as a result. One such expert, Jeff Asher, who runs a data analytics website focused on crime statistics, notes, "NCVS and UCR disagree from time to time about crime's direction even though the two measures have been in strong agreement over the long term. This is to be expected given the methodological differences in how each metric works and the inherent challenges in tracking crime trends. Crime data is hard and can sometimes tell complicated stories which only serves to highlight the need to always caveat appropriately ... ."[28]

Often politicians, advocacy organizations, or companies that are trying to influence audiences will attempt to selectively highlight statistics to support their point of view. For example, politicians who believe (or can benefit from) the idea that crime is getting worse are more likely to cite statistics that show crime going up, while politicians who believe (or can benefit from) the idea that crime is declining will publicize parts of these reports showing crime going down. But because of the transparency of the government reporting, reporters and citizens can dig more deeply into the data and draw their own conclusions.

There's good evidence that when public information is available, people act on it. You may have experienced this, for example, if you chose airline flights based on on-time statistics that are posted on the websites of airlines and travel providers like Expedia. Researchers Weija (Daisy) Dai and Michael Luca tested the value of transparency by working with the online site Yelp to post restaurant hygiene scores from the San Francisco Department of Public Health.[29] After Yelp included the scores in its pages on restaurants, those with poor scores saw a 12% decrease in purchase intentions.[30] Restaurants with poor scores publicized on Yelp were less likely to get a second poor rating, which is evidence that the poor scores caused the restaurants to take action.

Regrettably, a lack of transparency from government sources can have serious consequences. Consider what happened with the water supply in Flint, Michigan. After a change in the source of the city's water, residents including LeeAnn Walters noticed that the water in their taps had turned orange and that children in their households began to suffer serious health problems and developmental delays.[31,32] When Walters tested her tap water, the results showed concentrations of toxic lead between 104 and 397 parts per billion (ppb), at least six times the EPA's allowable concentration of 15 ppb. After she reported the problems to the EPA, a manager there raised alarms that Flint's water supply could include dangerous levels of lead.[33] When Walters and an environmental engineer from Virginia Tech distributed test kits to concerned citizens, 17% of 271 kits showed unsafe lead levels.[34]

Even so, the Michigan Department of Environmental Quality (MDEQ) maintained that, based on its own testing over the whole of the Flint water system, there was no systemic problem. How could the MDEQ have come to such a different conclusion? Only concerted digging into the city's data collection methods explained the difference. The city's MDEQ-advised testing told households to flush the cold water for five minutes before collecting the sample, and the sample bottles had such small openings that they could be filled only with faucets open to a narrow trickle.[35] While these procedures were allowed by federal law, they also significantly reduced the chances of detecting dangerous lead levels.[36] MDEQ's testing procedures had missed a dangerous – and expensive to fix – problem with the public water supply.

The task force commissioned by Michigan Governor Rick Snyder stated that "MDEQ misinterpreted [the federal clean water regulation] and misapplied its requirements . . . As a result, lead-in-water levels were under-reported and many residents' exposure to high lead levels was prolonged for months."[37] Until the MDEQ's testing procedures were transparently revealed, there was no way to explain why it had missed dangerous levels of toxins in the city's drinking water.

Public Opinion Researchers Must Clarify Their Data's Limitations

Responsible pollsters and survey researchers who are members of the American Association for Public Opinion Research (AAPOR) are embracing its set of transparency principles.[38,39] When they sign on to the organization's Transparency Initiative, they are required to disclose who sponsored the research, who conducted it, how the data were collected, what measurement tools they used (such as the text of survey questions), what population they were studying, and how they generated and recruited the sample they used. They also disclose when they collected the data, the size of their sample, whether data were weighted to better match the population, and how they processed the data.

A key element of transparency programs is not just disclosing how survey researchers collected and analyzed the data, but exposing the limitations of the conclusions. For example, an election poll of people in Iowa, conducted online, should make it clear that some error could be introduced by sample bias from people who don't have Internet access.

These limitations can be exploited by political campaigns and then exacerbated by hyped media coverage. For example, suppose that two candidates, call them Able and Baker, are running against each other for a seat in the Senate. Of 10 polls, nine show Able with a lead of five to 10 percentage points. The tenth poll shows Able leading Baker by only one percentage point. If Able's actual lead over Baker is, say, eight percentage points, it's certainly possible just by sampling error that one of the polls would underestimate that lead.

But in campaign ads, both Able and Baker are likely to highlight the closer poll, not the ones showing a large lead. And media organizations may be more likely to present the results showing a close race because it's more exciting. Voters hearing about such a tight race may be more likely to contribute to their preferred candidate ("Able needs your help!" or "You can push Baker over the top!") and to vote on Election Day to turn the tide.

Even if the pollsters transparently reveal the limits of their surveys, candidate advertising is unlikely to point voters to a balanced collection of all the state polls. This is why a data-savvy consumer of election poll data will, before drawing any important conclusions, look to unbiased sources of reporting (not the campaigns), including transparent and fact-forward disseminators who present careful analysis across multiple polls and provide full details on study methodology and limitations.

Transparency in Financial Data of Publicly Traded Companies

Companies whose shares are publicly listed on stock markets must report their financial results quarterly, including revenues, expenses, growth, assets, and liabilities. These reports are regulated by the Financial Accounting Standards Board's Generally Accepted Accounting Principles (GAAP), a set of accounting rules that specify, for example, what sorts of receipts can and can't be reported as revenue.[40] Auditing firms like Deloitte, PwC, EY, and KPMG verify companies' compliance with GAAP. The auditing firm's job is to check the numbers reported and verify for investors that they are accurate.

Some company executives have attempted to boost their stock prices – and their own compensation – by distorting financial data about their companies. For example, a company that misclassifies revenue or hides costs can make itself appear more profitable, especially if auditors are lax in enforcing accounting rules. Such lack of transparency about true revenues and expenses can mislead investors and, when eventually revealed, cause precipitous drops in stock prices that cost investors millions.

You may have heard of notable examples like Tyco and Enron. At the industrial conglomerate Tyco, the CEO Dennis Kozlowski and CFO Mark Swartz were found guilty of 22 counts of grand larceny, conspiracy, falsifying business records, and violating business law, including concealing more than half a billion dollars of self-dealing fraud.[41] Tyco paid $2.92 billion to shareholders duped by its lack of transparency, and its auditor, PwC, paid $225 million in damages.[42] The energy and financial company Enron fooled investors and regulators by concealing billions of dollars in fake holdings, off-the-books loans, and concealed losses.[43] When its opaque dealings caught up with it in 2001, Enron reported a $618 million loss, wrote off $1.2 billion in asset values, and declared bankruptcy. The huge and historically respected accounting firm Arthur Andersen, Enron's auditor, was convicted of obstruction of justice for destroying evidence in 2002 and disbanded shortly thereafter. In the wake of the scandal, Congress passed the Sarbanes-Oxley Act in 2002, requiring new levels of transparency in corporate financial documents.[44]

The Challenge of Algorithmic Transparency

Transparency in reporting is at least theoretically possible in research, government statistics, and finance. But now that complex algorithms and AI are processing data and generating results in all sorts of fields, there's another imperative: algorithmic transparency. Algorithmic transparency is the principle that even complex algorithms should behave in documented and explainable ways, and that in particular they should not operate in a way that creates harm or deception.

Algorithms can certainly be designed to deceive. Perhaps the most notable example of this was the algorithm built into the engines of Volkswagen diesel vehicles in 2014, a year in which Volkswagen controlled 70% of the US market for diesel passenger cars. Like all auto manufacturers, Volkswagen was required to comply with emission tests limiting the amount of nitrogen oxide pollutants present in the vehicle's exhaust.[45] But limiting exhaust fumes could also have the effect of reducing performance. So Volkswagen engineers included engine control algorithms in more than 10 million cars that could detect when vehicles were being tested for emissions and change the engine's characteristics to simulate compliance with emissions rules. These deceptive algorithms were embedded in more than 100 million lines of computer code controlling the engine. In a 2016 settlement, Volkswagen settled the charges by agreeing to a $10 billion buyback program and compensated owners with checks of more than $5,000, reflecting the diminished resale values of the cars. Volkswagen's CEO Martin Winterkorn resigned as a result of the deception.

Algorithmic bias can also appear in marketing practices. Researchers have shown that across major digital search engines, the algorithms that deliver personalized online advertisements to people browsing the Internet target ads with negative personality characteristics toward women (i.e., advertisements geared toward impulsive investors are disproportionately shown to women while advertisements geared toward disciplined investors are shown more often to men).[46] According to a study by Latanya Sweeney, Harvard researcher and former CTO of the Federal Trade Commission, online searches for African American names were more likely to show ads for services that track down arrest records.[47]

And this kind of algorithmic bias has morphed into outright discrimination in the form of "weblining." Weblining – a digital form of redlining – involves using online data and algorithms to treat certain groups of people differently. For instance, a bank or lender might offer less favorable rates or deny services entirely based on a person's social media activity or online shopping habits rather than their financial history. Algorithmic transparency would eliminate weblining and help sellers, researchers, regulators, and consumers ensure that markets are open and fair to everyone.

Of course, pursuing and achieving algorithmic transparency presents several thorny challenges. Commercial algorithms are a form of intellectual property, and revealing too much about them can compromise the owner's competitive advantage. Most consumers have little patience of comprehension for discussions of source codes. And as the technology becomes increasingly complex, especially with machine learning algorithms, not even the developers are entirely sure how they work. Even if you could fully explain an algorithm, you may empower bad actors to game it.

One way around these challenges is by implementing "explainable AI" (xAI) systems that analyze the inputs and impacts of decision-making algorithms and provide clear explanations of the most significant factors influencing outcomes.[48] This technique allows for transparency without revealing proprietary source code or raw data. For instance, a bank that uses an algorithm for loan approvals might tell an applicant that their interest rate was based 40% on their credit score, 30% on their debt-to-income ratio, 20% on their employment history, and 10% on other factors. (I discuss AI in greater depth in Chapter 10.)

Research suggests offering users a "medium" level of transparency builds trust more effectively than either low or extremely high technical transparency.[49] This involves providing basic insights into how algorithms work without overwhelming users with technical details. In practice, this might look like a social media app providing users with a simplified explanation and possibly some control of how their feed is curated: "Your feed is personalized based mainly on: (1) accounts you interact with most, (2) topics you engage with frequently, (3) posts similar to ones you've liked recently. You can adjust these factors in your settings."

One real-world example of this type of algorithmic transparency is FICO's credit score interface myFICO, which shows the various factors that cause a person's credit score to go up or down, along with a qualitative sense of their relative importance in the algorithm (how much more it affects your score if you open a new credit card account compared to if you are late with a mortgage payment). Similarly, Facebook and Google have features that tell people why they are seeing certain content, including ads. While these are noteworthy examples, there is also concern that even the approach to transparency (and the degree to which it is provided) can be manipulative.[50]

A related approach would be offering a tiered system of transparency, where regulators and auditors have access to higher levels of technical information to ensure fairness and compliance, while end users receive more digestible explanations of algorithmic decision-making processes that still protect a business's intellectual property and guard against gaming.[51] For instance, an autonomous vehicle company could offer users a clear, non-technical explanation of how the car makes decisions, focusing on key safety features while giving regulators detailed technical documentation, including source code and training data, to verify safety standards and algorithmic fairness.

You can see how all three of these approaches would bring organizations more in line with regulations like the EU's General Data Protection Regulation (GDPR), which mandates users' rights to explanations of some algorithmic decisions,[52] while also addressing the technical challenges of transparency in modern AI systems. Already, the UK's Information Commissioner's Office has released guidelines on how companies using AI systems should explain the way their systems make decisions about individuals, as has the OECD's Observatory of Public Sector Innovation.[53,54] A balanced strategy acknowledges the complexity of modern AI while still prioritizing fairness and accountability in algorithmic decision-making, thus helping organizations build trust in their AI systems, identify and address potential biases, and provide meaningful transparency without compromising the effectiveness or proprietary nature of their algorithms.

Transparency Is Central to the Data Ecosystem

Without transparency, there can be no trust in the data ecosystem. And without trust, the data ecosystem ultimately collapses.

Transparently conducted research will always report how the subjects were recruited (or more generally, how the data were captured) and how the data were analyzed, as well as the limits of the conclusions. Trustworthy researchers will also report who funded and conducted the research, to make data consumers more aware of potential sources of bias. Researchers who follow these principles become part of the community of research producers and can expect others to build on their findings.

Producers of data and statistics have a responsibility to explain in as much detail as possible where their numbers come from, ideally sharing both the raw, de-identified data and the statistical techniques so others can vet them.

Disseminators of data, including media companies, must maintain a skeptical attitude. They should never quote a statistic lacking its accompanying provenance.

To be data-savvy consumers, we must be disciplined in examining how the data we consume were generated, by whom, and with what intent. While we may not spend our own time generating statistical analyses, we can certainly see if data producers have shared information on the data's provenance and how they reached their conclusions, and with a little experience, use that information to determine whether a set of results are useful to us. Transparently shared methods and data make it far more likely that others will be able to challenge – or confirm – results. And that should be a requirement for any data we plan to use to make important decisions.

6

The Paradox of Data Neutrality

IN A TELEVISED address on March 19, 2003, President George W. Bush explained why he wanted to invade Iraq. Iraqi leader Saddam Hussein had stockpiled weapons of mass destruction that would threaten the Persian Gulf and the peace of the world. "The people of the United States and our friends and allies," he explained solemnly, "will not live at the mercy of an outlaw regime that threatens the peace with weapons of mass murder."[1]

But the entire war was justified based on a tragic miscalculation drawn from of highly questionable evidence, assembled with a bias toward one point of view. Everyone making decisions, from President Bush on down through his cabinet, military leaders, and the leaders of his intelligence agencies, pursued one ultimately inaccurate conclusion. Starting the Gulf War was a very expensive decision; the direct and indirect costs could approach $2.2 trillion.[2] The war also cost the lives of 4,488 US service members and more than 180,000 others, including 134,000 civilians.

How did this happen?

After the terrorist attacks of September 11, 2001, the Bush administration dedicated itself to the "war on terror," attempting to find and punish those responsible. As Bush later wrote, "My blood was boiling. We were going to find out who did this, and kick their ass."[3] Bush,

Vice President Dick Cheney, and others in his administration became convinced that Saddam Hussein was involved; as a result, shortly after 9/11, Bush told other world leaders that he would soon "hit" Iraq.[4]

Starting with this firmly held conviction, the Bush administration leaders charged the vast American intelligence apparatus to find evidence of Iraq's weapons of mass destruction. Leaders didn't tell intelligence officers what conclusion to reach, but they did relentlessly ask the same questions – one CIA staffer told Congress that the "hammering" by senior Bush administration officials exceeded anything in his 32-year experience.[5] Sure enough, as anyone under such intense pressure would, intelligence analysts attempted to find what their leaders were asking for.

Their evidence included testimony of an Iraqi defector about biological weapons, evidence that Iraq was procuring thousands of aluminum tubes appropriate for use in making nuclear weapons, and documents suggesting that Iraq was procuring uranium ore. All later turned out to be subject to more benign interpretations or outright forged.[6]

Pressure from the top determined which point of view would prevail. Countervailing evidence was argued away as intentional deception.[7] Despite what a later investigation described as the "gossamer nature" of the intelligence, Bush's team ignored the doubts and used the questionable evidence to justify an invasion.

The administration's top weapons inspector later testified that "we were almost all wrong" in believing that Iraq had weapons of mass destruction.[8] George W. Bush and all of his top officials had known in their gut that Hussein was a threat to the world. Unfortunately, gut feelings like that can lead anyone astray, even the president of the United States.

Maintaining Neutrality Is Difficult, but Essential for a Fact-Forward World

While the disastrously failed assessments that led to the Iraq War are likely among the costliest misinterpretations of data ever, regrettably, dangerous mistakes in the world of data are not unusual. But data-savvy researchers, disseminators, and consumers must resist them. The cause of these errors is researchers and those interpreting their research who fall victim to what I call "the paradox of data neutrality." The paradox results from the two contradictory qualities that make excellent research possible:

- Dedicated researchers often start from a belief, based on past experience, that a given hypothesis is true.
- Neutral researchers must give at least equal weight to evidence proving their hypothesis is false.

Remember, researchers are human beings. Research is hard and expensive work. Unless a researcher is setting out to find a fascinating result, why even make the effort? And yet, if you start with a fixed conclusion in mind, you've lost your objectivity, and you may miss crucial evidence that would *disprove* your original theory.

That is exactly what happened in the search for weapons of mass destruction in Iraq. The belief that Saddam Hussein was a threat led the administration to seek evidence that confirmed their belief and ignore evidence that contradicted it. Even if the CIA and other intelligence agencies were diligent in collecting evidence on both sides of the issue, the higher up the chain of command they got, the more they were continually exposed to officials' desire for one-sided evidence against Iraq. The administration cherry-picked the bits of data that supported their desire, tossing neutrality out the window.

People generally believe they are sensitive to bias. In the NORC Data-Savvy Survey conducted in 2024, 70% of respondents agreed that research findings presented in a neutral and unbiased way had an impact on how much they trusted the research.

Even if people believe this, one of the human qualities that leads us to seek and interpret evidence in a way that supports our own existing beliefs is *confirmation bias*. It applies whether we are ordinary people reading numbers in the news or the president of the United States making a decision about war. It's a powerful human prejudice, because it eases our daily lives – no one wants to reverse a belief and cast doubt on all the decisions they've made based on that belief. But while confirmation bias may make psychological sense in our brains, it has harmful effects that undermine objectivity, distort data, and lead to flawed (and sometimes disastrous) decisions. Confirmation bias that distorts accurate and neutral perceptions of truth is a constant danger for decision-makers in politics, in science, in business, and everywhere people use data to make decisions.

A personal anecdote might be revealing here. I recently had an early morning meeting at which my attendance was essential. I awoke that morning, looked at my clock, and was startled to see that I had overslept and missed the start of the meeting. My wife and I had agreed that she, being an early riser, was going to wake me up; she didn't. I noticed that it seemed much darker than I expected it to be at that time of morning, and I was surprised that my dog wasn't bugging me to get fed. As I put on my watch, I was annoyed to see that it either had stopped or was running an hour behind. I said to myself, "Wow, it's going to be one of those mornings, isn't it?" I walked into the kitchen, mightily annoyed, and said to my wife (in a tone of voice that is generally not advisable to use with your spouse), "Why didn't you wake me up?"

"Because it's 6:15," she said. I looked at the time on my mobile phone and saw that she was indeed correct.

Apparently, I'd hit the wrong button on the clock the previous night and had inadvertently set it an hour ahead.

But at the moment when I woke up, after one glance at the clock, I had been certain I was late. I ignored the fact that my wife wouldn't forget to wake me up. I ignored the darkness outside. I ignored that the dog didn't bug me for food. I concluded that my watch had stopped, when it hadn't. Basically, I put the "evidence" from the clock on my nightstand above all of the other evidence, which I systematically ignored – until it became obvious that I was wrong.

You may think I was just being stupid (I will confess to being sleepy), but the fact remains that confirmation bias is a powerful force that often blinds each of us to the need to be balanced and weigh evidence in a neutral way. And the powerful lure of confirmation bias means that everyone in the data ecosystem – those producing research, those disseminating it, and those consuming it – must be wary of seeking out only the data that confirm our beliefs. This leads to what I call the fundamental principle of data neutrality:

> *Each of us must be equally diligent in seeking out data that contradicts our beliefs as we are in seeking out data that conforms to them.*

Types of Data Advocacy

The opposite of data neutrality is data advocacy. Data advocacy means conducting research in a way that is designed, from the outset, to confirm or support a belief. But not all forms of data advocacy are the same. Some are intentional, others are not. Even when data are collected in a neutral way, decision-makers can be biased in which data they decide to consider (cherry-picking) and in how they interpret the data (motivated reasoning). And the very structure of how research works lends itself to a bias toward finding and publishing interesting results (p-hacking). Let's explore these dimensions of data advocacy in more detail. (To be clear, the descriptions that follow are not mutually exclusive; many instances of data advocacy fit into several of these categories.)

Intentional Advocacy

Intentional data advocacy is all around us. If you watch Fox News or MSNBC, you know that the commentators on such channels are far more likely to be citing facts and research intended to support their preferred political point of view. And the public remains quite aware of potential bias in media. In a 2023 poll, NORC found that a third of American adults report encountering biased journalism, misleading news headlines, and false claims from politicians daily.[9]

But it's not just politics. If you watch a Chicago Cubs game on the channel controlled by the team, you expect the announcers to interpret what they see in a way that favors the Cubs and their fans. Research conducted by the auto industry is likely to support the economic value of private cars, just as the research for the tobacco industry that I cited in Chapter 2 failed to find evidence of health problems with cigarettes.

A few years ago, the party of a sitting US president sent a poll to its mailing list of his supporters. It started with this question:

How would you rate the job President [name deleted] is doing for the American people?

- Great
- Good
- Okay
- Other

This is a good example of intentional data advocacy. The poll was sent only to the president's supporters and the choices are slanted toward only positive results. If the president's party were to publicize this poll, you would be justified in treating the resulting data very skeptically, because the poll is not even close to neutral – and is not even intended to be so.

Inadvertent Advocacy

Most research doesn't set out to be biased. Even so, the researchers may produce results that support a point of view that coincides with their own beliefs. As the noted physicist Richard Feynman once said, "The first principle is that you must not fool yourself – and you are the easiest person to fool."[10]

Researchers may design an experiment, a data collection, or the analyses of the data in a way that conforms to their mental model of the world and pre-existing beliefs of what the research will show – and inadvertently bias the results. Sometimes this can be a very obvious miss and thus represents sloppy research, like a drug trial that recruits only the very sickest patients. But it is often more subtle than that. Take an example where a researcher is dividing the population into age groups to look for differences in some metric of interest (for example, cognitive function). They find that when grouped one way, there are no statistically significant differences by age, but using an alternative specification of the age groups, the differences by age become statistically significant. If the researcher is expecting to see differences by age, they will tend to discount the results from the first grouping and focus on the results of the second grouping.

A deeper approach, before deciding that the second age grouping is the correct result, would be to use some more advanced statistical techniques to explore more fully the relationship between age and cognitive function. But it's a lot more work, and takes a lot more of time, and the researcher already got the expected result. You can see how this is a tricky problem – this researcher didn't manipulate the study to produce the expected result, but they stopped short of fully exploring the results they did get. These researchers may feel they're doing everything they can to be neutral but still fall victim to their own background assumptions.

The same is true of those who disseminate data. The reporters at a given newspaper may have inadvertently acquired a similar set of perspectives, which they then reflect in the choice of data they share in the stories they write. And even the most balanced reporters and editors have another obvious bias: They rarely broadcast or write stories about how everything is fine, because more people tend to read stories about how a problem or crisis is brewing. (The very definition of "news" is that you're going to hear about something "new.") This may explain why weather forecasters on television always seem to be warning of big storms that don't quite live up to the weather reports.

And each of us that consumes data is subject to our own biases, believing stories that confirm our prior ideas and ignoring or finding fault with those that seem out of line with our prior expectations (just as I did when I assumed my alarm clock was correct despite all of the other evidence to the contrary).

Cherry-Picking

The term "cherry-picking" means publishing or reporting only those results that confirm a specific point of view.

Politicians are adept at cherry-picking. For example, in 2008, an ad for presidential candidate Barack Obama said that his opponent John McCain "voted to cut education funding," and that he "even proposed abolishing the Department of Education."[11] While McCain did in one instance suggest abolishing the department, his record in the Senate was supportive.[12] In two decades in the Senate, McCain generally supported increasing education funding and strengthening the Department of Education. But one time, in 1995, McCain called for a 1% cut in the department's budget, and that was the instance that Obama's campaign chose to highlight – as opposed to the 33% increase he'd voted for in 2001.

The media includes various mechanisms for investigating and correct unbalanced claims, such as Fact Checker in the *Washington Post* or the Poynter Institute's PolitiFact. Such fact-checkers strive for a thorough, unbiased, and dispassionate review of the evidence on a particular topic or controversy. Unfortunately, even when fact-checking reaches an audience, the research shows that it often fails to change people's perspectives due to confirmation bias and motivated reasoning from people's existing beliefs and ideology.[13] As the Washington University political scientist Steven Smith points out, "Cherry-picking news and interpretations of events can grab and hold an audience, and this pattern is not lost on candidates and elected officials ... [Politicians] know that the audiences they care about will not see and hear the follow-up analyses offered days later or in a different location."[14]

Cherry-picking pervades the debate on global climate change. When the year 2011 turned out to be slightly cooler than 2010 and 2009, some cited it as evidence that climate change wasn't happening, even though the long-term trend over decades unequivocally demonstrates a warming trend (see Figure 6-1).[15] Although 97% of actively publishing climate scientists agree that humans are causing global warming, the remaining 3% get cited frequently in articles attempting to present a "balanced" viewpoint. A 2019 study found that climate change contrarians who are not scientists are featured in 49% more media articles than climate-change scientists.[16] While this may obey some notional idea of balance, it certainly doesn't adhere to the general idea of "the preponderance of the evidence."

There is an active debate about what constitutes appropriate balance in journalism. Journalists and other media figures may feel they've been fair by giving approximately equal weight to opinions on both sides of an issue. But while this is the easiest way to write about a controversy – you just contact spokespeople for each side and quote them fairly – it's not necessarily the most effective in terms of representing truth. Media figures who subscribe to this technique can be accused of "bothsidesism" – regardless of whether both sides have any facts to support them. If there's clear data that pickleball injuries are

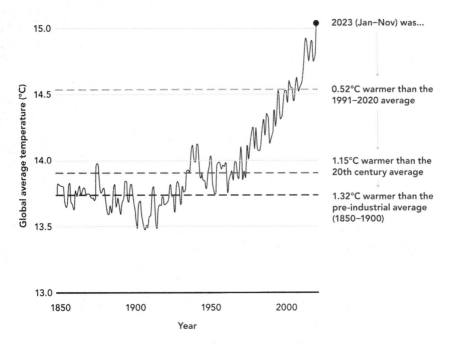

Figure 6-1: Despite yearly variation, there is a clear upward trend in global average temperature.

Source: "What's in a number? The meaning of the 1.5-C climate threshold" by T. Di Liberto, January 9, 2024, on Climate.gov. NOAA Climate.gov graph, based on data from NCEI.

on the rise, there's no need to quote a (hypothetical) pickleball spokesperson saying nobody ever gets hurt playing pickleball.[17] More importantly, if there is evidence supporting both sides but one side has more effective and/or more substantial evidence than the other, simply reporting both sides implies (incorrectly) that the two points of view are equivalently valid. As David Rapp, psychologist and learning scientist at Northeastern University explains, "When both sides of an argument are presented, people tend to have lower estimates about scientific consensus."[18] And as Geneva Overholser, former *New York Times* editorial board member, explains, journalists are not serving the truth "when we're so devoted to 'bothsidesism' that we don't want to look like we're favoring anything. It is not a symmetrical situation, yet we act like it is."

This is not just advice for journalists, either. Every data consumer needs to evaluate competing claims for credibility. When there are two opposing viewpoints, believe the one presented with more evidence, not the one that fits your preconceptions.

And remember, it's not just people who cherry-pick data. It's algorithms, too. The algorithms of popular social media sites like Facebook, Instagram, X (formerly known as Twitter), and YouTube are designed to show people what they want to see. If you're conservative, you'll see facts, data, and reporting that support conservative viewpoints; if you're liberal, you'll see liberal-skewing information – a phenomenon known as a "filter bubble."[19] Search engines like Google work the same way: They observe what you click on and feed you more of what you seem to like. And AI algorithms like ChatGPT learn from the dialogue that users have with them and will explicitly seek out what you are asking for, even if it's one anomalous fact in a sea of contradictory evidence. (My organization, NORC, is currently developing a model to detect and mitigate algorithmic bias. That effort is funded by Amazon Web Services' Health Equity Initiative.)

Motivated Reasoning

Data producers, data disseminators, and data consumers are also subject to the phenomenon known as motivated reasoning. Motivated reasoning is the analytical component of confirmation bias: Basically, if you believe x, you seek out data and analyses that justify x.

The analysts in the intelligence community who interpreted information contradicting the existence of weapons of mass destruction as evidence that Iraq was attempting to fool the world were engaging in motivated reasoning. They needed a way to square their beliefs with facts that challenged those beliefs, so they synthesized a sort-of conspiracy theory that absorbed and neutralized those contradictory facts.

Paul Krugman, the Nobel Prize-winning economist and *New York Times* columnist, often discusses the common problem of motivated reasoning in economics. Because the set of economic conditions at any moment in time is unique, there is no way to conduct scientific experiments with national or global economies to make economic predictions. Motivated reasoning fills that vacuum to explain what is happening with the economy over the short term. For example, in 2023, one group of economists, including former Treasury Secretary Larry Summers, predicted that inflation was going to persist at high levels and it would require a recession to bring it back down. Krugman believed that inflation was transitory and would decline on its own. He showed that economists in general tended to be either inflation pessimists (like Summers) or inflation optimists (like himself) and that they started from whatever their conclusion was and gathered and interpreted data to support that conclusion. As he pointed out, economists were throwing out the classic models and picking data to prove themselves right: a perfect example of motivated reasoning.[20]

P-Hacking, Data Dredging, and the File-Drawer Effect

Let's return to probability theory for just a moment. When unusual or unexpected events occur, people will often use this as "proof" that something notable or worrisome is the cause of the event. But a simple truth underlies all statistical analyses: Unlikely things occasionally happen. (For a quick review of probability and statistics, refer to Chapter 3).

For example, suppose we test 100 frequently used spices on sets of petri dishes infected with a common bacterium. Assume for the sake of argument that none of the spices has any actual effect on the infection, and that by "no actual effect," we mean that the infection would grow half the time and shrink half the time.

Out of the 100 spices, just by random chance, some will appear to reduce the infection. If you are a researcher conducting this experiment, you may look at those results and say, "Wow, this common spice appears to reduce the infection. Moreover, there is only a 5% chance that this would happen by chance." So you publish a paper that reports, say, that cinnamon reduces bacterial infections.

The act of looking for significant effects in different combinations of variables and subsets of data is called "p-hacking." The "p" in this expression is the reported probability of the effect. In the case of the randomly produced cinnamon therapy, the researcher might report that "$p < 0.05$," meaning that the effect would happen by random chance only 5% of the time. But if you review enough variations on the experiment, you'll inevitably find some that pass the gate of the small-probability p-value – and of course, those are the "interesting" results that get published.

Researchers Joseph P. Simmons, Leif D. Nelson, and Uri Simonsohn set out to show how this might apply in practice.[21] They conducted two intentionally silly experiments designed to demonstrate that it is "unacceptably easy to publish 'statistically significant' evidence consistent with *any* hypothesis." In the first study, the researchers were able to produce a statistically significant result that experimental subjects feel older after listening to a children's song, a result that they note is "unlikely." In the second study, the researchers produced a statistically significant result that when experimental subjects listened to the song "When I'm 64," by the Beatles, they actually *became* younger, a result that they note is "necessarily false."

The researchers explain how they produced these results, including the various ways in which they omitted key context, overlooked subjectivity in their decisions around study design (in this case, purposefully), and failed to disclose particular aspects of their methods. Despite these problems, the researchers pointed out "these two studies were conducted with real participants, employed legitimate statistical analyses, and are reported truthfully," and further pointing out that "the redacted version of the study we reported in this article fully adheres to currently acceptable reporting standards."

One way in which researchers can engage in p-hacking, without necessarily intending to, is when they engage in undirected data dredging, or data mining, which amounts to just looking for interesting stories to tell from data sets without a clear rationale or description of what they are trying to explore and why. Since there are typically countless possible ways to slice a complex data set, it's likely that at least some of them will generate statistically significant results.

While much of the time, such arbitrary results discovered in this way are not meaningful or useful in any practical sense, they are still potentially publishable. It can also be the case that the "discovered" statistically significant result actually does have some practical importance. In these instances, we don't necessarily want to ignore the result simply because it was discovered by data mining, but we would certainly want to use a different data set to try to replicate the results, and regardless, the researchers should be transparent about their methods.

The flip side of data dredging and publication bias is what's sometimes called the file-drawer effect. When a researcher does an experiment and *fails* to find anything interesting, the most likely outcome is not to publish anything. Going back to our original example, if chili powder and nutmeg have no effect on the infections in the petri dishes, the researcher is unlikely to publish a paper to tell the world about the ineffectiveness of chili and nutmeg therapies. That research goes in a file drawer and nobody else ever sees it. The net result is that positive results are far more likely to be published or reported on than negative results.[22]

Scientific literature discusses various methods to correct for publication bias and the file-drawer effect, but there is no single widely accepted approach.[23] A very broad-based implementation of scientific transparency – discussed in the previous chapter – is perhaps the most immediate way to mitigate the bias toward positive results. Specifically, this would mean that researchers report their intentions and expectations ahead of time (along with any potential conflicts), ensure that they comprehensively and accurately report their methods, and then make the data public regardless of whether they proved their hypothesis or not. However, this approach would still require journals and other scientific venues to overhaul their approach to publication, such as purposeful emphasis on publishing null results, and developing advanced disclosure and review of studies researchers plan to do and then submit for publication.

Replication studies can help identify when publication bias has led to the publication of a study that is actually wrong. When replication fails, the original results are called into question, and meaningful scientific debate occurs, often leading to additional replication studies that will ultimately allow a definitive conclusion. However, while replication studies can lead to the correction or retraction of published studies that are flawed, replication studies do nothing to eliminate the underlying bias toward positive results. And once again, replication is possible only when researchers are fully transparent in their methods and data.

Even when the scientific community corrects itself, there's a need to account for both data advocacy and positive publication bias for it in other elements of the data ecosystem. Media and other data disseminators are more likely to share startling positive results. For example, one study of the benefits of vitamin E on cardiovascular health looked hopeful but was eventually disproven. Even after the publication of papers demonstrating there was no effect, half of the articles about it cited the earlier hopeful, but debunked, study.[24]

This back-and-forth can be confusing for data consumers who see early positive results published – even if they might just be the result of random chance – and then see them contradicted later with more detailed study. Being aware of this dynamic is part of data literacy, as I will discuss in the next chapter.

Data Advocacy in the Sciences

Professional researchers typically know more about the phenomena that they study than anyone else. As a result, they tend to come to conclusions about the fields that they study based on their past experiments and data. It takes discipline to pursue research in a neutral way despite the biases that come from past experience.

A classic example of this in the field of psychology was the "marshmallow test," conducted by psychologist Walter Mischel. In experiments conducted between 1967 and 1973, he offered a single marshmallow to 4- and 5-year-olds and then told them, "You can have this marshmallow now, or you can wait and have two later." He kept track of which children gave in to temptation. Following up on the children decades later, Mischel showed that the kids who couldn't wait and ate the marshmallow right away were more likely to grow up to have problems: poor academic performance, drug use, mental health problems, and weight problems.[25]

The idea that behavior on a single task at preschool age determines our futures is certainly seductive. But later and more detailed analysis cast doubt on the experiment. Nearly all of the small group of preschool students Mischel studied had similar backgrounds and went on to be well-educated. Additional research showed that other factors, including the subjects' parents and their own assessments of self-control, were better predictors of the fate of the students than their ability to resist temptation. Further analysis showed that performance on the marshmallow test was no more predictive than many other factors.

Was Mischel predisposed to find what he found? According to UCLA behavioral economist Daniel Benjamin, "The marshmallow test ... fits into Mischel's whole outlook on psychology. Mischel considered the test, which allowed researchers to see how people acted in real situations, a better measure of behavior than answers on question-naires."[26] To his credit, Mischel conducted a follow-up experiment with Benjamin, with a more diverse set of children and a better experimental design. The resulting analysis found a far weaker set of correlations to later behaviors and success.[27]

As Mischel explained in 2015, "The idea that your child is doomed if she chooses not to wait for her marshmallows is really just a serious misinterpretation." This is a good example of how researchers can identify their own confirmation biases and act to modify or correct them.

The bias toward publishing interesting results occurs in the biological sciences as well. In one notable case, diabetes researchers Peng Yi, Ji-Sun Park, and Douglas A. Melton published a paper in 2013 showing that a molecule produced in the liver could cause proliferation of the pancreatic cells that produce the blood-sugar-regulating hormone insulin.[28] This breakthrough could have pointed to a potential treatment or cure for type 1 diabetes, a disease characterized by an inability to produce insulin. This would have been particularly meaningful for Melton, whose children both have type 1 diabetes.

Although Melton was a highly respected Harvard professor, his findings came into question from other researchers, including a paper published a year later that failed to duplicate his result. Working collaboratively with researchers in other labs, Melton retested the result with a "blinded" approach, in which researchers are unaware of which cells are receiving which treatments. When the collaborative research failed to replicate the molecule's effect, the original paper was retracted. As Jeffrey S. Flier, former dean of the Harvard Medical School, wrote, this is how science works at its best. "This case study is an example of a responsible scientist addressing a major error openly. The cause of the erroneous claim ... remains unknown, but it most likely resulted from a combination of a technical lab error and confirmation bias, causing initial enthusiasm to override scientific skepticism. Thankfully, following publication of a highly credible disconfirming report, this mistake was followed by an admirable effort to acknowledge it and to provide a definitive scientific answer."[29]

Regrettably, such errors continue to occur, especially when funding is at stake. "Whether aware of it or not (most certainly are), scientists prefer their experimental hypotheses to be true, especially when their grant proposals are justified by claims that they are," Flier writes. "When scientists face highly consequential grant deadlines, publication decisions, and impending promotions, some forgo best practices. Instead, they cut corners when selecting data to 'present a story'."[30]

There's also the understandable challenge that comes from "exploratory research," in which scientists naturally desire to find clinically interesting results that could point the way to helpful therapies. Unfortunately, as Flier writes, "results that are highly innovative and unexpected – and therefore potentially the most exciting – are more likely to be false positives and untrue."

These publication biases – and the sometimes contradictory news coverage that accompanies them – may have contributed to a decline in the public's faith in science. For two decades leading up to the 2020s, public faith in science was steady. But according to the General Social Survey (conducted by NORC and sponsored by the National Science Foundation), in 2022, only 39% of American adults reported a great deal of confidence in the scientific community, down from 48% the previous year (see Figure 6-2).[31] This is a substantial change in a longtime measure that had been relatively stable for many years. The shifting scientific narratives related to COVID-19 and politicians and government officials taking stances on preliminary studies that hadn't yet been tested likely contributed to this loss of confidence. It's worth pointing out that, even with this decline, trust in our scientific community is still higher than any other area measured except the military, which has the highest trust at 46%.

Finally, while we like to believe that important results will always see the light of day, what gets published depends in part on journal editors' and reviewers' attitudes and opinions, which is often based on a heavy ballast of belief in the status quo. I experienced this myself in a healthcare study I led in the 1990s in collaboration with seven colleagues. The study analyzed data on who was receiving kidney transplants in the US.[32] Previous studies had shown that there were

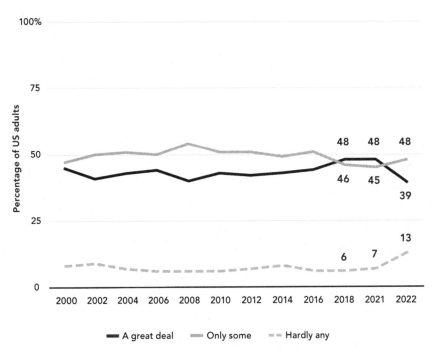

Figure 6-2: Americans' confidence in the scientific community declined in 2022. Survey question: "I am going to name some institutions in this country. As far as the people running these institutions are concerned, would you say you have a great deal of confidence, only some confidence, or hardly any confidence at all in them? (Scientific community)."

Source: AP-NORC. (June 15, 2023). "Major declines in the public's confidence in science in the wake of the pandemic." Data from GSS, conducted by NORC.

demographic differences in who received the transplants – men, people with higher income, and white people were more likely to get transplants. At the time, medical experts typically explained that effect by noting that women, people of color, and lower-income people also were more likely to have health conditions like heart disease or obesity that made them poor risks for a transplant. What was new about our study was that we had a unique data set that had detailed data on other health risks (beyond kidney failure) as well as the demographic data. We were able to show that lower-income patients, women, and nonwhite patients were significantly less likely to get transplants, even when correcting for the presence or absence of additional health risks.

My colleagues and I knew these were important results, but we debated about where we should publish them. We were concerned that since this study refuted widely held medical "wisdom" (and made clear that the allocation of kidney transplants was inequitable), we would have a hard time publishing it in a top medical journal, especially since – viewed from one limited perspective – all the study was doing was replicating previous results. My more senior colleagues were particularly worried about this, having seen this sort of thing happen multiple times in their careers. It was a true learning moment for me. Fortunately, we identified an editor at a top journal who agreed to review and ultimately publish the paper.

The Worrisome Challenge of Data Advocacy in Government

It's fair to say that most researchers don't set out to be biased. While the instances of data malfeasance and falsification make the news, most of the time advocacy in the sciences takes the form of biases from designing experiments based on what you expect, looking for significant results, and publishing what seems interesting.

But in government, the guardrails are less well established – as we saw in the case of the nonexistent weapons of mass destruction in Iraq. People in Congress or political appointees in the executive branch typically have an agenda and are looking for data to support that agenda. There's a far greater need to be skeptical when looking at data disseminated by government officials who are directly connected to political parties. This is one of the reasons the United States has a strong set of federal statistical agencies whose work is largely overseen by career civil servants, whose professional lives are not directly tied to political outcomes.

I have observed instances of political appointees engaging in data advocacy firsthand. In one instance, I was having a routine conversation with a health policy expert (a political appointee) in the Department of Health and Human Services about some of the possible research my organization, NORC, might be able to do to inform the programmatic work that she was overseeing. Her response was to share a set of conclusions that she and other senior political officials in the department were expecting to find and to ask me whether we could do research to that would support those conclusions. As a nonpartisan, neutral research institute, this was not work NORC could undertake.

Another time I was discussing NORC's work with a former high-level Congressional staffer who told me that unless NORC's research came out through his pre-vetted partisan sources, he wouldn't believe it. He said this knowing full well that the whole purpose of organizations like NORC is to do our best to produce unbiased factual results on important societal topics. I suspect – but am not certain – that he also knew that his partisan sources will generally only publish research findings that support their political point of view; this is often referred to as a partisan echo chamber. I said, "Look, we're producing facts and figures for the American people, not facts for Democrats or facts for Republicans." His response? "Not interested." Starting with a conclusion in mind, or only being willing to believe information that has been filtered through a partisan lens is the very definition of data advocacy.

All too often, in government circles, politics is as important as data in shaping policy. There may be no better example of motivated reasoning than the way that genetically modified organisms (GMOs) were regulated in the European Union (EU).

GMOs are foods that were created through genetic engineering to, for example, provide grains that are more resistant to mold or fruits that are easier to ship. They're also at the center of a firestorm of public opinion, not all based on facts.

In Germany, a poll showed 80% opposed to GMOs, despite a lack of scientific evidence of harm. In the UK, which was at the time part of the EU, Prince Charles stated that genetically engineered foods took humanity into "realms that belong to God."

But based on the results of more than 3,000 scientific studies and the judgment of 284 technical and scientific institutions globally, GMO foods are safe to eat.[33] As the European Food Safety Authority itself wrote in 2010, "The main conclusion to be drawn from the efforts of more than 130 research projects, covering a period of more than 25 years of research, and involving more than 500 independent research groups, is that biotechnology, and in particular GMOs, are not *per se* more risky than e.g. conventional plant breeding technologies."

But even without evidence, public opinion caused European food regulators to rule according to the "precautionary principle," which states that any substantially new product must be tested for safety. Starting in 1990, any company wanting to grow GMO foods in Europe needed to submit an environmental risk assessment.[34] And regulators pandering to public opinion created onerous authorization tests that only applied to GMOs. As Italian researcher Giovanni Tagliabue described, "[Plant products that] express the same trait, for example tolerance of rapeseed to weed-killers or rebalanced starch content in potatoes, are subject to radically different authorization procedures, depending on whether they are created using one method rather than another: token analysis for 'non-GMOs', almost never-ending for 'GMOs'." The regulations remain, regardless of the lack of data showing harm, largely because Europeans don't like the *idea* of genetically modified foods.[35]

More recently, in the UK, ministers have similarly used questionable statistics to justify policy. In the first half of the 2010s, government statistics appeared to show that half of all international students in the UK were overstaying their visas.[36] The UK Home Office launched a major effort to identify illegal immigrant students. Meanwhile, the UK Office for National Statistics took a closer look into the data and found that they'd been misclassifying many students on visas and that there was no actual evidence of students remaining in the UK after their student visas had expired – but that was of little solace to those who'd been hounded by the authorities.

According to House of Commons Library statistician Georgina Sturge, policy based on faulty statistics and analysis is commonplace. The UK government's austerity agenda launched in 2010 originated in part based on a mistake in an Excel spreadsheet. The original analysis showed that countries with public debt that exceeds 90% of gross domestic product saw their economies shrink by 0.1% – a strong argument for reducing government spending. The authors later corrected the error and found that such countries economies' *grow* by 2.2% – hardly an economic collapse.[37]

Among the most fundamental of statistics generated by government are economic statistics, for example, measurements of inflation and unemployment. In the United States, many of these statistics are generated by the Bureau of Labor Statistics (one of the federal statistical agencies I discussed previously) based on long-established and well-documented methodologies – methodologies that are standardized specifically to withstand politicians' tendency to present biased perspectives.[38] But such standards are not always followed by governments elsewhere in the world.

Argentinian inflation statistics are a particularly interesting case of the battle between data neutrality and data advocacy. As described by political scientists Roberto Aragão and Lukas Linsi, starting in 2006, the Argentinian government minister Guillermo Moreno systematically attempted to influence official Argentinian inflation statistics for electoral goals and to reduce required government interest payments.[39] Moreno met with technicians at the Argentinian National Institute of Statistics and Censuses (INDEC), which was responsible for compiling inflation numbers. He asked about the shops and items in them for which INDEC was tracking prices, likely with the intent to pressure the shop owners to report fewer price increases, but the INDEC technicians explained they were legally prohibited from sharing the information. He suggested changes to how INDEC computed the inflation numbers, but soon realized that because of the transparent process by which the data were compiled, manipulation would be difficult to hide. He then argued that the methodology was "unpatriotic" and that INDEC should make changes to "improve" the inflation statistic, but the technicians again refused to comply.

By 2007, the government had sacked the leader of INDEC and replaced her with a more compliant and loyal administrator. The new administration changed the data they compiled, excluding all prices that increased by more than 15% and replacing them with alternate data sources. But the discrepancies between the official numbers generated by such cherry-picking and what ordinary citizens experienced was so great that Argentinians lost faith in the numbers, as did press and analysts comparing official numbers to contradictory data from other sources. By 2013, global financial institutions like the International

Monetary Fund ceased to find INDEC's statistics credible, undermining the government's ability to participate in the international financial system.

Although many US economic statistics may be relatively free from advocacy and manipulation, one area where we see the opposite, especially recently, is the reporting of statistics on crime. As described in the previous chapter, there are two predominant data systems on crime in the US. The National Crime Victimization Survey (NCVS), conducted by the US Department of Justice's Bureau of Justice Statistics (BJS), is based on a survey, while the FBI's Uniform Crime Reporting Program (UCR) is based on a compilation of statistics from local law enforcement agencies who voluntarily report data to the FBI. Those agencies don't collect data the same way or with the same frequency, and not every agency "volunteers" its data, so UCR data are always incomplete. At the same time, the UCR data are more standardized because they are based on administrative records, whereas the NCVS are survey data reported by the victims. Another key difference between the two data systems is when the data are reported: Data releases from the UCR are generally much more recent (by a year or more) than the NCVS, because survey data takes much longer to collect.

The differences in the two crime reporting systems allow politicians to cherry-pick the results that support their worldview and advance their political agenda. As of the time of this writing (2024), Democrats are heralding reductions in crime that have occurred recently, based on UCR data, whereas Republicans are focusing on increases in crime that happened earlier in President Biden's term, based on NCVS data.

For example, when Florida Governor Ron DeSantis launched his presidential campaign in 2021, he reported that under his administration, Florida's crime rate had reached a 50-year low. In fact, less than 10% of the law enforcement agencies in Florida had reported crime statistics to the FBI that year, enough missing data to render DeSantis's statement highly questionable.[40] Similarly, when the former mayor of Wichita, Kansas, Brandon Whipple, claimed that violent crime had been cut in half during his term, his data source at the FBI was missing half of Wichita's violent crimes due to data synchronization issues between the Wichita Police Department and the FBI during the switch between the old and new systems discussed above.

Of course, cherry-picking of results by politicians to advance their own ends is not the same as actual data advocacy on the part of government staff who produce and analyze the data. But since the line between the government agencies and the politicians is often blurry, it can be difficult for the public to know the difference. In the end, a greater investment in improving the two data systems and harmonizing the results from them will reduce the opportunity for biased actors to spin one set of statistics or the other. As John Roman, director of the Center on Public Safety & Justice at NORC, said, "The data itself shouldn't be controversial. The more we can improve the crime data, the less controversial it is, and the more we can have policy debates that are based on different approaches to solving the problem, rather than debates about what the facts are."[41]

How to Be Data Neutral in a World Full of Data Advocacy

Challenges to data neutrality are a problem because every biased statistic undermines our trust in the data we depend on. Those challenges are trickier to deal with than it might first appear, because even when we've sensitized ourselves to the most obvious and blatant sources of bias and advocacy, we may still find bias in data produced by researchers and analysts who created the results with the best of intentions.

But if the stories in this chapter have any lesson, it's that, as Shakespeare said, the truth will out. Argentina's inflation will continue regardless of official statistics. More research will reveal if there is any actual harm from GMOs. Purported cures for diabetes, if they don't work, will be revealed as false hope. And let's hope that, going forward, the world will be much slower to use highly politicized assertions based on ambiguous intelligence data as the basis to launch a devastating war.

Our job – as data-savvy producers, disseminators, and consumers of data – is to identify advocacy and fight our own tendencies toward confirmation bias. If we do it well, we can improve data neutrality and shorten the time it takes to reveal misleading data advocacy. Each of us can make a difference. Here's one set of reasonable recommendations:

- **Data producers should be transparent about their research plans and make them publicly available.** The transparency measures I described in the previous chapter will go a long way toward allowing researchers to check each other's work for bias – for example, by looking for questionable patterns in published data. To guard against their own unconscious biases, researchers must go further. There are a range of best practices (they vary based on the type of data and research) that are designed to mitigate unconscious bias. Researchers need to be assiduous about following them and adopting them as standards. And responsible data producers can adopt principles that will guard against the tendency to publish statistically significant results that happen just by chance. More than 80 prominent scientists have endorsed a regime in which researchers register their research plans with journals *before* the research gets underway – explaining what effects they are testing for – and avoid some of the perils of p-hacking and data dredging after the fact to find "interesting" results.[42] And research journals can reduce "file-drawer" bias by accepting and publishing negative results: papers that show what effects were tested and found *not* to exist.[43]

- **Data disseminators should account for advocacy.** Too often, news organizations strive for balance – for example, citing spokespeople on either side of an issue. This is problematic because it often highlights views that are unsupported by scientific evidence or that are based on very weak or faulty evidence. Media should spend more effort striving for accuracy in scientific results, reporting the facts of what the evidence actually supports. This means revealing who is funding research and what their interests and advocacy might be. It means digging deeper into methodologies of cited statistics to examine where biases might have been introduced. And it means looking at larger patterns in previously published research to put any numbers in a broader context. Finally, it means applying extreme skepticism to statistics cited by obviously biased parties, such as politicians, and applying fact-checking techniques as rapidly as possible to point out questionable statistics. (Daniel Dale, a reporter at CNN, has become adept at this, fact-checking politicians in real time to provide instant context.) As I'll show in the next chapter, the discipline of data journalism – in which statistically skilled reporters deeply examine and analyze data sets to create new insights – add more sophistication to disseminators' presentations of data and statistics.

- **Data consumers should adopt a healthy skepticism of "scientific" findings reported by people and organizations that have a vested interest in the result.** In the next chapter, I'll go into more detail about data literacy and how data consumers can apply it. But based solely on what I've described in this chapter, you can take measures to protect yourself from both intentional and inadvertent data advocacy. For example, when you hear of statistics cited by politicians, be cognizant of fact checkers' ability to add context to those numbers. Be skeptical of numbers that neatly line up to reinforce the publisher's worldview. When you hear of new "miracle" medical treatments, consider the data provisional – withhold judgment until additional research confirms or contradicts the new findings. And above all, be aware of your own confirmation bias. Each of us knows how we believe the world is, and now that we have news sources and social media confirming our biases, it's easy to fall into a one-sided data trance. Question your own preconceived notions and ideas, even on topics you've thought about a lot. Actively seek out data that contradicts your own assumptions and jolts you back from the dangers of confirming your own prior assumptions.

7

Fostering Data Literacy

THE STUDY OF Data carries a reputation for being dry, boring, and difficult to comprehend. But an understanding of data is crucial to make decisions. One way to solve this problem is to make data into a living experience that people can interact with.

That's the province of data journalists, a unique set of data disseminators who turn data into vivid, interactive experiences, embedded in the websites of newspapers and other information suppliers.

Consider the ongoing coverage (as of the time of this writing) of drought in California created by Sean Greene for the *Los Angeles Times*, with additional reporting by Thomas Suh Lauder and Hayley Smith and supported by a small team of graphic design and software professionals. Greene and Lauder are assistant editors focused on graphics and interactive design, while Smith is the paper's climate reporter.

The *LA Times* includes regular articles about challenges or fluctuations regarding water supplies (and as evidenced by the movie *Chinatown*, water supplies have been a big issue in Southern California for more than 100 years). Every article includes a link to a page titled, "Tracking California's water supplies" featuring a series of interactive maps and displays.[1] Readers can track the year's precipitation as compared to the average, see how precipitation has varied over 20 years in any part of the state, and even track their own local community's

131

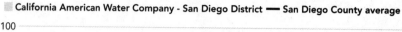

California American Water Company – San Diego District

Statewide residential water use (gallons per person per day)

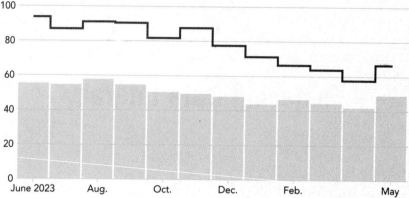

■ California American Water Company - San Diego District ▬ San Diego County average

Figure 7-1: The *LA Times* water usage data journalism project shows water use by county and supplier.

Source: LA Times and California State Water Resources Control Board; used by permission of the *LA Times*.

residential use. Since many parts of California are under state orders to conserve or reduce water consumption in periods of drought, this is a useful tool to see if such reductions are actually happening in a given location (see Figure 7-1).[2] Like many of the interactive graphics in the article, the underlying data comes from public sources, in this case, the California State Water Resources Control Board.

It's also possible to see at any given time how much water is stored in any of the key reservoirs that serve California. For example, Figure 7-2 shows the status of water in Nevada's Lake Mead as of the months leading up to July 2024, which is at an alarming 33% of capacity, well below the historical average.

Finally, the article includes a color interactive chart of historical drought conditions, with the ability to examine any date (see Figure 7-3). Even when much of the state is not experiencing drought, as is the case as I'm writing this in the summer of 2024, the chart makes it clear that drought has recurred more and more frequently since 2002.

Why does this matter? Because it allows the residents of California to be more data literate. On reading an article about, say, new water

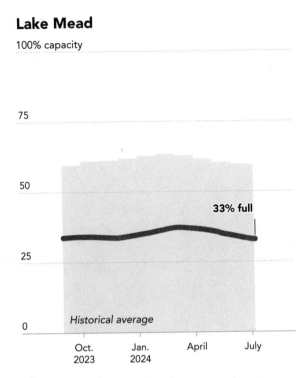

Lake Mead

Figure 7-2: The *LA Times* graphically shows historical and current water levels in key reservoirs. Note: The shaded area represents the historical average for the time of year.

Source: LA Times and US Bureau of Reclamation; used by permission of the LA Times.

restrictions or proposals to gain access to new water sources, the reader becomes a data-savvy consumer who can easily see historical trends or examine what's happening in with the water suppliers and consumers in their own community. They may use this information to decide which people and measures to vote for, or just to inform their own decision about whether it's a good idea to water their lawn or wash their car.

Data journalism like this brings data – especially public data like the water supply, consumption, and drought data for California – and makes it into an interactive explorable resource for data consumers. It's dynamic: Any consumer can check up-to-date local or statewide information at any moment. And that goes a long way toward supporting a fact-forward society.

Drought in California since 2000

Percentage of area in each US Drought Monitor category

Abnormally dry   Moderate drought   Severe drought   Extreme drought   Exceptional drought

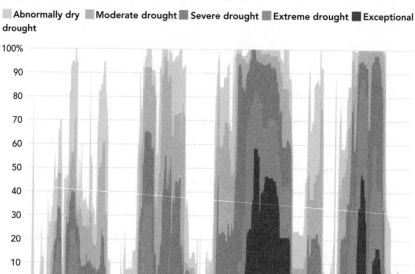

Figure 7-3: A color-coded chart reveals historical drought patterns.

Source: LA Times and US Drought Monitor; used by permission of the *LA Times*.

Data Literacy Creates Clarity Across the Data Ecosystem

Data journalists like the *LA Times* team behind these interactive features are contributing significantly to media's role as a key data disseminator. But we need more of them to help raise the fact-forward contribution of journalism in our increasingly data-driven world.

And as I'll show in this chapter, the value of being skillful with data certainly doesn't stop with data journalists. All data disseminators – including the mass of regular journalists who quote statistics and track down facts for a living – need a basic mastery of data literacy. Corporate workers who frequently come in contact with data sets must know how to analyze them. Ordinary citizens need to know how to interpret the data they encounter fairly and skeptically, a skill I strongly believe they should learn in high school and college.

In the rest of this chapter, I'll examine the fact-forward impact of data literacy on data journalists, other reporters, industry, government, and individuals, including students.

What Is Data Literacy?

I am one of the early adopters of the term data literacy, having been writing and speaking about it for more than a decade. A key theme in this work is that barriers have fallen, barriers that once kept data as the domain of an educated and highly trained elite. Access to data has been democratized, which is great, but the necessary accompaniment to democratized data is widespread societal data literacy. Put simply, as more and more data become more readily available to everyone, each of us needs to develop essential skills in how to understand and use data.

Here's my working definition of data literacy:

Data literacy means understanding the appropriate uses and limitations of data: where data sets come from, what makes them valid and applicable to the question at hand, how to fairly summarize or analyze them, and how to draw relevant and meaningful conclusions from them to inform decisions.

The specifics of data literacy, or at least which aspects of data literacy a person needs to focus on, depends on what role the person is playing in the data ecosystem. If you are a data producer and analyzer, data literacy means you need to use statistical and data science best practices to collect and analyze data fairly to produce statistics and insights. If you are a data disseminator, you're responsible for understanding the uses and limitations of the data others produce and interpreting those results fairly and in context as you publicize them. If you are a data consumer, data literacy means understanding the basics about data and the importance of concepts like integrity, transparency, and neutrality to help you develop confidence about which data are worth trusting and which are suspect. Not every journalist or consumer needs to become a trained data scientist. But each of us needs to gain additional savvy to ensure that we're acting on trustworthy information.

Data Journalism Illuminates New Facts About the World

Consider the career of one highly active data journalist, Andrea Fuller at the *New York Times*. As she explains, "I had never heard the term 'data journalism' when I was at Stanford . . . I got my Excel skills from passable to great, and started learning to work with databases . . . I could kind of carve out this own space for myself – I didn't know a lot of other people doing it until I dove into the data journalism world, and so it was a really fortuitous turn of events that I ended up loving all this."[3]

Data journalism is a powerful tool that requires far more effort than a typical news story. As Fuller relates, "I will spend weeks and weeks on a big investigative data story, checking numbers, thinking about ways that the numbers could be wrong, worrying about what-ifs, . . . [T]he most important skill for a data reporter isn't actually math or programming ability, which are not necessarily the things I'm best at, but it's carefulness. Being meticulous is essential. It's an incredible amount of work on the backend."

The results of all that work are fact-forward, data-centric stories that would never have existed otherwise. Unlike other news stories, such journalistic efforts often include graphics and interactive features like the tool in the *Los Angeles Times* story that lets you analyze water use by location and historical drought conditions by date. Here are some notable examples of data journalism from the hundreds of projects published in major publications in the past few years:

- In a January 2017 article, "How America's Thinking Changed Under Obama," journalists Reuben Fischer-Baum and Dhrumil Mehta at FiveThirtyEight aggregated, analyzed, and presented data from more than 7,000 polls conducted during the Obama presidency.[4] An interactive chart allows readers to examine attitude shifts on 32 major issues (see Figure 7-4). For example, the proportion of people who believed that marijuana should be legal increased from 38% to 58% over eight years, but approval of Obama's foreign policy dropped from 59% to 43%. Any given poll reflects only a snapshot in time but aggregations of this kind reveal broad and fascinating shifts in attitude.

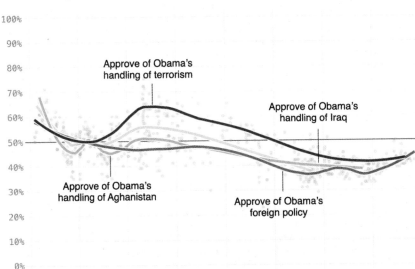

Figure 7-4: FiveThirtyEight uses aggregated poll averages to show shifting voter attitudes.

Source: "How America's thinking changed under Obama," by D. Mehta & R. Fischer-Baum, January 18, 2017, on FiveThirtyEight. Used by permission.

- In November 2023, nine international journalists for the UK's *Financial Times* provided a dramatic visualization of how thousands of mosques in China have been altered or destroyed as part of the nation's crackdown on Islamic culture.[5] They painstakingly created a data set of 2,312 mosques by using photos from Chinese mapping sites like Baidu Maps and Google Earth satellite imagery. Dozens of before-and-after photos make it clear how mosques had had their distinctive and religiously significant domes and minarets removed, completely altering the character of their architecture. A map shows sites across China, and a chart reveals how areas with the most Muslims have also suffered the greatest share of mosques with altered appearance (see Figure 7-5).

- The site Our World in Data includes an amazing array of interactive data charts based on publicly available data on topics from the spread of automated teller machines to child mortality. One notable interactive chart shows how the cost of healthcare

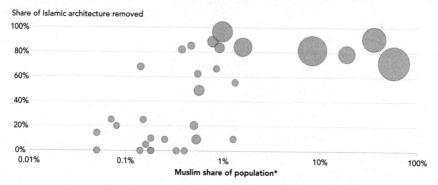

Mosque modifications were more systematic in areas with larger Muslim populations
Dots represent regions, sized by number of mosques with Islamic features analyzed

Share of Islamic architecture removed

* Includes all census-defined ethnic groups that traditionally practice Islam

Figure 7-5: *Financial Times* **data journalism shows patterns in which mosques have Islamic architectural features altered.**

Source: "How China is tearing down Islam," November 7, 2023, in the *Financial Times*. Used by permission.

has increased and its relationship to life expectancy for dozens of countries; the spending versus benefits in the US while once very similar to other Organisation for Economic Co-operation and Development (OECD) countries are now clearly on a different path (see Figure 7-6).[6]

Data-Literate Journalists Must Inject Context into Their Work

For every expert data journalist, there are hundreds of other journalists producing stories that include data points. Such articles may include survey results, data compiled and shared by corporations, results of clinical trials, or economic data released by the government. But without appropriate context, such data may be hard for readers to understand or trust. Providing that context is the job of every journalist, not just data journalists.

Alberto Cairo, Knight Chair in Infographics and Data Visualization at the University of Miami's School of Communication and author of four successful communication books, is concerned that many

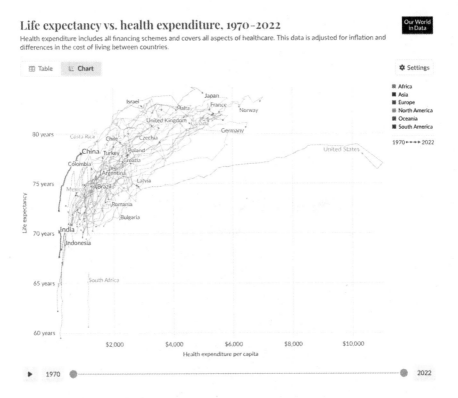

Figure 7-6: Our World In Data reveals decades of data on how nations' health expenditures and life expectancy.

Source: OurWorldInData.org. *Data Source:* UN, World Population Prospects (2024); OECD Health Expenditure and Financing Database (2023). Health expenditure data is in international dollars at 2015 prices. Used under a Creative Commons CC BY license.

journalists are uncomfortable with this responsibility. "If you know absolutely nothing about math or statistics, even the very basics, I can't see how you can work as a journalist," he states flatly, suggesting that a journalist's lack of data fluency is "the equivalent of not knowing grammar."[7] He told me, "Knowing how to reason about numbers and statistics, at least at a very elementary level, should be essential to the work."

Not all journalists are ready to assume this responsibility. John Wihbey, assistant professor of journalism and media innovation at Northeastern University, studied journalistic attitudes for his book *The Social Fact: News and Knowledge in a Networked World.*[8] Wihbey is very

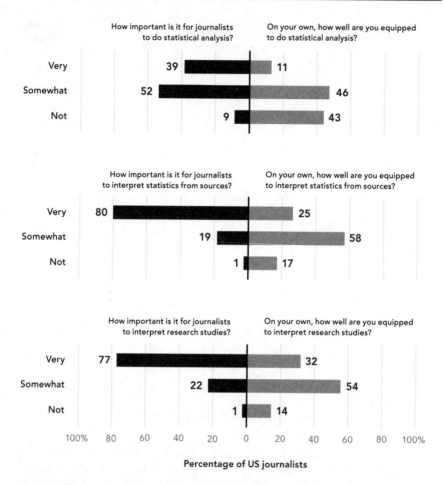

Figure 7-7: Journalists believe their data skills are limited relative to their importance.

Source: 2015 survey by John Wihbey of Northeastern University. Used under a Creative Commons CC-BY-ND license.

transparent in describing that his survey used a nonprobability sampling approach, but the design is nonetheless fit for his research purpose, and it overcame many of the barriers to reaching this notoriously difficult to survey population. Among more than 1,000 journalists he surveyed in 2015, 80% said it was very important that they and their colleagues were able to interpret statistics from sources, but only 25% felt they were well equipped to do so. Similarly, 77% felt it was very important to be able to interpret research studies, but only 32% felt well equipped to do that (see Figure 7-7).[9] As Wihbey wrote, "[W]hen a police department makes a claim about reducing crime, or a health care provider touts progress on patient safety, skeptical journalists with good data skills will have a greater ability to analyze the data themselves, see through faulty claims and call out misinformation."

Journalism education has historically failed to emphasize the statistical side of journalism. A 2016 study determined that only 19% of such programs required journalism majors to take a statistics course.[10]

As more pools of data flood the world, the journalists tasked with interpreting them for the public will see greater and greater demands on their data literacy. Their journalistic instincts already drive them to find opposing viewpoints for statements of opinion by public figures; they must apply the same scrutiny to results that purport to be based on data. Any journalist must provide context – how robust, transparent, and unbiased are the methods used to derive the conclusions from the data, and what other analyses bear on those purported conclusions?

Adept journalists also learn to tap the value of unbiased experts whose data literacy exceeds their own. Independent and respected academics in a given field, such as medicine, physics, or economics, can provide context and scrutiny for results from studies they're not affiliated with. Journalists "should at least have the ability to interrogate the data in collaboration with experts," suggests Cairo.[11]

Data producers that conduct large-scale surveys, like NORC, often have data that can provide context for polls and consumer research. In the field of taxes, for example, the nonpartisan Urban-Brookings Tax Policy Center typically analyzes the impacts of candidates' proposed tax plans.[12]

As described earlier, any journalist dealing with data must provide context; the purpose of this context is of course to enable the reader to apply their own thinking to a piece of journalism and form conclusions, which from a conceptual and cognitive standpoint is labeled "understanding." So, context must go well beyond citing opposing viewpoints. Readers need to know where the data come from, who is reporting them, how dependable they are, what flaws they might have, how they relate to the rest of the field to which they are relevant, and their overall context. Such an analysis requires more reporting and legwork, but it is the only way to ensure the journalist's role as data disseminator is providing insight and not just numbers to plug into a slot in a story.

Therefore, journalists have a responsibility to develop good data skills. Helping journalists develop effective data skills is the responsibility of their employers, sure, but also of society more generally through educational and training opportunities. I discuss this in detail in Chapter 9.

Data Literacy Has Become a Corporate Imperative

One force elevating the visibility of data literacy is its high profile in corporations. For decades, corporations have been hiring and training specialists who understand, work closely with, and generate insights from data. Prior to the recent frenzy about AI, the hot cross-industry business topic was data science and data analytics, and it remains a primary focus in the business world. Today, data science is the key to effective business intelligence. It focuses on assembling, analyzing, visualizing, and acting on business data. For example, a service company might monitor the performance of a customer service team in the hope of finding ways to be more efficient or to serve customers more quickly. Or a manufacturing company might use a dashboard to monitor inventory, defects, and downtime in its manufacturing processes to reduce waste and increase profit.

Analytics is another discipline that has now pervaded all elements of business in companies of any size. For example, marketing staffers might examine advertising and email programs to see which programs are most likely to get customers clicking and which reach the most profitable customers and generate the highest return on investment for the corporation. As author and analytics expert Brent Dykes writes, "[D]ata in the hands of a few data experts can be powerful, but data at the fingertips of many is what will be truly transformational."[13] This is the corporate dimension of data democratization. Analytics is big business; Gartner has forecasted that software for business intelligence and analytics will become a $13 billion market by 2025.[14]

But as digital data have flooded into every business process, the task of understanding and acting on that data has expanded from data specialists to a much larger class of managers and staff. Their access to data, combined with easily mastered tools like spreadsheets and dash-boards, has greatly expanded the number of employes who analyze data. And that creates new demands for data literacy for rank-and-file employees.

A study conducted by Forrester for the technology vendor Tableau projected that 70% of employees in large companies will use data heavily in 2025, up from 40% in 2018.[15] Forrester's survey included 1,032 people with at least three years' experience at compa-nies with more than 500 employees, along with 1,032 decision-makers in those companies. Among the decision-makers, 82% said they expected at least basic data literacy of all employees in their departments. This result was consistent across departments, includ-ing finance, human resources, marketing, and operations. But only 40% of the employees said their organization has provided the data skills they need. Even so, nearly three-fourths of the decision-makers expect employees to improve those data skills on their own. As the report concludes, "The big disconnect between employer expecta-tions and the data training employees actually get presents a serious obstacle to creating the data-driven cultures many organizations desire. A telling example is that 69% of decision-makers say a lack of data skills stops employees from using data effectively in decision-making." And eight out of 10 employees in this study reported that they're more likely to stay at a company that trains them for the data skills they need.

Data Literacy in Government

Government agencies are among the organizations for which data lit-eracy is most important. Their workers must frequently deal with and make sense of streams of data, such as tax information, labor and employment data, inflation and economic growth, crime statistics, and healthcare statistics. Two Asia-Pacific countries have recently taken action to increase the data literacy of their government workforces. In Australia, the government created a "Data Literacy Foundational Pathway," which Australian public service workers can complete to learn about the uses of data, trust, foundations of data research and analytics, statistics, and how best to communicate insights from data.[16]

In Singapore, more than half of the officers in 70 agencies completed baseline data and statistics training.[17] These initiatives are as much about culture as knowledge. Weng Wanyi, director of Singapore's Government Data Office, said that the training initiative would help the government policy and planning to be more data-driven and evidence-based and better able to deliver government services that meet the citizen's needs.

While the trend toward greater amounts of data analysis in companies and governments may not have much immediate relevance for construction workers or retail clerks, data now pervade more jobs than ever. Large farms use data to analyze yields and make weather-related adjustments; media companies tweak the news they publish and the entertainment they stream based on where the clicks are coming from; travel companies plan routes and optimize prices based on analyses of consumer behavior. The demand for data literacy among an ever-increasing proportion of workers will spread throughout the economy, boosting demand for college programs, secondary school data literacy programs, and adult education.

Most Consumers Lack Data Literacy, and They Know It

As described in Chapter 2, we fielded the NORC Data-Savvy Survey of 1,071 adults in June 2024 and included several questions on data literacy. People in the survey have at least a surface-level appreciation of the principles of data integrity, data transparency, and data neutrality as described in Chapters 4–6. They generally state that they're more willing to trust research that has a clearly presented methodology and is presented in an unbiased way (see Figure 7-8, which was also shown as Figure 5-2 in Chapter 5). Sources matter, too: 68% are more willing to trust research shared by a person or organization they trust, 54% are more likely to trust it if the research source is mentioned, and 44% are more trusting if the research funder is also mentioned. (However, 62% are more likely to trust research if the findings are aligned with other research they've already seen, an indication of confirmation bias.)

But Americans are less confident in their data literacy skills. Only 52% agreed they were extremely or very capable of evaluating

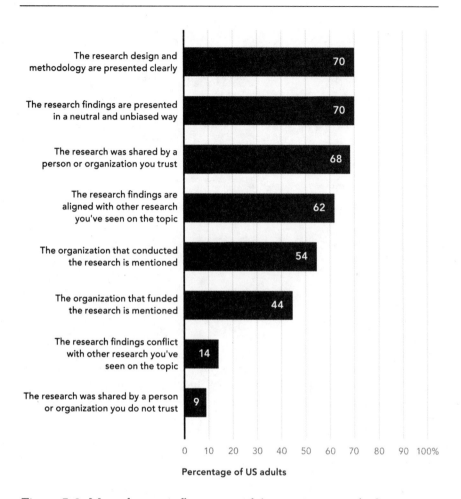

Figure 7-8: Many factors influence people's trust in research. Survey question: "Think about times when you read, watch, or hear about a research study on a topic of interest. How much does each of the following factors impact your trust in the research?" Chart shows: Increases your trust a lot/a little.

Source: NORC Data-Savvy Survey of 1,071 US adults via AmeriSpeak panel, June 2024.

information for accuracy, and 51% thought they were extremely or very capable of understanding and using statistics (see Figure 7-9). And these answers were skewed by age: Among those 60 or older, only 39% expressed confidence in their skills in either area.

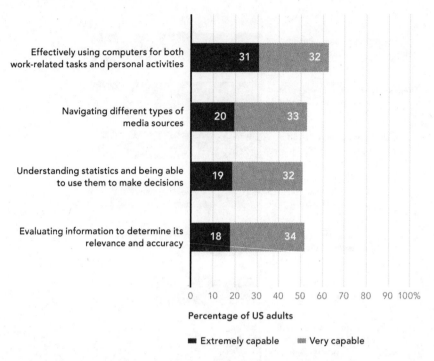

Figure 7-9: About half of US adults feel they are capable of understanding statistics or evaluating information for accuracy. Survey question: "How would you rate your skill level for each of the following?"

Source: NORC Data-Savvy Survey of 1,071 US adults via AmeriSpeak panel, June 2024.

We also surveyed more than 1,000 US teenagers ages 13–17 to gather their perspectives about data skills in the NORC Data-Savvy Teen Survey, conducted in September 2024 using NORC's AmeriSpeak Teen Panel. We found that teens recognize the importance of data skills but do not feel they are getting trained in them (see Figure 7-10). Virtually all teenagers in the study – a full 91% of them – said it is very (42%) or somewhat (49%) important that high school students graduate knowing how to interpret statistics, with very similar results when it comes to interpreting research studies. Around half of the teens believe they are "somewhat equipped" to do this interpretation, but very few of them (21% or less) say they are very well equipped for such tasks. As the volume of data bombarding teens increases daily, these results suggest we are not doing enough to help our young people become data savvy.

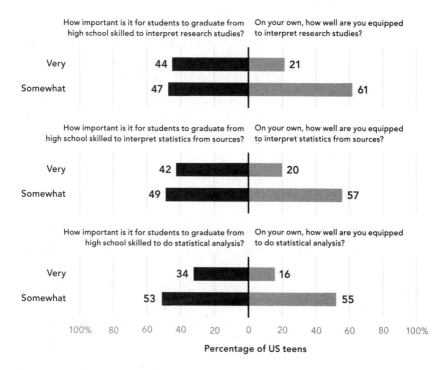

Figure 7-10: An overwhelming majority of teens feel data skills are important, but only around one in five feel very well-equipped with such skills. Survey questions: "How important is it for students to graduate from high school skilled in each of the following?" and "On your own, how well equipped are you to do each of the following?"

Source: NORC Data-Savvy AmeriSpeak Teen TrueNorth Survey of 1,037 teens ages 13–17 years, September 2024.

Education at All Levels Will Create the Foundation for Data Literacy

According to the National Center for Education Statistics, the number of US students graduating with a degree in data science has grown substantially in recent years, going from fewer than 100 in 2020 to more than 800 in 2022. And about 6,000 US college students graduated with a degree in statistics in 2022, up from about 4,500 in 2020 and 3,600 in 2018 (no data are available for data science degrees in 2018).[18] While it is encouraging to see increases in the number of college students graduating with data skills, these numbers are only a tiny fraction of the millions of people who graduated from college during those years. By themselves, a few thousand data scientists and statistics graduates won't move the needle much on data literacy.

More encouraging, perhaps, is the 17% of high school seniors in 2019 who took at least one statistics course in high school[19] (for college students, approximately 30% of undergraduates took at least one statistics course[20] based on 2017 data; the years are different for high school and college because the data sources are different). But that is far less than the approximately 85% of 2019 high school seniors who completed advanced algebra, or the 40% who completed precalculus.

There's certainly a case to be made that for typical students, unless they're going on to become engineers, basic knowledge of how to understand and perform data analysis is likely to be considerably more useful than learning the formulas that describe parabolas and hyperbolas in an advanced algebra class. Even so, I was unable to find any evidence of a university program that required data science for undergraduate degrees, even for engineering or science majors.

There's already some evidence that a college education helps some people with data literacy. In the NORC survey I cited in the previous section, 67% of respondents who had graduated college said they were extremely or very capable of understanding and using statistics, nearly twice as many as the 37% of high school graduates who never went to college. But even among college students, about one in three feel they lack competency in understanding statistics.

The point is not simply that we need to increase the percentage of students who take a single data science or statistics class to fulfill a requirement. We need to rethink what we teach – in college and earlier – to create a foundation of data literacy for future citizens. No college would dispute that every student should graduate with a competency in expository writing and basic mathematics. Why are there no requirements that our students achieve basic data literacy? Learning to appropriately evaluate data appears to be an essential basic competency that colleges and universities have neglected.

And we shouldn't limit our goals to college students. In K–12 education, data science should be built into the curriculum and integrated into the teaching of basic math, science, and finance. To have a data-literate population, we need to develop data skills far earlier in the educational experience, especially since a large portion of the population does not go to college. We need to focus more time, attention, and funding on creating data literacy in middle and high school students, regardless of whether they plan to attend college. This idea meshes nicely with the trend in K–12 education of requiring financial literacy courses in high school students, with state legislators increasingly recognizing that understanding finances is a much-needed real-world skill.[21]

Interestingly, people who consider themselves more data-savvy put a higher premium on these skills. Among people who say they are very or extremely capable of understanding statistics and data, 66% feel skills in data literacy are essential for high school students versus only 39% among those who say they are not too or not at all capable.

People already intuitively know this, even if they haven't yet articulated it to their school districts. In the June 2024 NORC survey I mentioned earlier in the chapter, 89% of respondents asserted that it was essential or important for students to graduate from high school with data literacy skills – a similar number to those who were in favor of requiring better-known skills like financial literacy, digital literacy, government literacy, and media literacy (see Figure 7-11). While teens were less enthusiastic about additional course requirements, one in three said they would sign up for a data literacy class (see Figure 7-12).

Importantly, classes aimed at developing basic data literacy will be useful every day, whether the student is assessing different measures of inflation relative to their personal experience, talking to a doctor about the odds of the effectiveness of a treatment, or understanding shifting attitudes as reflected in opinion polls. In other words, data literacy is an overarching analytic skill – not only is it intrinsically useful, but it enhances similar (and highly valued) skills like financial and media literacy.

One of the most promising initiatives on this front is the American Statistical Association's *Guidelines for Assessment and Instruction in Statistics Education* (GAISE). This program includes materials for both

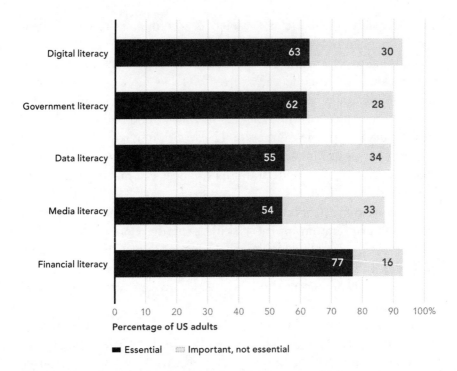

Figure 7-11: A majority of US adults say it is essential for students to learn data literacy skills in high school. Survey question: "How important is it for students to graduate from high school skilled in each of the following?"

Source: NORC Data-Savvy Survey of 1,071 US adults via AmeriSpeak panel, June 2024.

K–12 and college-level teaching. GAISE is built on the following principles[22]:

- Teach statistical thinking. Teach statistics as an investigative process of problem-solving and decision-making; give students experience with multivariable thinking.
- Focus on conceptual understanding.
- Integrate real data with a context and purpose.
- Foster active learning.
- Use technology to explore concepts and analyze data.
- Use assessments to improve and evaluate student learning.

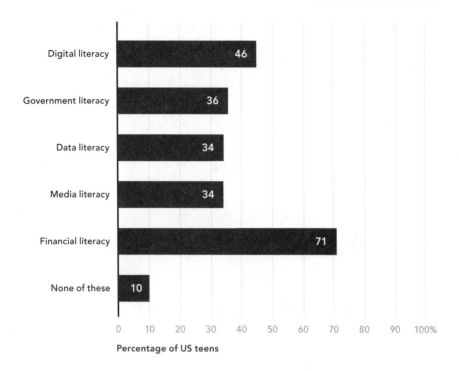

Figure 7-12: While one in three teens would take a course in data literacy, they're more open to financial and digital literacy coursework. Survey question: "If your school offered classes on each of the following topics, which classes, if any, would you sign up to take? Please select all that apply."

Source: NORC Data-Savvy AmeriSpeak Teen TrueNorth Survey of 1,037 teens ages 13–17 years, September 2024.

GAISE reflects an encouraging focus on concepts that will be of practical use to students gaining data literacy. Among the goals included in the guidelines are "Students should become critical consumers of statistically based results reported in popular media, recognizing whether reported results reasonably follow from the study and analysis conducted," and "Students should recognize and be able to explain the central role of variability and randomness in the field of statistics."

The GAISE program for school students embraces this practical approach. Its K–12 report states, "Every high-school graduate should be able to use sound statistical reasoning to intelligently cope with the requirements of citizenship, employment, and family and to be prepared for a healthy, happy, and productive life." GAISE includes exercises with practical information, such as conducting experiments about plant growth or interpreting surveys about popular music. It also helps students learn to create and interpret graphics and charts based on data. And it doesn't stint on teaching when and how interpretations of statistics can be wrong.

Milo Schield, a statistics professor affiliated with the University of New Mexico, has a parallel approach that shows promise.[23] In his new course on statistical literacy, he suggests teaching students to answer seven refreshingly basic questions about a statistic they are evaluating (my commentary follows each point in italics):

- How big/how much/how many? (What is the absolute magnitude?) *The most important element of a quoted statistic is the total amount of the quantity in question.*
- Compared to what? (Can you put the statistic in context?) *Whether a change is large or small, important or unimportant, is a lot easier to evaluate when you can compare it to similar numbers in other fields, or other time periods.*
- Why not a rate? (Can it be stated as a percentage of a larger base?) *An important element of context is how a number compares to a base number – a change in a price is best understood as a percentage of the original price, for example.*
- Per what? (Is this the right base? Or is it distorted by a "diabolical denominator?") *Changes over time can be annual, quarterly, or monthly. And quantities that double or triple might not be all that significant if it's based off a small original number.*
- How were things defined, counted, or measured? (What is the methodology?) *This relates to the transparency measures I described in Chapter 5.*
- What was taken into account? (What was controlled for?) *Did the person sharing the statistic or result account for variables like race, age, gender, or income, for example?*
- What else should have been taken into account (controlled for)? (Are there missing, possibly confounding variables?) *What other variables might have caused the cited effect?*

Based on student feedback, the course was successful; 95% found it valuable, 78% would recommend it to a friend, and 32% felt it should be required of all students. These are encouraging results, given that the course was taught partly remotely due to the COVID pandemic.

As Steven Levitt, co-author of the bestselling book *Freakonomics*, said, "I believe that we owe it to our children to prepare them for the world that they will encounter – a world driven by data. Basic data fluency is a requirement not just for most good jobs, but also for navigating life more generally, whether it is in terms of financial literacy, making good choices about our own health, or knowing who and what to believe."[24] To that end, he is a founder of a new coalition called Data Science 4 Everyone, whose aim is "advancing data science education so that every K–12 student is equipped with the data literacy skills needed to succeed in our modern world. Equitable access to data science education is an opportunity to open doors to higher education, high-paying careers, and an engaged community."[25]

As should be clear from what you've read in this chapter, I wholeheartedly agree with this proposition. I'd simply add that we also need to pay attention to the adult population as well. Data skills are becoming so essential for successful navigation of our world, and as I have noted, most adults today feel they lack essential data literacy. Fortunately, it appears that this need is starting to be addressed in the form of numerous continuing education classes and professional trainings in data science and basic data skills that have emerged over the past several years. When I first started developing the ideas for this book several years ago, there were very few such programs. This is an encouraging development.

8

Standards and Privacy

IN 1980, THE total number of airline passengers worldwide was 800 million. By 2019, that had ballooned to 4.6 billion passengers.[1] What accounted for this rapid expansion?

Deregulation, of course, was the driver that started off this enormous growth.[2] But in addition to airplane fuel, the airline industry is powered by data. It's an enormous task to translate the industry's massive amount of transactional and logistics data into information that ends up putting passengers in the seats of airplanes. And the key to this task is data standards.

The story of data in the airline industry goes back to the 1960s, when some airlines were using computers, but with many different systems. American Airlines and IBM, perceiving an opportunity to computerize the reservation business, introduced a much more comprehensive system called Sabre.[3] As electronic reservations became more common, the industry trade group for the airlines laid out a common data standard for reservations and classes of fares. This set the stage for a far more rapid expansion.

By the 1980s, Sabre began to pitch travel agencies to include computer terminals in their offices to make reservations. At first, agencies needed a separate terminal for each airline. Realizing that this was wasteful, the airlines further standardized their data formats and systems, enabling Sabre to put a single terminal in each travel agency that could make reservations on most airlines and, crucially, to enable reservations that tied together flights from different airlines.

This standardization proved to be essential when the Internet arrived. In 1994, Alaska Airlines launched the first website that allowed customers to make a reservation online. Soon after, in 1996, the online sites Expedia and Travelocity went live with flight information from all major domestic airlines. The online reservation business was off and running, an advance that was built directly on the standards and systems originally created for the travel agency terminals.

Because of shared data standards and infrastructure, the travel industry's technology continued to expand. You can now book train reservations, international flights, hotels, and rental cars through these same travel systems. Mobile airline and travel apps function only because of the common reservation standards. Other data systems have been built on top of this solid, standardized infrastructure, enabling any consumer to sort flights by duration, schedule, or price; see which flights are most or least likely to land on time; track and gain benefits from loyalty programs; and even get information on the legroom and comfort of individual airline seats. These systems don't just benefit consumers. The travel companies use them to constantly manage their inventory of flights and plan new routes based on what searches consumers are making on their computers and smartphones.

Henry Harteveldt, CEO of Atmosphere Research Group, is a travel analyst who has studied the evolution of the industry over more than four decades. As he explains it, "The internet had completely disrupted how the travel industry does business, but now it enables airlines to do far more."[4] Sixfold growth in passengers in 40 years required more planes, bigger airports, and more employees, but none of that would have been possible without the standardized data formats that the industry was built on.

Expanding the Usefulness of Data Depends on Standards and Privacy Protections

As I'll show in this chapter, creating comprehensive data standards is a necessary prerequisite for making data more useful. When data are standardized into common formats, systems can interoperate, like the disparate airline systems that were combined under the Sabre reservation standard. The same applies to many other forms of data. For example, various government data sets and statistics can be combined in powerful ways, but only when there are common, standard definitions for terms like income, inflation, race, family, and debt.

Data standards start with *metadata*, which is information about data. The definitions of fields within data sets are metadata. For example, if the data collection is a block of airline reservations, the metadata might describe what dates they covered, where they came from, and the definition of terms like airline, flight number, departure time, class of service, price paid, and passenger name. If metadata is compatible across data sets, the reservations can become part of a larger and more comprehensive system, which is exactly what happened with the airline industry.

Of course, in addition to the time and money involved in creating standardized data, combining data and systems comes with risks, too. If a data collection includes, say, information about who was diagnosed with a set of diseases and that information is combined with who is qualified for an increase in credit limit, there's the potential for abuse: A financial institution could in theory bias their decisions about who gets credit based on private health information. Any increase in standardization and combination of data sets demands more careful attention to privacy concerns. In fact, without firm and audited rules about privacy standards, there's no safe and appropriate way to combine data sets from multiple sources. In this way, privacy rules are just as important as data standards in enabling the appropriate uses of data to grow.

In this chapter, I'll describe how data standards are fueling growth in the usefulness of data and explore how privacy standards are equally essential to enabling that growth. I'll also discuss some of the inherent tensions between making data easier to use and more accessible while also keeping it secure and (where necessary) confidential.

Examples of How Growth Emerged from Data Standards

The airline industry is far from the only example of standardized data leading to an explosion of new ways to gain functionality and insight. Another fascinating example comes from the financial services industry.

After the instability that caused the stock market crash of 1929, the government moved to enforce standardized quarterly financial reporting for companies in 1933. Stock trading used to be conducted in a "pit," with buyers and sellers negotiating prices and shares, but the prices were reported on an electronic device called a stock ticker that was present in many brokers' offices. Electronic trading took off starting in 1971 with the launch of NASDAQ, the first fully electronic stock market.

As the Internet became prevalent in the mid-1990s, the US Securities and Exchange Commission required the standardized reports about public companies' revenues and profits to be posted in an online database called EDGAR. Just as in the travel industry, this was followed by tools that allowed consumers to consume the standardized information and buy and sell shares on online platforms like E*Trade without the need to work with a dedicated stockbroker. Stock trading volume rose almost 10,000-fold, from 1.1 million shares annually in 1973 to 10.1 trillion shares in 2023.[5]

It now seems completely normal that you can get information on every stock, option, mutual fund, or security in hundreds of apps from information companies like Dow Jones or trade any asset instantly on your phone with established brokers like Fidelity or startups like Robinhood. But this change is all pretty recent, over the course of the past three decades. Many of us are old enough to remember when the best you could do was look at the previous day's results for a small sample of major stocks and mutual funds that were reported in the newspaper every day – back when most of us read physical newspapers. A huge share of the economic growth of the finance industry is built on a foundation of standards, including some mandated by the government, like uniform reporting standards for public companies. These standardized data streams make modern finance possible.

Data standards are essential to creating platforms for innovation. Consider what the MBTA, the transit authority for greater Boston, did with its data stream. In 2014, the planners at the MBTA realized that data from their internal system for tracking the locations of subway cars, trolleys, and buses – built on GPS data and transponders in mass-transit vehicles – would be extremely useful for the traveling public.[6] A mobile app was clearly the ideal mechanism for sharing these data, so that commuters could check their smartphones to see transit schedules and whether buses or subways were running on time. But rather than build its own app, the MBTA published a set of standards for accessing its data stream. The result was an explosion of transit apps from private companies, supported by various business models. The apps competed on the ease of their interfaces. This generated exactly the result the MBTA had hoped for – a proliferation of convenient and steadily improving apps – without the transit authority having to invest in and maintain any apps on its own. Similar transit data streams now power apps all over the globe.

Standardized Formats and Definitions Are Central to Government Data Infrastructure

Standards are central to making data more accessible. Two surveys may use different definitions of terms like income, citizen, or ownership. (If the bank holds a loan on your truck, do you "own" it?) Standards are particularly important for combining data from different sources. As a report from the National Academy of Sciences (NAS) and the National Science Foundation (NSF) on data infrastructure suggests[7]:

> Data have to be exchanged across users and should be comparable over time, space, and subpopulations. For example, interoperability in healthcare means separate systems, devices, organizations, and entities can exchange and appropriately use health-related data. Comparability means the unemployment rate in Los Angeles should have the same meaning as that in rural West Virginia. The unemployment rate in March 2022 should have the same interpretation as the unemployment rate in January 2018. Unemployment among those 18–25 years old should mean the same as unemployment among those 45–60 years old. Interoperability and comparability rest on the consistent application of standards for data elements, classification schemes, documentation, time periods, and more.

This standardization starts with metadata: specifically, standardized data labeling. Consider, for example, the assembly of health statistics from multiple sources. Medicare, the government insurance program for people over 65, pays for a wide range of medical treatments tied to specific illnesses or conditions for which healthcare providers get reimbursed. For the providers to correctly code their bills for payment, there need to be established definitions of the set of diagnoses and symptoms that constitute a particular illness, together with established definitions of what constitutes a relevant medical treatment for that service.

The US government standardizes definitions of metropolitan areas, occupations, and industries for labor statistics. For example, the NAICS – the North American Industry Classification System – standardizes the reporting and classification of businesses, making analysis of business results like profit and employment by sector far easier. And another set of standards, the recently revised Statistical Policy Directive 15 on Standards for Maintaining, Collecting, and Presenting Federal Data on Race and Ethnicity,[8] will enable a more sophisticated analysis of racial patterns across all federal data efforts. As Richard L. Santos, director of the Census wrote in 2024, Directive 15 is "providing us with a more nuanced and dynamic understanding of our population's complex and rich diversity of communities and identities . . . I encourage you to . . . think about how you can [now] portray your whole self when answering future race/ethnicity questions in our surveys and censuses."[9]

The late Katherine Wallman, former chief statistician of the United States and a valued colleague of mine, suggested that data standards like these create essential incentives for those with data to share it with others, enabling all sorts of insights from new comparisons and data combinations.[10] Standard definitions enable private and academic sources to generate compatible results based on government definitions, which can then feed back into government statistics, enriching the data and creating more insights for all.

The quest to standardize everything will always run up against the ingenuity of researchers in creating new forms of data that are related in new ways to existing data. As an old joke among data scientists suggests, "The nice thing about standards is that there are so many of them."[11] But even as new forms of data proliferate, various industry and government bodies are hard at work trying to rationalize as many data formats as possible. Here, from the NAS/NSF report, is a short list highlighting a handful of important standardization efforts[12]:

- Statistical Data and Metadata eXchange (SDMX): A standard for formatting multidimensional data and metadata into a framework for automated data exchange
- The United Nations Economic Commission for Europe family of standards: A collection of standards used by European government bodies and data producers
- The Data Documentation Initiative (DDI): An international standard for stages in the planning and creation of data
- The National Information Exchange Model (NIEM): A common vocabulary including terms, definitions, relationships, and formats for data exchange across organizations
- The International Organization for Standardization (ISO) and the International Electrotechnical Commission (IEC) 11179: Conceptual models for managing data classification schemes
- International and domestic standards for electronic data interchanges: Including ANSI X12 for electronic data exchange and the SEC's XBRL for financial reporting
- The Federal Geographic Data Committee (FGDC): The lead government entity for geospatial (location) data

Without Privacy Protections, Combining Data Is Problematic

You can't just heedlessly combine data about people or businesses – that sort of thing tends to upset people and can lead to harmful disclosures of people's private information unless there are some sort of guardrails in place. This is the role of privacy rules.

Privacy is both an enabler and an impediment to the expansion of public data availability. Privacy objections derail data combinations. But solid privacy regimes and structures create standardized privacy protections, allowing people to be more comfortable sharing data about themselves. Addressing the concerns of Internet users is essential; according to a 2021 NORC survey of 1,004 American adults, 38% are not yet satisfied with the government's efforts to protect their privacy and secure their personal data, while 61% want the federal government to devote a high level of effort to improving online data privacy and security.[13]

In this vein, one groundbreaking regulation is the Health Information Portability and Accountability Act (HIPAA), which created a set of detailed regulations on when and under what circumstances health data can be shared. Pretty much every patient in the United States has by now had the experience of signing a HIPAA release form, so those patients are at least theoretically aware that there are rules for the sharing of health information. Those rules ensure that health data are shared only under certain carefully delineated conditions and for specific and useful purposes, such as coordinating care and public health monitoring.[14]

Similar regulations include European General Data Protection Regulation (GDPR), which specifies the rules by which European citizens can give consent to have their data collected and creates regulations on how companies must protect that data, for how long they can keep it, and how, on request from a consumer, they must share or delete that information. The California Consumer Privacy Act secures a similar set of protections for citizens of the state of California. As I write this, Congress is considering the American Privacy Rights Act, a comprehensive privacy regulation with bipartisan support.[15]

By creating ground rules for the collection and sharing of information, these sorts of regulations prevent indiscriminate sharing of data, while enabling some data aggregation and sharing under specific circumstances. They're a necessary prerequisite for building the infrastructure to allow beneficial data sharing that would generate useful analyses while still safeguarding individual privacy. Privacy rules create a scaffolding to prevent an individual's private information from being shared inappropriately. They also establish a best practice framework for research. For example, HIPAA and similar health regulations are essential for ethical medical research.

Corporations are in many ways at the epicenter of this tension between data sharing and protection of privacy. There's a great temptation for companies to hoard data, combine data from multiple sources, blend it with public data, and use the resulting aggregations for the purposes of targeted marketing. But without privacy

protections, such combinations can easily create troubling viola-
tions, from revealing to people what their spouses are buying for
presents to targeting people based on proxies for race or disease conditions. In one notable case, a woman alleged gender discrimination
in the way the Apple credit card determined credit limits.[16] When
algorithms based on combined data are not transparent, the results
can be harmful. These concerns were instrumental in leading the
European Parliament to implement the GDPR.

Even when companies obey privacy regulations with regard to
data, there is still a risk for criminals to exploit weaknesses in data
systems to prey on anyone whose data they can access. There were
more than 3,200 data breaches and compromises in 2023, with an
impact on more than 350 million people.[17] When data are combined
without privacy protections, such breaches can reveal information
that could be used to exploit, financially or otherwise, the people
whose data have been compromised.

Privacy regulation cannot, of course, prevent all such problems,
but appropriately conceived, it can lessen their negative impacts by
reducing the disclosure risk when breaches do occur. Privacy regulations interact with data security protections put in place by the organizations and people in charge of data systems to try to keep people's
data safe.

The Promise of Federal Information Sharing Depends on Updated Privacy Regimes

The federal government collects massive amounts of information.
Each data set has been designed to fulfill a specific information need,
and in general, each data set does that reasonably well (of course each
data set has strengths and limitations, as discussed throughout this
book). But without a data sharing infrastructure in place to combine
these data sources, we miss out on innumerable opportunities to
explore what may be the most powerful insights the data sets have to
offer. Combinations like that provide perspective, for example, illuminating how socioeconomic trends are connected to disease conditions
by geography. But to obey privacy regulations, such combinations
require scrupulous attention.

For example, in its statistical and analytical work, NORC must follow rules including HIPAA, GDPR, the Federal Information Security Management Act (FISMA), the Confidential Information Protection and Statistical Efficiency Act (CIPSEA), the Family Educational Rights and Privacy Act (FERPA), and the Children's Online Privacy Protection Rule (COPPA). These privacy regulations are designed to protect the population, but there's a need to update them to make the work of combining and gaining insights less onerous. Federal stewards of data must now pay diligent attention to legislated privacy rules because of concern about making errors that would violate individuals' privacy or subject their agencies to legal risk. In the absence of such modernization, data often remain in silos that resist efforts to combine them for greater knowledge.

There has been progress. For example, it used to be the case that the only way to get access to sensitive census microdata (data about individuals) was to visit one of the nation's 33 carefully monitored Federal Statistical Research Data Centers in person. It's now possible to access the data remotely and relatively easily, even as the Census continues to monitor the data use to ensure adherence to privacy and confidentiality restrictions.

All of this demonstrates the inherent tension between protecting data and enabling access and use of the data. On the one hand, making data maximally available increases their utility for the largest possible group of decision-makers; on the other hand, if the data are not kept private, confidential, and secure, there will be negative consequences for the people who provided their data, and they will be less willing to provide the data going forward. I'll describe in the next chapter new government efforts to create a framework to maintain privacy while easing some of the more onerous restrictions.

One potential solution to this conundrum, which is being used throughout the government, is to create nondisclosive public data extracts – that is, aggregated collections of data that are designed to make it very unlikely that any individual's information could be identified and retrieved. For example, the IRS has created such data collections about tax returns, enabling nonprofit organizations like the Tax Policy Center to analyze the potential impact of proposed changes in the tax law.[18]

The National Academy of Sciences, the National Science Foundation, and other agencies have funded research into what steps would be necessary to better enable "blended data," that is, combinations of data across multiple agencies.[19] As their report states:

National statistical agencies, researchers, the private sector, and the public increasingly rely on blended data to produce the evidence needed for informed policymaking and to understand various aspects of society. Blended data (i.e., data combined from multiple sources of previously collected data) have numerous benefits. They can enable rich analyses impossible with any one data set alone; increase the accuracy, granularity, and timeliness of analyses; improve data equity; and reduce response burden and cost to the public. The benefits are increasingly attainable as computational and statistical methodologies advance, making data integration feasible even with massive and distributed data sources.[20]

The NAS privacy report recommends carefully analyzing both the benefits and potential risks of any planned blended data project. It also recommends comparing methods and estimating the required resources to minimize the chances of a breach of confidentiality. Any such effort also demands a maintenance plan, because as data sources change, both the benefits and the disclosure risks may shift.[21]

I'm certainly not advocating for the government to release personally identifiable information in ways that would violate privacy and create risks for the people who provide their data. But there is so much potential here if laws, policies, and regulations can be modernized. These are my main recommendations:

- **Modernize outdated privacy rules.** For example, Title 13 requires the Census Bureau to protect information (such as addresses) that are now widely available; it requires the Census Bureau to withhold business names for 30 years, even though most businesses pay large amounts of money to publicize their names. New rules for the Internet age could make such data far more useful.
- **Rationalize privacy rules with legislation.** Pass laws to rationalize privacy rules across departments and ease the process of

different parts of government sharing data aggregations in ways that do not threaten privacy. Build bureaucratic support for clearer communication among data holders to better enable them to understand and manage trade-offs between usefulness and the risk of inappropriate disclosures.[22] The NAS privacy report emphasizes that any such data sharing framework must be dynamic, adjusting to changes in policy needs, data availability, and technology.[23]

- **Focus on increasing sample size over diversity of information collected.** Our national data sets contain many esoteric questions. These questions offer relatively limited information content and are analyzed and used very infrequently. At the same time, we often face the "small cell size problem" where we want to look at the data with finer levels of granularity but find that there are not enough people with a particular combination of characteristics for us to draw meaningful conclusions about them. Re-examining the emphasis on content over sample is a worthwhile exercise. If the resources spent on collecting esoteric content was instead directed to increasing the number of people surveyed, analysts would be able to draw finer and more interesting conclusions by analyzing different slices of the data. And in most cases, the risk of disclosure or identification of an individual goes down as sample size goes up, simply because there are more individuals with any particular set of characteristics.

- **Explore opportunities for data combinations with lower privacy risks.** This begins with "anonymizing" data sets, that is, removing information that would enable the identification of any individual's data records. Unfortunately, clever data scientists with malign objectives can sometimes still identify records that have been anonymized. To reduce the risk of these sorts of actions, agencies should explore techniques that enable data analysis while protecting privacy. Here are some possible approaches: (1) Generating synthetic data that simulate actual data collections without including any actual respondent information. (2) Releasing "perturbed" data with small, random changes introduced to make it harder to identify individual records. (3) Secure multiparty computation (SMC), a technique that allows the analysis of blended data without any individual data set leaving its secure server.[24] (4) Homomorphic encryption, which allows statistical analysis of encrypted data without risk of revealing the underlying data; for example, IBM researchers were able to use homomorphic encryption to do machine learning from a data set of encrypted banking transactions.[25] (5) Privacy-preserving record linkage (PPRL), which links data applying to the same individual without using any of that individual's personally identifiable information, a useful technique to limit privacy risks for medical research, for example.[26] (6) Data enclaves: applications that make it possible for a small set of carefully vetted and authorized individuals to get access to sensitive data sets, with all of their queries monitored.[27]

- **Engage with private data creators.** Encourage private sector companies and nonprofits to contribute useful data under this same comprehensive privacy regime. For example, taken together, all of the nation's public utilities have a vast collection of useful data about Americans' energy use. Combining such private data collections with the government's own data sets could benefit researchers and decision-makers throughout both the private and public sectors.

Standards and Privacy Are Building Blocks for Public Data Infrastructure

The best term to describe the improved world of data that I'm proposing is *public data infrastructure* – that is, a set of assets, tools, and standards that will greatly improve the insights we can all get from the data that both companies and governments are collecting. In the next chapter, I'll explain the other elements that will make public data infrastructure powerfully beneficial for the world.

9

Public Data Infrastructure

ONE OF THE most effective ways that we, as a society, can become fact forward is if multiple sectors work together to create a public data infrastructure that fosters data savviness and data literacy across the population. At NORC, a research organization whose every activity centers around the creation, management, analysis, and dissemination of data, it is a core part of our mission to both demonstrate and promote the value of a public data infrastructure. One of the most effective ways for us to do this is to make it easier for citizens from all walks of life to access, analyze, and share our data. The following case is an example of how we try to do just that.

The General Social Survey (GSS), a large-scale nationally representative survey of people living in the United States, is one of our most informative national data sets. It is primarily funded by the National Science Foundation and conducted by NORC. Fielded every other year, and with historical data going back to 1972, the GSS tracks shifts in respondents' behavior and attitudes on dozens of interesting subjects, including God, government, education, health care, civil rights, and the economy. The breadth, rigor, and timescale of the GSS has made it one of the most cited sources of data on the American public. But while small extracts of GSS data had been used in classrooms and cited in major news publications, the structure and format of the GSS data sets made it difficult for anyone but sophisticated researchers with advanced data analysis skills to analyze the full richness of the data. Or, as NORC senior fellow Felicia LeClere put it, GSS data were "murky and hard to use, with data availability problems across its multiyear time frame."

To me and my colleagues, the fact that a such a valuable data set – and one under our charge – was difficult to use was simply unacceptable. I asked LeClere to build a "GSS Data Explorer," a full set of online tools to make it far easier to share GSS data with the widest possible range of users, from true data experts to curious students in grade school.

Her team analyzed potential audiences and worked to make the GSS data more accessible. By 2016, they had created a comprehensive, searchable codebook and a table generator visualizing trends for 25 popular survey questions since 1972. This effort sparked significant interest, with the GSS Data Explorer receiving over half a million hits in its first week.

Recognizing the need for further improvements, we invested in developing custom code and data interfaces, while simplifying access for less technical users like teachers, students, and journalists. In 2022, we launched an updated GSS Data Explorer at gssdataexplorer.norc.org. The Explorer is now integrated into the workflow of researchers and data scientists managing the survey, while also providing interfaces for analysts with varying skill levels. Users can conduct basic analyses on the site or download data sets for more advanced work. The updated Explorer makes it easy for people with minimal data skills to create accurate, understandable charts of consumer attitudes and behaviors over time, significantly enhancing the accessibility and utility of this valuable data set. Here are some examples. The following charts, which anyone using the GSS Data Explorer can easily produce in a few clicks, show shifts in gun ownership by education, different age groups' attitudes about gay sex, perspectives on the death penalty by race, and how men and women feel about whether preschoolers suffer if the mother works (see Figures 9-1 through 9-4).[1] In each case, transparent details about the methodology and question wording are provided along with the online chart.

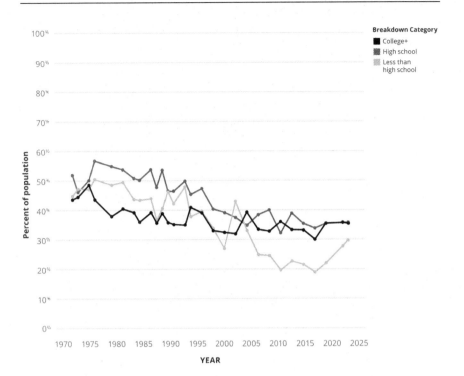

Figure 9-1: Trends in gun ownership by education level, 1972 to 2022. Survey question: "Do you happen to have in your home or garage any guns or revolvers?"

Source: GSS Data Explorer.

As a quick aside (because as a researcher I can't help myself from commenting on the results just a little bit), one of the fascinating things shown by all of these charts is how similarly American public opinion has evolved over time: regardless of demographic subgroup (age, gender, race, education level), Americans' attitudes all move in the same direction over time.

The GSS Data Explorer has been a major success in raising the visibility and utility of the GSS data. The GSS is the second-most-cited data set in the United States, after the US Census. The Data Explorer has opened up the possibilities and use of the GSS data for the public, and it has raised NORC's visibility and reputation as an organization that can generate new forms of insight into public opinion.

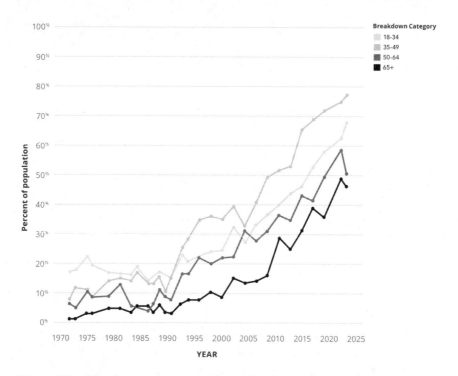

Figure 9-2: Trends in acceptance of sexual relations between same-sex adults by age group, 1972–2022. Survey question: "What about sexual relations between two adults of the same sex – do you think it is always wrong, almost always wrong, wrong only sometimes, or not wrong at all?" Chart shows: Not wrong at all.

Source: GSS Data Explorer.

Public Data Infrastructure Is Worth Billions, Perhaps Trillions

I provided all this detail on the GSS Data Explorer as one small example of the possibilities when data stewards focus on making their data more accessible. This one data system example won't change the world. But I do believe that a concerted effort, across society, to make data more accessible and usable can generate major benefits. The future should be one in which *the overwhelming majority* of data sets are broadly available like this – and all users have increased skills in understanding data and using it effectively.

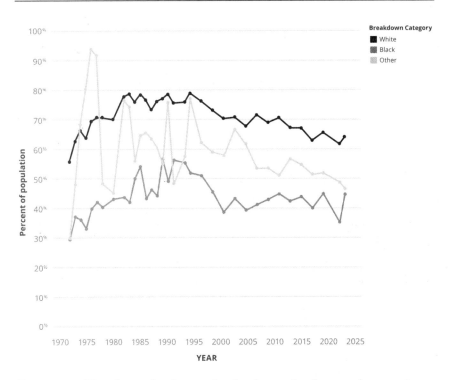

Figure 9-3: Trends in who favors the death penalty for murder convictions by race, 1972–2022. Survey question: "Do you favor or oppose the death penalty for persons convicted of murder?" Chart shows: Favor.

Source: GSS Data Explorer.

This is what I call public data infrastructure, and it is essential that we, as a society, invest more time and resources in building a good one.

Look at it this way. Traditionally, the way governments improve the economy has been to invest in infrastructure. The infrastructure of the public highway system and airports makes the nation run better, quicker, and more effectively. The infrastructure of the Internet has transformed how all of us access information. Infrastructure investments like GPS allow us to better navigate our vehicles and businesses to improve logistics as they track their fleets of trucks, trains, and planes. Consider support for public data infrastructure the same way: as an investment the government makes, together with

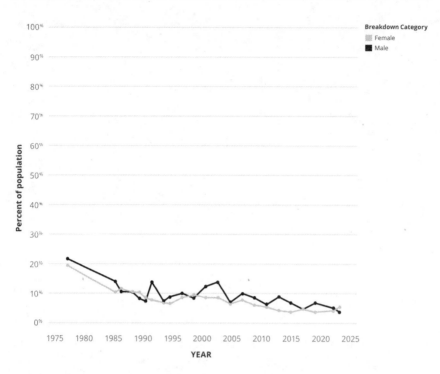

Figure 9-4: Trends in who says preschool kids suffer if the mother works, by gender, 1977–2022. Survey question: "Please tell me whether you strongly agree, agree, disagree, or strongly disagree. A preschool child is likely to suffer if his or her mother works" Chart shows: Strongly agree.

Source: GSS Data Explorer.

private companies, nonprofit organizations, and educational institutions, to enable all of us to benefit from more accurate, relevant, and timely data.

Is investing in public data infrastructure worth it? In 2013, McKinsey & Company estimated that the total economic value of open data – that is, making public data from government or other sources available for any organization or individual to access – would reach $3 trillion.[2] This includes about a trillion dollars of value from education, more than $700 billion in transportation, and more than $500 billion in consumer products. The benefits McKinsey quantified included increased efficiency, reduced waste, improved convenience for consumers, more effective consumer segmentation, better decisions, improved productivity, and improved price transparency for consumers. Joel Gurin's book *Open Data Now* explores this theme in more detail, with examples of how startups, financial companies, nonprofits, and all sorts of other organizations are benefitting from the trend toward more open access to data.[3]

In the rest of this chapter, I'll describe the elements of public data infrastructure. I'll show some more examples of how data producers and disseminators, from research companies to private industry to the government, are taking steps to build the infrastructure to promote a fact-forward world.

What Are the Elements of Public Data Infrastructure?

We're used to thinking of public infrastructure as facilities maintained for the benefit of all of us, like highways, parks, or public water distribution systems. But we need to think more broadly. You can expand the idea of public infrastructure to include institutions we all benefit from, like schools, law enforcement, and fire departments. You could broaden the idea further to include the legal code, which is essential to the government's role in preventing damaging behaviors like theft and fraud that would help the public.

Just as all these diverse elements are part of how society sets itself up for the mutual benefit of all citizens, there are also a varied collection of elements that would make up a public data infrastructure: a set of facilities created and maintained to enable all of us to benefit from data. With these efforts, society can support and maintain the data-savvy practices I've described so far and enable all the data producers, analyzers, disseminators, and consumers to effectively participate in the data ecosystem. It also enables the creation of new insights from combinations of publicly accessible data (including, by the way, the insights that are increasingly being generated by AI, as I describe in the next chapter).

The more we build the public data infrastructure, the more the benefits of data will accrue to all of us. Figure 9-5 provides a summary view of key elements of a public data infrastructure and how this infrastructure fosters the data-savvy skills described throughout this book.

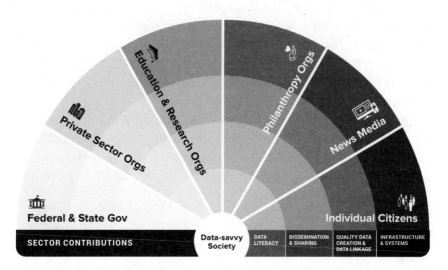

Figure 9-5: An overview of sector contributions to a data-savvy society.

Looking at public data infrastructure broadly, it includes:

- **Enhanced and better-integrated standards for data formats and privacy.** As I described in the previous chapter, standards and privacy protections make it possible to combine data sets to generate new insights. But we will all derive more value from data if the standards are revised and updated. Newer standards will enable more effective linking and sharing of data. When many of the current privacy laws were written, we lacked sophisticated tools, methods, and computational technology that expand both the opportunities and risks associated with data. What's more, many of the types of data currently available didn't exist. Updated privacy regulations will ensure that we continue to protect each individual's data in the context of these changes.
- **An educational system, including schools, academia, and research organizations, that creates data-savvy consumers.** This starts early with a lifecycle approach to data literacy for citizens of all ages, as I described in Chapter 7. As data literacy becomes a greater focus of our educational system, the societal benefits of a data-savvy citizenry will accrue more deeply and more substantially. Moving from the current state, where most people have very limited fluency with data and statistics, to a

	Data Literacy	Dissemination & Sharing	Quality Data Creation & Data Linkage	Infrastructure & Systems
Federal & State Gov	Fund programs, create standards, promote literacy with national data sets	Make data accessible and usable; adopt dissemination policies, standards	Harmonize data standards; foster linkages; bridge conflicting privacy regulations	Fund, support, and promote integration of government data systems
Private Sector Orgs	Train and develop workforce data skills; educate customers about industry data	Commit to transparency; publicly share data and methodologies	Partner across industry to promote consistent best practices	Invest in shared systems; partner with government on standards
Education & Research Orgs	Educate K–12, college students, adults; use best research practices	Convene communities; promote data-savvy dissemination	Teach best practices; foster data source linkages	Conceptualize, design, support cross-sector systems
Philanthropy Orgs	Fund data literacy programs, public awareness	Model effective dissemination initiatives; fund innovation	Incentivize multi-sector linkages, quality standards	Identify and support multi-sector data systems
News Media	Support data journalism, model data literacy practices	Report data with transparency, objectivity, balance; showcase data journalism	Report on privacy practices and uses of combined data systems	Make case for value of systems in a data-savvy society
Individual Citizens	Pursue, practice data-savvy skills; demand data literacy education	Responsibly share quality data; seek out and encourage fact-forward actors	Use and demand best practices when creating and linking data	Adopt and embrace new standardized systems, tools

Figure 9-5 (continued): Details on sector contributions to a data-savvy society.

state in which each of us understands the core principles of good science, data integrity, data transparency, and data neutrality will lead to better decisions and better outcomes across society. Not-for-profit organizations, especially research organizations and those whose missions are centered around data, can contribute by making data more available and easier to analyze, while simultaneously advancing data-savvy thinking with all of their audiences.

- **Federal, state, and local governments that support public data.** Governments produce large amounts of high-quality public data, such as the census, labor statistics, and health statistics. That means they have a central role in providing consistent standards and policies for creating and disseminating public data. Such entities can also take the lead in building methods for linking data sources while maintaining privacy, as I described in Chapter 8. I explore the role of open data in the government sector in detail in the second half of this chapter.

- **Private sector companies that participate in and promote public data sharing and analysis.** Companies are skilled at analyzing their proprietary data, like customer data and loyalty data. They also often join forces with private research companies to generate industry data, for example, as Nielsen does when it combines point-of-sale data from multiple retailers. Technology sector companies like Meta (with Facebook and Instagram) and Google (with its search function, maps, and YouTube) are notably amassing, analyzing, and exploiting masses of data from their customers. Private companies that are able to contribute non-proprietary portions of their data will benefit from other players that build on those data, generating new combinations and new sources of insight. (There is ample precedent for this sort of contribution to public knowledge by private companies; many companies like Microsoft and IBM benefit and derive profits from contributing to shared open-source coding projects, for example.) Companies can contribute to public knowledge about what consumers want, how they behave, where they go, how they shop, how much time they spend online, and how they interact with their devices. In the long run, if they wish to avoid onerous regulations and damage to their brands, it will be in their best interest to police against the pernicious use of data and algorithms that help promote false information or promulgate biases. To benefit fully from the value of data, companies must create and fund training and professional development opportunities for the workforce to develop data skills and share their own data in public whenever feasible (as Google does with Google Trends, for example). Because so much learning about data takes place in companies, not just in educational institutions, those companies will benefit by embracing the principles of data integrity, data transparency, and data neutrality.

- **News media embracing their role in responsible data dissemination.** Because of their essential role as data disseminators, news organizations that want to preserve their audiences and reputations will benefit from an unwavering commitment to truth in reporting, data transparency, data integrity, and data neutrality. There is a constant tension for media companies here, resisting the temptation to report alarming but questionable statistics that will drive audience engagement and instead presenting numbers in a balanced, skeptical, and analytical way that is more focused on insight than sensationalism. Investing in investigative and revealing data journalism, as I described in Chapter 7, is essential, and so is intelligent reporting on statistics in everyday stories on topics like crime, health, and the economy. Media has a fact-checking role in calling out public officials, politicians, candidates, private companies, and even other journalists who distort the presentation of data. It will also be essential for news media to report on what it means for us to have – or miss out on – a truly data-savvy society. If we are going to harness the collective will and resources necessary to build a more effective public data infrastructure, the public needs to understand the benefits of doing so – and the consequences if we fail.

- **Philanthropic sector organizations contributing to public data.** As they do in every other arena, philanthropic organizations should seek ways to augment, supplement, and fill gaps in data collection from governments and private companies. With so many philanthropies focused on education as a means to improving society, they should increase their focus on fostering data literacy across K–12 and post-secondary education.

■ **Citizens behaving as responsible participants in the data ecosystem.** At the end of the day, people are the fundamental participants in all public infrastructure. They make ethical contributions by participating in juries, voting in elections, driving safely, consuming water and electricity responsibly, and so on. The choices they make (or don't make) and the demands they place on both their elected representatives and the companies they patronize to advance a fact-forward world will ultimately determine our level of investment in public data infrastructure. They are the ones embracing new systems and approaches to becoming data literate and data savvy. They are responsible for evaluating and sharing appropriate facts and statistics online and calling out false and distorted information. As everyday people become more aware of the benefits of an effective public data infrastructure, and the risks of not having one, they will start to become the most powerful change agent for creating a fact-forward society, especially as they strive to raise data-savvy children.

Around the World, Governments Are Creating Public Data Infrastructure

The US government creates, compiles, and disseminates a vast amount of data. And, as we'll see later in the chapter, it is making slow but steady progress on the essential task of making all of the data easily accessible to researchers and consumers.

Around the world, other nations are also making progress on this task. In Canada, the government agency Statistics Canada is charged by law with collecting data and serving the nation with high-quality statistical information – and has been doing so since 1918. This includes the once-every-five-years Canadian census, along with 350 surveys on every possible aspect of Canadian life.[4] A visitor to the Statistics Canada website can review statistics in 31 different categories, from agriculture to travel and tourism.[5] A few clicks and you'll find yourself viewing, say, a historical chart of new motor vehicle registrations by fuel type and province (see Figure 9-6)[6] or a table of frozen ham exports by province and to which country they were exported (the Philippines apparently loves Canadian ham).[7] Because of Canada's comprehensive approach to data collection, much of the data is viewable in the form of interactive charts, with downloadable data tables on each page. Statistics Canada also provides access to public-use "microdata" files, including a full set of records for each data collection, so that statistically sophisticated users can go deeper in analyzing the data from various perspectives.[8] The agency clearly publishes its standards for transparency and accountability so that users can assess the data collection on those dimensions.[9]

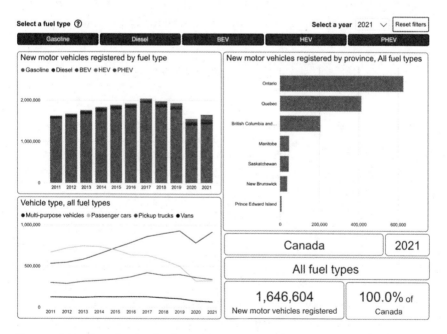

Figure 9-6: Canadian vehicle registrations, 2021.

Source: Statistics Canada website.

What other nations are embracing public data infrastructure? The Organisation for Economic Co-operation and Development (OECD), an international body dedicated to establishing evidence-based standards and solutions to an array of international challenges, scores 40 different nations on how open, useful, and reusable their data are – a fair reflection of each country's public data infrastructure.[10] As its report states, "Open government data has become a vital instrument for tackling both longstanding and emerging policy issues [and] is critical for strengthening democracy in the digital age." OECD rates nations on the availability of data sets, the accessibility of those data as measured by variety of formats and transparency, and the extent to which national data collection agencies promote reuse of data within and outside their governments. South Korea, France, and Poland led the index by demonstrating a comprehensive approach to open data initiatives. (While there are many open data initiatives in the US government, OECD stated that the comprehensive information required to rate the US was not supplied[11]). Based on OECD's methodology, there appears to be much room for improvement on this aspect of data infrastructure: OECD found that only 48% of high-value data sets were available as open data across all the countries surveyed.

American Public Data Infrastructure Successes

Public data infrastructure in the United States is slowly but steadily growing. But already, there are notable successes. Air quality measurement is one example.

Because of open data, I can tell you that as I am writing this in May 2024, the air quality index in Southern Texas is 103 (unhealthy) due to a wildfire, but less than one month ago, it was 48 (good). This information is instantly accessible through the US government website www.airnow.gov. AirNow compiles data by partnering with nine US federal agencies (including the Environmental Protection Agency, US Forest Service, National Weather Service, National Park Service, and NASA), all 50 states, 32 Native American tribes, and partners in both Mexico and Canada.[12] The algorithm is based on data from thousands

of monitors across the country.[13] As a result, it's possible for researchers, businesses, and ordinary consumers to access accurate, consistently
formatted air quality data from more than 500 US cities, as well as
historical data.

The federal government makes a lot of data publicly available. For
example, at data.gov, the government has published more than
300,000 data sets, including data on electric vehicles, banks that have
failed, small businesses, greenhouse gas emissions, produce prices, and
disease incidences.[14] There are 82,000 earth science data sets, 71,000
related to the oceans, 47,000 from the Department of Commerce, and
531 related to the climate.

The government maintains other open data repositories as well.
For example, usaspending.gov documents all the money the federal
government spends and where it goes. Using this resource, you can
find out that the FBI budget for fiscal year 2024 is $11.8 billion,
including $4.5 billion for counterterrorism, $4.2 billion for investigating and prosecuting criminals, and $2.0 billion for intelligence.[15]
At performance.gov, you can gather data on how well the various
government departments are accomplishing their measurable goals
and how various government statistics are varying. For example, this
site documents that gross domestic product per person, corrected for
inflation, has risen from $19,400 per person to $61,000 per person
in the 60 years leading up to 2020, or that the percentage of the
population receiving social security disability benefits has risen from
0.9% to 5.2% in the same time period.[16]

The challenge with this vast data collection is in finding what
you're looking for and understanding how it relates to other data. For
the most part, it's not an *accessibility* problem, it's an *organizational and
interpretation* problem. One organization attempting to help with this
is USAFacts, a nonprofit organization started by former Microsoft
CEO Steve Ballmer in 2015. USAFacts attempts to make sense of the
information from 90,000 federal, state, and local governments, often
in incompatible formats that make analysis challenging. USAFacts
publishes topical analyses, for example, tracking whether fentanyl
overdose deaths are rising on a state-by-state basis and which ethnic
and social minorities have experienced an increase in hate crimes.[17]

USAFacts is an exemplar of how private nonprofit organizations can take advantage of government data infrastructure to create value for the communities they serve.

There is hopeful progress in collecting and analyzing data on other fronts – like tracking and reducing injuries and violence from firearms. So far, there is public reporting on fatal shootings, but there's no simple way to track people who are shot but don't die. As NORC senior fellow John Roman wrote, "Data on issues such as how shootings are distributed across jurisdictions and among different demographic groups, or what determines whether victims of gun assault and robbery are killed, wounded, or threatened would go a long way toward developing evidence-based policy to reduce gun violence. In an age of intense partisanship, shared facts pave the way to building a shared purpose: improving public safety."[18]

With funding from Arnold Ventures, NORC convened a panel of experts to catalog all available sources of firearms data.[19] The panel's report recommends building a public data infrastructure to harmonize firearms data across systems and levels of government while collaborating to facilitate rigorous research designs. A follow-up report suggests a Federal Firearms Data Agenda, including recommendations for the federal government to create systems for tracking nonfatal gunshot injuries, surveying gun owners, and building resources to enable state and local governments to integrate their health, social service, and criminal justice efforts to reduce public harm.[20] It also recommends that state and local governments standardize their reporting efforts through the National Incident-Based Reporting System (NIBRS). Following this blueprint could generate evidence that would better inform legislation, licensing, and law enforcement priorities to reduce gun violence.

Steps Toward America's Public Data Infrastructure

As you might imagine, individual steps like the tracking of air quality, government spending, or firearms violence ought to be part of a more comprehensive effort to build public data infrastructure. The National Academy of Sciences (NAS), with funding from the

National Science Foundation (NSF) have published out a series of reports under the header, "Toward a 21st Century National Data Infrastructure." The first report sets the stage by noting that the United States needs a "national data infrastructure that blends data from multiple sources to improve the quality, timeliness, granularity, and usefulness of national statistics, facilitates more rigorous social and economic research, and supports evidence-based policymaking and program evaluations."[21]

Perhaps not surprisingly, many individual Americans tend to agree. In a 2021 AP-NORC survey of 1,004 individuals, 34% agreed that "Increasing information-sharing across different agencies to streamline online services" would have a major impact on them personally.[22] Anyone who's had to deal with data from multiple government agencies can probably relate to the frustration this statistic reflects.

However, over the course of more than a decade, the federal government has steadily moved in the direction of creating this common infrastructure that would create a powerful foundation for all sorts of data analysis from combining data from federal, state, and private data sources. From the outside, such progress may appear slow, but given America's ever-shifting political climate, the vast amounts of data involved, and the need to maintain safeguards on privacy, the progress has been substantial. (See the sidebar "Federal Data Infrastructure: A Chronology" for more details on this progress.)

As Jason Saul, executive director of the Center for Impact Sciences at the University of Chicago's Harris School of Public Policy, points out, one key benefit of this governmental investment in infrastructure would be to significantly improve transparency in the government's operations. "There should be a common outcomes taxonomy for tagging all federal programs," he stated.[29] "The average person should be able to look at how much we've spent on each outcome that matters to them, understand the 'cost per outcome' for every funded program, and see how that compares to others." We all deserve this sort of insight into our government's investments, which would go a long way toward illuminating what the nation's legislative priorities ought to be.

Federal Data Infrastructure: A Chronology

Over the past decade, the US federal government has undertaken various initiatives aimed at developing a common data infrastructure. These efforts have focused on facilitating data analysis by combining data from federal, state, and private sources while addressing challenges such as shifting political priorities, managing huge volumes of data, and maintaining privacy safeguards.

Key Milestones

2013

- President Obama issues an executive order creating an open data policy.
- Freely available, machine-readable data becomes the default for federal government-produced data.[23]

2016

- Bipartisan support leads to the creation of the US Commission on Evidence-Based Policymaking.
- The Commission envisions efficient creation of rigorous evidence as a routine part of government operations.

2017

- The Commission on Evidence-Based Policymaking issues a report with 22 specific recommendations, including[24]:
  - o Creation of a National Secure Data Service (NSDS)
  - o Appointment of chief data officers throughout the federal government
  - o Standardization of state-collected data
  - o Secure access for external researchers to confidential government data
  - o Enhanced privacy protections

2018

- The Foundations for Evidence-Based Policymaking Act ("Evidence Act") is passed.[25]

- Key provisions include:
  - o Federal government policies should be based on factual statistical evidence.
  - o All government agencies must develop open data plans that make data public by default.
  - o Annual plans required from each agency describing evidence-building for policies.

2021–2022

- The Advisory Committee on Data for Evidence Building (ACDEB) issues two reports.
- These reports detail plans for advancing and coordinating evidence-based data use in government.

2022

- The National Science Foundation (NSF) launches America's DataHub as an open-data demonstration.
- The mission of America's DataHub is to[26]:
  - o Develop new ways of acquiring and linking data to yield valuable insights into critical issues
  - o Support cutting-edge data infrastructure
  - o Build data security capabilities to further increase privacy protections and public trust
  - o Provide novel and innovative analyses
  - o Share lessons learned for similar activities across the federal government[27]
- The CHIPS and Science Act establishes a five-year NSDS Demonstration project (NSDS-D) (see vision description after this list).

2023

- The NSF announces $7.5 million in funding for new data infrastructure projects, including:
  - o Synthetic data research

(continued)

(continued)

> o Platforms for federated data usage
> o Expanded access to restricted-use data through "Federal Statistical Research Data Centers"[28]
> o Enhanced access to vital national statistics through new and improved standards for data quality, metadata, definitions, systems, and technologies

The Vision for a National Secure Data Service (NSDS)

Informed by the ACDEB reports and lessons learned from the America's DataHub demonstration project and with funding from the CHIPS and Science Act, the NSDS Demonstration project (NSDS-D) aims to provide a platform of shared services to:

- Streamline and innovate data access
- Enhance data linkage capabilities
- Strengthen privacy protections
- Support expanded data use

Key goals include:

- Collaboration across all levels of government and with non-government stakeholders
- Development of a comprehensive data ecosystem
- Support for evidence-based decision-making, especially in public policy

The NSDS-D project will:

- Inform decisions about the establishment and form of a permanent NSDS
- Determine necessary and effective shared services
- Identify innovations to support the NSDS mission

As this infrastructure develops, it promises to significantly improve transparency in government operations and provide valuable insights into national legislative priorities.

A Powerful Vision Emerges

Momentum is building for a public data infrastructure that can help create a data-savvy citizenry. Much of the effort happening now within the federal government involves combining different forms of data. Most government agencies now source some data from private sources or combine data from multiple government agencies. The Bureau of Economic Analysis (BEA) taps 142 private sector data assets, the Energy Information Administration (EIA) uses around 80, and the Census Bureau uses at least 20.[30] As I described in the previous chapter, data combinations like this can be expensive, raise privacy issues, and run afoul of incompatibilities in definitions and data redundancy. There may be problems with transparency because private sector organizations may not be willing to reveal the details of their methods, making these sources into "black boxes." When these data are combined with official statistics, the resulting methodology may be hard to explain or suspect. And private sector organizations can change their methods, causing problems with consistency or comparability with official statistics.

Even so, statisticians and data scientists inside and outside the government are exploring creative ways to resolve many of these problems.[31] For example, the government agency tasked with tracking construction starts used satellite data to identify new construction rather than attempting to rationalize construction permits from thousands of local jurisdictions.

The National Academy of Sciences report, discussed at the start of this section, lays out seven attributes of the new National Data Infrastructure[32]:

- Safeguards and advanced privacy-enhancing practices to minimize possible individual harm
- Statistical uses only, for common-good information, with statistical aggregates freely shared with all
- Mobilization of relevant digital data assets, blended in statistical aggregates to provide benefits to data holders, with societal benefits proportionate to possible costs and risks
- Reformed legal authorities protecting all parties' interests

- Governance framework and standards effectively supporting operations
- Transparency to the public regarding analytical operations using the infrastructure
- State-of-the-art practices for access, statistical, coordination, and computational activities; continuously improved to efficiently create increasingly secure and useful information

The recommendations of the NAS reports are both comprehensive and tangible, and the vision is expansive:

Information about the welfare of the population – its health and safety, educational achievement, occupational skill distribution, employment status, wealth, housing status, and hundreds of other attributes – guides the assessment of a country's well-being. Information about the status of the economy similarly prompts judgment.... To assess current conditions as well as the performance of elected officials and the policies they pursue, citizens of democracies require authoritative and trustworthy statistics. The absence of such facts can leave citizens vulnerable to misinformation and disinformation – a threat to democracy itself. . . .

The Far-Reaching Benefits of a Growing Public Data Infrastructure

If the federal government succeeds in its efforts to embrace a new public data infrastructure, the benefits will be powerful. We will all gain data-based insights into how to solve the nation's most pressing problems, such as immigration, healthcare costs, inflation, unemployment, the costs and priorities of education, global warming, crime, political polarization, and the spread of false information. We'll be able to make better decisions and have principled arguments based more on facts and data and less on heartfelt, but hard-to-agree-upon emotional perspectives on what ought to happen. The benefits will include more timely data, better use of existing information, increased transparency, and improvements in the insights that the nation relies on for decision-making. Put simply, more people will have better access to more relevant, detailed, and transparently created data.

But as necessary as they are, the efforts of the federal government and other big data collectors are not in themselves sufficient. These efforts will bear fruit only if we concurrently invest in a data-savvy public, as well as committing to integrity, neutrality, and transparency in all elements of the data ecosphere. Powerful and connected data is only as good as the ability of those using it to understand it and make better decisions with it.

In its broadest and most advanced state, a comprehensive public data infrastructure is an idealistic concept. However, what we have seen from this chapter is that at a practical level, creating a modern public data infrastructure is not only doable, but is being done – at least partially – across government, educational and research institutions, businesses, and philanthropy. Enhancements to our existing data infrastructure continue to accrue, as do the benefits of the evolving infrastructure. We have a clear idea of what's necessary to create a data-savvy world. Now we just have to commit the resources to keep building it.

10

The Promise and Challenge of Artificial Intelligence

WHAT FOLLOWS IS the transcript of a dialogue with ChatGPT.[1]

Hi, Dan. What can I help you with today?

I wanted to talk about artificial intelligence (AI). Is that a topic on which you can have an interesting and informative conversation?

Absolutely, Dan. Artificial intelligence is a fascinating and rapidly evolving field, impacting various sectors from healthcare to finance. Whether you're interested in understanding its basics, exploring specific applications, or discussing ethical considerations, I'm here to provide insightful and concise information. What aspect of AI would you like to delve into?

Let's start with this. How much will AI affect the things people see and read in the future?

AI will significantly impact what people see and read in the future by personalizing content, improving search algorithms, and generating news and media. This technology can tailor information to individual preferences, streamline content discovery, and even create articles or stories, enhancing user experiences and potentially raising concerns about the authenticity and diversity of the content consumed.

Researchers are using AI to analyze their data. What sorts of new insights might emerge from such techniques?

Using AI to analyze data, researchers can uncover patterns and correlations that were previously undetectable, predict future trends with greater accuracy, and automate complex data process- ing tasks. This can lead to new insights in areas like disease pre- diction, climate modeling, and social behavior analysis, ultimately enhancing our understanding and enabling more informed decision-making across various fields.

That all sounds great, but not everything is as wonderful as you make it seem. Isn't it true that AI-generated content often contains errors (also known as "hallucinations")?

Yes, that's true. AI-generated content can sometimes contain errors or "hallucinations," where the AI produces inaccurate or nonsensical information. This happens because AI models pre- dict text based on patterns rather than understanding context or facts. These inaccuracies highlight the need for careful oversight and verification when using AI-generated content, especially in critical applications like news, healthcare, and scientific research.

What are the best ways to avoid these hallucinations? Can we ever eliminate them entirely?

To minimize AI hallucinations, it's essential to use high-quality training data, implement rigorous validation processes, and employ human oversight to verify outputs. Techniques like fine- tuning models for specific tasks and using hybrid systems that combine AI with rule-based approaches can also help. However, eliminating hallucinations entirely is challenging due to the inherent limitations of current AI technologies, so continuous monitoring and improvement are necessary.

AI often generates results without much transparency into how they were created. Large Language Models and neural networks can't really tell you how they got their answers, can they?

You're correct. AI methods like Large Language Models and neural networks often operate as "black boxes," providing little transparency into how they arrive at their results. This lack of explainability can be problematic, especially in critical applications. Researchers are working on developing explainable AI techniques to make these processes more transparent, but achieving full transparency remains a complex challenge.

How can we fix the problem of bias in AI systems?

To address bias in AI systems, it's crucial to use diverse and representative training data, implement fairness-aware algorithms, and conduct regular bias audits. Involving interdisciplinary teams, including ethicists and domain experts, can help identify and mitigate biases. Continuous monitoring and updating of AI models are necessary to ensure they remain fair and unbiased over time.

Bad actors are using AI to create false content, including "deepfake" videos. Is there any way to stop these, or to detect them so people can tell they are fake?

To combat deepfakes, researchers are developing advanced detection algorithms that analyze inconsistencies in videos, such as unnatural facial movements or lighting anomalies. Implementing digital watermarking and blockchain technology can help verify content authenticity. Public awareness and education on recognizing deepfakes are also crucial. While detection methods are improving, staying ahead of increasingly sophisticated deepfake technology remains a continuous effort.

When it comes to people being smart about data, is AI really an improvement? Will AI actually contribute to a deeper understanding about data, or is it more likely that it will flood the world with fake and misleading content?

AI has the potential to enhance data understanding by uncovering complex patterns and providing actionable insights, contributing to smarter decision-making. However, it also poses risks of generating fake and misleading content if not properly managed. The key lies in responsible AI development, incorporating robust ethical guidelines, verification mechanisms, and continuous monitoring to maximize its benefits while mitigating potential harms.

Thanks for an evenhanded explanation of a complex topic.

You're welcome, Dan. I'm glad I could provide a balanced perspective. If you have any more questions or need further clarification on AI or any other topic, feel free to ask.

How to Think About AI

When I first considered it, it seemed like a mistake to include a chapter on artificial intelligence in this book. Books are written at a specific point in time, and AI technology is evolving incredibly rapidly. In less than two years leading up to the moment I'm writing this chapter (June 2024), ChatGPT burst upon the world and evolved through several major sets of improvements. Meanwhile, Microsoft, Google, Meta, and Apple not only announced AI features but built them directly into their search engines, productivity tools, social networks, and computing devices. One long-tenured technology analyst who has tracked everything from the internet cloud to social media to smartphones over the last three decades described AI as "the fastest moving topic I've ever covered."[2]

But failing to acknowledge this dramatic and far-reaching set of shifts would be irresponsible for a book about how to be data savvy. So let's concentrate on what *isn't* changing. Even as AI evolves rapidly, the *principle* behind it remains constant:

Artificial intelligence tools detect patterns in large data sets and then use those patterns to generate results that mimic the existing data.

This is how an AI tool can review millions of mammograms, some with images reflecting cancer and some without, and use those patterns to identify potential cancers.

It is how an AI model can read thousands of articles on, say, Supreme Court decisions, and write a summary of those articles when a user prompts it with, "Describe Supreme Court decisions about the limits of executive power."

It is how an AI tool can absorb hundreds of thousands of pop songs and generate potential new hits.[3] Or, after reviewing masses of animated videos, create a new video based solely on a script description.[4]

The mechanism that these tools use is typically a neural network: a huge collection of computing resources designed to detect patterns in masses of data and render those patterns into terms the machine can process and then use to create new content. This ability to generate new content is why such models are typically called "generative AI." In the dialogue at the start of this chapter, ChatGPT-4o, a large language model (or LLM), has consumed all the text from what are likely hundreds of thousands of pages of information about AI and used the patterns in that information both to parse my prompts and to generate summaries of the information it read. The result is a plausible simulation of what it would be like to talk to an extremely knowledgeable expert who can patiently explain any aspect of the topic.

As I write this, owners of copyrighted content and developers of AI tools are wrangling and exchanging lawsuits regarding whether it's permissible to scrape masses of web content and use it to fuel AI systems. Regardless of how that battle turns out, it's crucial to understand that even though AI systems have absorbed and detected patterns in the masses of data they consume, they don't actually *understand* anything.[5] AI models are simply able to simulate understanding based on sophisticated pattern analysis.

When AI tools make mistakes or "hallucinate," it is due to that lack of understanding. Because Thomas Edison was such a well-publicized inventor, they may claim that he invented the stock ticker, even though Edward Calahan actually invented it (and Edison improved it a couple years later). They might recommend eating a small rock every day, because they haven't distinguished dependable sources about nutrition from the source of that advice, which is the satirical site called *The Onion*.[6] The problem of making sure that things are true is far more difficult than the problem of making sure that generated output is grammatical, logical, and convincing, because truth is not a pattern-matching problem.

As the content and creativity expert Jay Acunzo memorably put it, "AI has read the internet. It has not read the room."[7] Reading virtually the whole Internet gives AI tools access to nearly everything people have written, spoken, drawn, photographed, filmed, or coded. It doesn't give them access to common sense or the subtleties of human interaction.

Here's a slightly more technical explanation of how generative AI works. It creates new content with predictive models. As ChatGPT itself explains in response to a query, these models "are the results of complex machine learning algorithms . . . the model predicts the next word or sequence of words in a given context that makes the most sense." This means that, while there are enormous amounts of computation and data involved, at the end of the day, all of the content that generative AI provides is probabilistic in nature. The words "makes the most sense" really mean "have the highest probability of being correct, based on predictive models." Recall that we've already described the strengths and limitations of probabilistic information throughout the previous chapters of this book.

We know that probabilistic information has a level of confidence associated with it. Here's what ChatGPT has to say about this: "Thus, while the responses [of generative AI] can be very accurate and contextually appropriate, they are fundamentally based on probabilistic predictions rather than deterministic rules or factual databases. When AI gets something wrong it is usually because the model has incorrectly predicted the next word or sequence of words."

In this chapter, I'll help you to become data savvy about artificial intelligence: its immense power along with its tendency to sometimes generate inaccurate but highly plausible results. If you understand why AI tools do this, you'll be in a better position to use them and understand their results. And that is a set of principles that I hope will remain useful, even as the AI technology continues to improve. Since the state of the science of AI is evolving so rapidly, much of the information in this chapter is based on interviews with AI experts who work with the technology every day.

AI Has Great Potential to Improve the Analysis of Data

Artificial intelligence tools have almost unlimited potential to create new insights from data. This includes the ability to draw conclusions quickly from data sets, suggest previously unrecognized patterns, and detect anomalies. AI can also analyze data sets that were previously too lacking in structure to afford useful analysis, such as collections of photos, masses of documents, or billions of social media posts and comments.

Let's start with the mass of information that the federal government collects, as I described in the previous chapter. AI could help with one of the biggest problems: finding the *right* information in this huge pile of data. As Richard Coffin, chief of research and advocacy for the data compilation site USAFacts, put it, "Government in the US is the biggest data creator and provider in the world . . . AI-driven access to data in the federal government is an absolute necessity. It must happen."[8] Imagine if you could ask a tool, "Find me the most reliable information on changes in crime statistics for felonies over the last five years" and get an answer without a need to have detailed knowledge of which agency collected the data and where they have published it.

I mentioned AI's ability to read mammograms and generate diagnostic information that is similar in accuracy to what a radiologist observing a scan can do.[9] Cynthia Rudin, a computer science professor at Duke, is among those working on this problem. As she explained, training such models takes collaboration with radiologists. For example, one tool helps analyze breast lesions by comparing parts of those lesions to parts of other lesions from the training set, enabling doctors to draw conclusions about a current case based on past cases.[10] This shows how AI algorithms tend to advance: not just with large sets of training data but in collaboration with human experts. The upside is enormous: Because a well-trained AI system can scan tissue and find comparable cases much more quickly than a human. Dr. Rudin is also working on automated tools that will generate a risk score for women without cancer by pinpointing subtle asymmetries between the left and right breasts.[11]

Charlene Li is a *New York Times* bestselling author whose new book *Winning with Generative AI: The 90-Day Blueprint for Success* advises corporate executives on how to leverage AI.[12] She expects rapid advances in data analysts using AI on corporate data collections to generate new insights. "When people get access to these tools, what are the questions they ask, that nobody else thought to ask?" she wonders.[13] "I often say that the biggest constraint of us using this technology to its full capacity is imagination and curiosity. We've never had access to this power and data."

Li has already multiplied her productivity with AI tools. "I am planning to generate all my audiobooks with the AI using my voice, rather than reading and recording every single word," she says. "I also will have it simultaneously translated to 20 different languages."

Katia Walsh, Li's coauthor and the chief digital officer of the Harvard Business School, expects AI to supercharge the utility of search.[14] It could answer difficult questions like, "Where can I get a necessary medical procedure by a provider with a good reputation at the minimum possible cost in my health plan?"

Michael Franklin, University of Chicago computer science professor and co-director of the university's Data Science Institute, points out how AI tools can conduct searches of unstructured data that were never before possible.[15] Franklin is among the cocreators of Palimpsest, a system that optimizes searches of unstructured databases like legal documents assembled from discovery processes, medical documents, and real estate photos.[16] For example, Palimpsest would enable a user to search through a database of real estate listings for midcentury modern architecture – a quality that isn't tagged in the database but could be identified by AI pattern-matching on photos.

Ensuring Accuracy Remains a Major AI Challenge

Results from AI tools are often accurate. But they do make mistakes and offer dubious or even dangerous information. For example, I had been researching on the Internet how to correctly wire a 220-volt piece of woodworking equipment. The results were confusing, and I wasn't sure I had the correct answer. Out of curiosity, I asked ChatGPT. It quickly told me just what to do, without caveats or cautions. The wiring that ChatGPT told me to use was one that quite a few of the Internet sources I consulted said was correct. It was also one that a number of people on other sites said was dangerous. So what did I do? I called my electrician! He was able to tell me the correct wiring (and not the one recommended by ChatGPT, which he said was definitely an electrocution risk), but only after I gave him a lot of additional detail, and even then, the answer he gave me was based on understanding my specific preferences in terms of what I wanted to accomplish.

In my experience, ChatGPT is not very effective at asking for more details so that it can provide a better answer (I have not been able to get it to do that, even when I have asked it fairly ambiguous questions). When discussing the possible qualifications, limitations, or uncertainty associated with its answers, ChatGPT generally provides very vague statements that often amount to, "Well, the actual answer depends on many things, so this might not be correct."

When ChatGPT produces incorrect results, it's often because of problems with the data on which AI tools were trained. As well-known technology analyst Maribel Lopez (founder of Lopez Research) explained, "One of the biggest issues in generative AI is that it's unclear if people are using the right data. If you are a business that had bad data issues before, your results will only get worse with AI. . . . It accelerates everything that was already wrong, and worse, it accelerates it with confidence, presented in perfect grammatically correct results."[17] This is the well-known principle of "garbage in, garbage out" but with a dangerous new twist – the stuff that comes out doesn't *look* like garbage.

Perhaps bad data is what led to a notably misleading corporate chatbot on the website of Air Canada. The chatbot told a bereaved traveler heading to a funeral that he could book a full-fare ticket and apply after the funeral he had traveled to for a partial refund under the airline's fare rules. This advice was wrong: The bereavement fare was available only at the time of booking. As PV Kannan, the CEO of chatbot company [24]7.ai and author of the AI book *The Age of Intent* commented, "I don't know how Air Canada managed to put that chatbot in front of customer."[18] Air Canada attempted to evade responsibility by claiming the chatbot was a "separate legal entity responsible for its own actions," but a legal tribunal rejected that claim. If your corporate chatbot makes an error, you're going to have to pay for it.

Algorithms that correct the biases in data can introduce other problems. For example, in an attempt to show more diversity in the images it generated, Google's Gemini tool at one point was creating pictures of America's founding fathers with invented racial characteristics and a pope who appeared to be a Southeast Asian woman.[19] Clearly, the effort to balance the pattern-matching tools' propensity to generate images of white men, while well-intended, had led to simply unrealistic (if perhaps thought-provoking) results.

All of these are examples of AI tools making inadvertent errors. But the same sorts of tools can be used for malign purposes, to deceive people.

For example, the branch manager of a Japanese company thought he was receiving a call from the director of his parent company. The director authorized transfers of about $35 million to finance an acquisition. But in fact, the call was not from his director but from a fraudster who had used AI "voice-cloning" software to fool the branch manager.[20] According to the Federal Trade Commission, the same sorts of software have also been used to fool people into thinking that their loved ones are in legal trouble and need cash immediately.[21]

"Deepfake" videos created with AI tools can fool people into believing false information about public figures, especially during elections.[22] Deepfake video circulating on social media in 2024 showed Moldovan president Maia Sandu, whose nation borders Ukraine, endorsing a party favorable to Russia and announcing that she would soon be resigning. In fact, Sandu had no plan to resign and supports Ukraine in its war with Russia. Officials in Moldova suspect that Russian "threat actors" are behind the fakes. In fact, deepfakes may be the most recent use of AI for cyberattacks, but we know that AI bots designed to deceive voters have been deployed on social media by nation-states since well before the 2016 US presidential election.

And in Bangladesh, a fake video showed Rumeen Farhana, an opponent of the ruling party, in a bikini. This was perceived as scandalous by many in the Muslim-majority nation.

Tools to detect deepfakes continue to improve, but they have a long way to go. NPR tested several prominent deepfake detection tools in 2024 and found that, despite claims of more than 90% accuracy, they missed many examples of faked simulations.[23] As with the rest of AI, these tools will become much better over time as their "training" becomes more sophisticated. In addition to AI detection tools, additional safeguards against deepfakes are emerging via industry self-regulation[24] and federal and state government regulations.[25] The regulatory framework is in its early stages, but it offers promise.

Researchers are working hard to improve the accuracy of AI tools. Bo Li, a professor with appointments at both the University of Illinois at Urbana-Champaign and the University of Chicago, is one. In one paper, her team investigated ways that AI tools can be misled to generate inaccurate or biased outputs or to cough up private information from their training data.[26] In another, she and her coauthors proposed a framework of guardrails that can help prevent models from generating harmful results.[27] While none of these methods is dependably accurate yet, Professor Li believes that they will become much more so over the next several years.

Distrust and Verify

While these examples of AI tools generating false or harmful information ought to raise concerns, let's take a step back from the AI frenzy for a moment. AI is a tool. And tools always have the potential to generate errors.

Consider a tool like Google Search. Google has always used pattern matching to surface sites that match the user's query. Some of those sites have always contained bad information or fakery. The difference is that if you see that a result is from the Babylon Bee or Comedy Central – or a biased site like the Daily Wire or the Palmer Report – a media-savvy consumer knows to be suspicious. The same applies to unsourced "news" you might encounter on Facebook, X, Instagram, or TikTok.

The difference with AI tools is that they generate extremely smooth and convincing text, pictures, sound, and video. In many cases, it's not clear where the information comes from. As a result, the right attitude toward AI output is always suspicion.

In the 1980s, President Ronald Reagan described his suspicious attitude toward Russian nuclear disarmament claims with the phrase, "Trust but verify."[28] Maribel Lopez of Lopez Research describes her similarly suspicious attitude toward generative AI as "Distrust and verify."

"Because you don't know if it is accurate, the first thing you need to do is ask, does this image look right?" Lopez asks. "These are powerful tools in the hands of the average individual. They are really powerful tools in the hands of nefarious individuals."

Remember that AI is optimized to match patterns that you are used to reading or viewing. That makes it quite persuasive. As a result, it taps into your confirmation bias. And that means that everyone using AI – data producers, data disseminators, and data consumers – must be extra careful in evaluating what the AI tools generate.

"Distrust and verify" is a very good place to start.

Throughout the AI Ecosystem, a "Human in the Loop" Is Essential

AI has the potential to revolutionize many kinds of work, including data science and journalism. The potential to generate new insights, faster and more often, is virtually limitless. But as with all technical advances, there are potential pitfalls. The sections that follow describe how all ecosystem participants – data producers, data disseminators, and data consumers – can more safely take advantage of the new AI tools. A common theme is the need to keep a "human in the loop," rather than allowing automated tools to simply generate and publish at will. Someone with expertise and judgment must distrust and verify, vetting the results, checking them for validity, and putting them into context. Just as an expert radiologist should review an AI analysis of a mammogram, an expert data scientist or skilled journalist should review AI-generated results before unleashing them on the public.

For Data Producers, AI Demands a Continued Focus on Transparency and Neutrality

Data producers now have a powerful new tool with the ability to analyze new and uncharted data collections. AI can be used to produce data very quickly, both from traditional sources and from new data pools. This includes so-called "big data" collections that would previously have been too complex or massive to use as data sources, like every click on a website, or all the vehicle movements detected by traffic cameras in a city.[29]

These analyses will also extend to correlations among data sources. An analyst could, for example, look at a thousand variables about every customer a company has and identify which factors predict whether a customer is likely to increase their business with the company or switch to a competitor.

AI tools also promise to help automate data scientists' tasks. One example is the Automatic Statistician project, which "aims to automate data science, producing predictions and human-readable reports from raw datasets with minimal human intervention."[30] Applied to a data set, various types of automatic tools not only generate basic statistics and graphs, but compare the results of different statistical models.

But as with the output of any automated system, such results should never be taken at face value without a human data scientist in the loop verifying their validity.

The challenge for data scientists is to figure out which patterns and statistics are real and which are just random chance, generated by the vast number of possible outcomes that a model can review. Recall the discussion of p-hacking in Chapter 6. The technique of casting about for something interesting to publish, regardless of whether it reflects a real effect, is about to get far easier and therefore more tempting.

There are not yet standards for whether results surfaced by AI are significant or publishable, and there need to be. This is a frontier that the data scientists of the next few decades must apply themselves to.

While it's too soon to come up with definitive guidelines, here are some ideas that could eventually become part of such guidelines:

- **Use retrieval-augmented generation (RAG) to improve accuracy.** Developed by research scientist Patrick Lewis and colleagues, RAG is a technique that allows large language models to give greater weight to content from a trusted set of sources. It doesn't eliminate hallucinations, but it reduces them. For example, an AI news generator could give greater credence to information from trusted sources like the *Washington Post* or the *Wall Street Journal* over reporting from unvetted and possibly undependable sources. The AI tool could go even further by giving more weight to news articles that practice the fact-forward approaches discussed in this book. A statistical model might lean more heavily on solid government statistics. The University of Chicago's Michael Franklin speculated about "the possibility that a reasonable set of criteria could be developed that constitute a seal of approval as being a higher quality information source. Or even beyond a seal, an enumeration of the degree to which a source adheres to best practices that lead to a reliable and high-quality source of information."

- **Question the robustness of data analyses.** AI tools will readily draw conclusions from very little data. The danger here is "AI-washing," that is, publishing results with the imprimatur of plausibility that comes from identifying them as the output of a model. AI conclusions based on weak or narrow data are worthless in the same way a consumer survey with a sample size of 10 is, but their weakness won't be as obvious. Researchers must query their AI tools about what sources led to their conclusions, and vet the dependability of those sources before asserting that any result is plausible. Government agencies and other trusted sources must be wary of publishing AI-generated data, because the choice to do so could indicate a level of confidence that's not warranted compared to other solid government statistics.

- **Use AI tools to check each other.** Different AI tools have different strengths and weaknesses; for example, some may be more rules-based, while others are based on pure neural network outputs. The diversity of methods creates an opportunity to use them to check each other and find inconsistencies, a method that's been tested by Sebastian Farquhar, a University of Oxford computer scientist.[31] Other AI tools attempt to identify fake photos, fake videos, and AI-generated text.[32] As described earlier, none of these tools is 100% accurate, but they continue to improve, and in the hands of wise data producers, they can help identify spurious content and results.

- **Be hyper-aware of biases.** As we discussed in Chapter 6, just because a data set is huge doesn't mean it's unbiased. AI, since it works with massive amounts of data, is subject to the same potential bias problems. For example, an analysis of English-language Internet comments on a topic will completely miss perspectives from speakers posting in Spanish, Chinese, Tagalog, or Haitian Creole. And models may have inherent algorithmic biases. For example, an AI weather model based on hurricane paths may become less dependable when applied to storms outside the usual hurricane season. In general, surprising conclusions that emerge from AI analysis of large data sets must be reviewed for reasonableness and compared against conclusions reached by other methods or with other models.

- **Require transparency.** As described in Chapter 5, it's becoming standard for researchers to publish their data sets and analysis methods so that others can verify their methods and catch potential errors. Data producers must extend this requirement into the realm of AI data analysis, sharing the model code or tools used and finding ways to give access to at least part of the large data sets they use. If other researchers can't verify the AI analyses and results, their utility and dependability is greatly reduced. In fact, AI companies facing pressure for greater transparency are already responding; AI models are increasingly showing which sources they used to arrive at results. Currently, this is relatively simplistic, but the detailed transparency outputs that AI models could be programmed to produce routinely (which sources, why, how they were weighted, levels of uncertainty or controversy, knowledge gaps, and so on) would make verifying the results provided by AI much easier for all users.

For Data Disseminators, Vetting Content Is a Major Responsibility

Data disseminators, including both journalistic publications and ordinary people using social media, now have a heavy obligation. They have the opportunity to share data-informed conclusions, including AI output, but they also have the responsibility to prevent the spread of poorly sourced, unvetted, AI-generated garbage.

The human in the loop is essential in these roles. Journalists have always exercised judgment in deciding which facts to trust and which to publish. Those skills must now rise to the challenges presented by AI.

Here are some methods that data disseminators should use when reviewing purported facts and statistics that may have been generated by AI.

- **Carefully scrutinize sources for credibility.** Peer-reviewed research is still the gold standard. Journalists must consider not just whether research results come from respected sources, but what methods they used. How were data generated? How were they analyzed? Did researchers check them with results from other models? If they used AI tools, did they publish the methods and data so others could review them? What biases or alternate explanations could explain the published results? Now that

AI tools are cheap and ubiquitous, almost anyone can analyze data sets and generate "insights," but that doesn't make those insights dependable.

- **Be alert for confirmation bias.** AI tools are designed to replicate existing patterns. As a result, they're basically machines for manufacturing confirmation bias. If dozens of articles purport to show that nuclear fusion is possible at room temperature, an AI summary tool like ChatGPT is likely to say the same thing. That doesn't make it true. And prompts can also bias output. If you ask a chatbot to take the position that inflation is rising, it will assemble results that support that claim; if you tell it to take the position that inflation is falling, it will do the opposite. This means that data disseminators must rein in the natural human desire to publish what they most want to believe, bringing a skeptical attitude to anything generated by AI.

- **Use AI tools to help, not to generate publishable information.** My team and I used AI to help create this book. For example, we used tools like Perplexity.ai to find sources for facts and opinions we wanted to cite, and ChatGPT to summarize long research papers. But *these were only tools*, used in the same way we might use a spell-checker, a Google search, or a data science application. We carefully checked everything the tools suggested, and only reported raw output as a means of demonstrating how AI works, not as accepted fact. In fact, as I write this today, one of the most important things to realize about generative AI is that it is much better at "being creative" than it is at reporting factual accuracy. For example, generative AI is very good at using all of the information available to it to produce synthesized content in a particular genre or style. You can ask it to write a "Shakespearean" sonnet on a particular subject. It's also good at automating tasks, as when Charlene Li asks it to translate her books into many languages. These are the strengths of large language models. But when it comes to factual accuracy, we are back to distrust and verify. All authors and members of the media should take the same approach. AI can vastly improve productivity, but it's still the primary responsibility of all data disseminators to find the truth, not to take an AI's word for it.

- **Debunk fakery.** Sites like PolitiFact and Snopes already identify false information, faked photos, faked videos, and other questionable content. Both the entities producing questionable content and the fact-checkers analyzing it for veracity are now armed with AI. Automated tools that detect fake news would make the job of such debunkers far easier, but humans in the loop are still essential. As International Center for Journalists Knight fellow Nikita Roy suggested, "fact-checkers should use the tools for 'language tasks' like drafting headlines or translating stories, not 'knowledge tasks' like answering Google-style questions that rely on the training data of the AI model."[33] Skeptics like Welsh scientist Sholto David and California microbiologist Elisabeth Bik already use technological tools to identify faked graphics in science papers.[34] Sites like PubPeer[35] and Retraction Watch[36] provide a platform for publicizing their efforts.

- **In corporate settings, put guardrails around AI output.** As Harvard Business School executive Katia Walsh warns, AI is now so popular that many companies are embracing it without a clear plan. "Fear of missing out is not a strategy," she emphasizes. Technology analyst Maribel Lopez suggests grounding AI analysis in the expertise of your company and putting your most knowledgeable human experts in the loop of data analysis. Restrict the reach of public-facing AI chatbots to avoid Air Canada-like gaffes. As she advises, "If I am a healthcare company like CVS, I want to make sure that if people are using the conversational interface, we are giving them drug information that [the manufacturer] has allowed, not random stuff from WebMD. It shouldn't answer questions about the weather, only answer questions about the prescription." Most data-savvy companies are already engaged in this type of work. Establishing clear guidelines for how and when AI can be used as part of the business, and for what purpose, is essential. But equally essential are internal review processes for pushing the boundaries so that the organization can still be curious and innovative in deploying AI.

- **Think like a journalist when using social media.** As I described in Chapter 2, each of us can now share information with our followers on Facebook, Instagram, X, TikTok, or LinkedIn. But malign actors are now using AI tools to crank out spurious data and fake statistics and posting them where others are likely to share them. Before you share that photo of a Fortune 100 CEO using hard drugs, or a statistic showing that over 20% of the population is LGBTQ+, or a story that concludes electric cars produce more emissions than cars with combustion engines, take the time to vet the source and verify the content. Of course, those examples are made up. In practical terms, even if the results seem highly plausible, you need to check them. You can use AI tools to track down and identify false information, just as a professional journalist would. Think of it as a way to keep your friends and family from swallowing fake news.

For Data Consumers, Identifying Accurate Content Will Continue to Be Challenging

Data-savvy consumers review the data they encounter for data integrity, data transparency, and data neutrality as we described in Chapters 4–6. But with AI, that job is becoming more complex.

As I write this in 2024, Americans are becoming increasingly aware of how AI will create challenges (see Figure 10-1). According to the NORC Data-Savvy Survey of 1,071 adults in June 2024, 59% indicate that they have a pretty good understanding of what AI is. However, 78% think AI-generated content should include a warning label, 35% feel that information generated by AI is often inaccurate, and only 25% feel confident they can identify AI-generated photos or video. Only 19% are confident they can tell AI-generated writing from text created by a person.

It's clear that the non-stop news coverage of AI since 2023, along with stories about deepfakes and other AI trickery in the 2024 election, will contribute to continued distrust of the technology in coming years. But AI is becoming omnipresent in our society, and despite calls from some voices to heavily regulate and/or tightly constrain access and use of AI, in the near term, any systematic or comprehensive effort to do so is highly unlikely.[37,38]

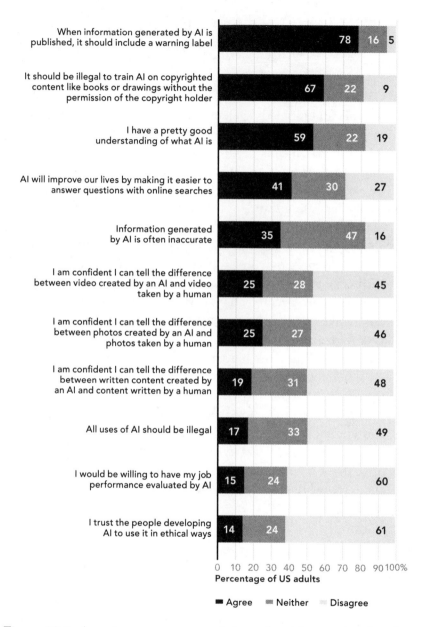

Figure 10-1: Americans are concerned about the risks associated with artificial intelligence. Survey question: "Do you agree, disagree, or neither agree nor disagree with the following statements about artificial intelligence?"

Source: NORC Data-Savvy Survey of 1,071 US adults via AmeriSpeak panel, June 2024.

The right response is to become as knowledgeable as possible. The data-savvy consumer in the 2020s must learn about AI. Here are some suggestions:

- **Gain experience with AI.** Many of us have learned to identify the true and misleading elements of tools like web searches and social media. Now it's time to apply similarly critical thinking to AI, and that means getting comfortable with it. There is no shortage of AI tools, now that it's built into Microsoft productivity software, Google Search, and mobile phone and smart speaker assistants. And, at least as I'm writing this, free versions of tools like ChatGPT and Perplexity Internet search are available to everyone. People hoping to become data savvy about AI should observe how these tools generate content and contrast it with what they're used to from human writing. (AI tools tend to write with an "accent" characterized by even tones, no sense of humor, banal word choices, and the lack of a story thread.)[39]

- **Use AI features to check AI content.** AI is constantly improving, so it will become harder to tell the difference as time goes on. Therefore, we will need to adopt the habit of using AI tools to detect AI-generated content (there are already many such tools available online for free). They should observe whether AI content includes links to its sources, a feature already found (and improving rapidly) in a number of AI systems. They should use AI tools to summarize their own content (emails, notes, audio recordings) and observe when the results are accurate and what they miss.

The Story Continues to Be Written – Rapidly

It's easy to be scared about the rapid rise of AI-generated content and the hallucinations and deepfakes that accompany it. But let's have some perspective. We've been here before with previous waves of technology, from radio, to television, to the internet, to mobile devices. Each came with benefits and each exposed obstacles to becoming a fact-forward society. As is common in these shifts, media coverage invariably tends to hype a technology and then point out its flaws.

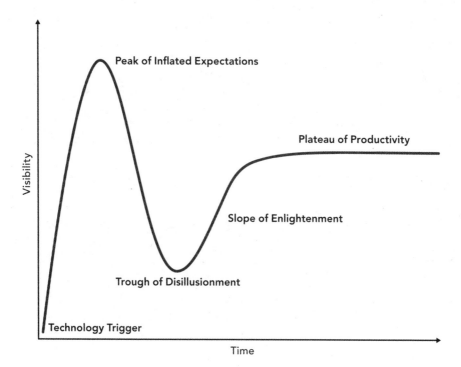

Figure 10-2: The Gartner Hype Cycle.

Source: This graphical representation is adapted from a diagram by Jeremy Kemp and is used under a Creative Commons CC-BY-SA 3.0 license.

This pattern of inflated expectations followed by disillusionment is so common that a leading technology research company has given it a name: the Gartner Hype Cycle (see Figure 10-2).[40,41] Recent examples include blockchain (and the subdomain of non-fungible tokens, or NFTs) and autonomous vehicles. But the final part of the Hype Cycle is the plateau of productivity, and AI is clearly heading for that end state.

For consumers to become data savvy about AI, we must add AI competence to the educational efforts for data literacy described in Chapter 8. Any data literacy program that does not include knowledge about AI and its strengths and limitations is incomplete.

The good news is that the accuracy of AI tools is likely to improve as they begin to police themselves. As computer scientist Michael Franklin explains, we are heading to a world of "safety for AI, and AI for safety." And AI and trust expert Bo Li predicts that by 2029, the output from AI will become more trustworthy, much less prone to errors, and much more transparent about how to use and interpret it. "The software will be safe enough," she says. "We will reach that end state in the next 10 years or so."

I continue to have high hopes for a fact-forward future in which each of us is more data savvy. What will that future look like? That's what the next chapter is all about.

11

The Data-Savvy Future

THERE ARE TWO paths ahead of us.[1] On the first path, we emerge as a far more data-savvy society in which most societal actors recognize the importance of reliable and trustworthy data and our collective responsibilities as users, suppliers, and disseminators of data. On the second path, data and information become inherently untrustworthy for everyone, and society becomes increasingly fractured.

One extreme version of a dystopic future based on this second path comes from the speculative fiction writer Neal Stephenson. His 2019 novel *Fall; or, Dodge in Hell* describes a world where there is so much disinformation that the average person has no way to know what is true and what is not. Vast swaths of America have become known as "Ameristan," in which disinformation is rampant and truth depends on who has attained the most influence.

In Stephenson's future, citizens who can afford it hire human "editors" to curate their news for truthfulness – or for whatever slant they desire. People whose editors have different perspectives might have diametrically opposed ideas of truth. And people unable to pay for a quality editor end up seeing whatever "facts" their social media algorithms show them.

Like all speculative novelists, Stephenson exaggerates for dramatic effect. But as we've seen throughout the preceding chapters, some of the dangers he foresees are real. Fabricated data are becoming more prevalent and more sophisticated. People with malign agendas – or in some cases, people just not paying close enough attention – are using data in inappropriate contexts, out of sync with the decisions for which they're being applied. Some people have given up on the idea that good decision-making requires high-quality, objective information, or even that such information exists. Algorithms are increasingly intermediaries between us and the data we see, and those algorithms may have unintended (or intended) biases. And with the explosion of new types of data – and new ways to publicize results – people are now capable of finding studies that reinforce whatever biases they may have started off with.

But the conclusion of all the research that went into this book is far more hopeful. The spread of deceptive (or simply sloppy) data practices can be counterbalanced by a wide range of actions and initiatives that – if we promote and encourage them – will lead to a data-savvy citizenry and a fact-forward society. So, let's look at some reasons why I am optimistic.

Individuals and Institutions Are Becoming More Data Savvy

For those of us involved in the creation and dissemination of robust, unbiased, transparently produced data, it's easy to think about the next few decades in existential terms. We are hopeful that the appropriate and accurate data will predominate and that the use of bad data and the misuse of data toward nefarious ends will decrease. But along with our hope comes the awareness that trust in data and science are not as strong as they once were, and we sometimes wonder if our hope is simply wishful thinking.

A careful examination indicates that our hope rests on a solid foundation. Reliable, accurate, and trustworthy data is profitable in the broadest sense. A medical study that accurately shows which treatment will cure a disease will, eventually, reward not only its discoverers but those who benefit from the treatment. A forecasting model that accurately predicts the movements of an economy – or an election, or the weather, or the prospects of a baseball player – will prevail, while an inaccurate model will be abandoned. A consumer who can identify and act on good data and spot and reject false data will make better decisions. And a government that can assemble and act on the highest quality information will have more prosperous citizens and a better negotiating position on the world stage. For individuals, a key aspect of the skills they need to hone to use data effectively is thinking probabilistically. This means understanding the implications of the inherent uncertainty that surrounds any data set – as discussed throughout the previous chapters – and using that knowledge to make well-informed decisions that take the uncertainty into account. Part of probabilistic thinking is open-mindedness to revising our conclusions, because the data on which we base the conclusions is often subject to revision. (If Wednesday's forecast said it would be cold on Saturday, we've learned to check the forecast again on Friday night when more relevant data are available.)

Researchers are comfortable with the idea that scientific results are never absolute – they are always subject to modification based on further investigation. With the democratization of data and analytic tools, more of us will learn to embrace this attitude. Part of being data savvy is to recognize that truth is subject to revision based on new information. In fact, the concept of updating your thinking or predictions based on new information is the essence of the very powerful and far-reaching field of Bayesian statistics.

The popular book *Thinking in Bets* by former World Series of Poker champion Annie Duke suggests how to use probabilistic thinking to maximize returns when you don't have all the facts.[2] We may not all be probabilistic thinkers yet, but increasingly, the world is training us in the value of thinking that way.

Furthermore, the degree to which people, regardless of their background and training, currently apply probabilistic thinking in their day-to-day lives might surprise you. As just one example, consider that roughly 50 million US adults (about 20% of the population) play fantasy sports.[3] This requires them to use their knowledge of the sport, along with a dizzying array of data and statistics about the teams and the individual players, to create a fantasy team that they believe will win their league, modifying the team as the season unfolds and the situation (including all of the statistics on the teams and players) changes. This boils down to a rather complex exercise in probabilistic thinking. It's reasonable to say that fantasy sports are actually a form of Bayesian analysis by millions of sports fans. If so many people can be effective Bayesians in their leisure activities, encouraging broader application of these skills to life's key decisions should not be terribly difficult.

Even as people are becoming more sophisticated, corporations are also upping their level of data savvy. They already use the most sophisticated algorithms for data analysis, simply because those algorithms pay off. For example, they use analytic methods and models to determine when their equipment is likely to need maintenance, which marketing and pricing strategies generate the most profitable returns, which compensation strategies will retain the best workers, and how much to pay to invest in or to acquire a potential partner company. Corporations also are poised to lead the way in sophisticated algorithms that combine private data, administrative data, and public data such as published financials and government statistics. It's logical for companies to be on the forefront of these advanced data analysis techniques.

With more and more people being exposed to data every day, there is increasing demand for information that clearly presents its quantitative basis. There's a reason that data journalism is becoming more popular in news media; analysis of data generates novel insights that help people make decisions on what degrees to pursue, where to live, and what policies to support. Data producers also now recognize that they must compete for attention and are learning use visualization tools and digital storytelling to package their insights in ways that improve transparency, credibility, and understandability for peer reviewers, data disseminators, and consumers.

As we know, some producers and disseminators will use these tools to create convincing-looking but misleading or flawed analyses. But as consumers become more data savvy, they will become more adept at determining which data sources are reliable and trustworthy and which are not, and they will develop the skill to assess fitness for purpose of any given source. Even if you don't agree with the *Boston Globe*'s political coverage, you might value its in-depth medical journalism (from the experts at STAT News). Or you might decide that the *New York Times*' "Wirecutter" feature, with its detailed product and price comparisons, is a useful source for making purchase decisions. Clickbait of questionable value may drive momentary advertising views, but sources that consistently excel at analyzing data and generating trust will prevail on loyalty.[4,5] And it's certainly the case that politicians who get surprised by incorrect results from flawed polls will demand more accurate ones the next time around.

Training and Infrastructure Are Evolving to Support a Data-Savvy World

As described in Chapter 9, infrastructure to support a data-savvy population is emerging in two areas: increasing sophistication in incorporating basic data science into school and college curricula, and improvements in the way governments, including the US government, assemble data sets and make them available. There's good reason to believe that both trends will continue to improve.

On the educational front in the United States, improvements will continue to happen from the top down as state governments, supported by federal government research and infrastructure, begin incorporating data science into curricula. One might think, with so many priorities competing for classroom time and resources, that yet another requirement for data science teaching would face a challenging road. But if the trends in financial literacy requirements are any indication, data literacy will soon follow (and in fact, data literacy is a more generalized version of financial literacy). Furthermore, it's reasonable to expect that much of the push for this additional training will start to come from parents and students.

The current passion for science, technology, engineering, and mathematics (STEM) education is rooted in parents' and students' desires to help young people to become successful in job markets. Data science is increasingly a part of STEM education. Science moves forward with data analysis. Technology depends on modeling and manipulating data flows. Engineering increasingly is an exercise in making improvements based on analysis of historical and real-time data. And statistics is a gateway to the mathematical elements that fuel all of these pursuits.

Competitive forces will influence educational priorities. States whose students are more data savvy will supply the workforce with individuals qualified for better jobs. Universities that train more data-savvy students will be able to better demonstrate the value of their undergraduate and graduate degrees. And nations that invest in data science education will attract investment from global corporations that can choose to locate their workforces anywhere.

Even as these investments in data-savvy citizens grow, governments will recognize the value of data infrastructure. As described in Chapters 8 and 9, America's and other nations' governments are investing in privacy, interoperability, security, and availability standards for government data. There's a reason for that. Governments are uniquely positioned to gather, combine, and analyze high-quality data to generate insights that will move entire nations forward. Weather data, economic data, public health data, and crime data become the fuel that powers smarter decisions for legislators, regulators, and bureaucrats. Take the US Federal Reserve, for example: When it makes its decisions about interest rates that affect the entire national economy, it needs detailed and dependable data about employment, growth, inflation, and debt. The same demand for quality data to support informed decisions applies to every branch of the US federal government, to state decision-makers, and to government of all nations.

The quality of such data infrastructure fuels private enterprise as well. Companies tapped into government data infrastructure can make better decisions about where to invest, what consumers can afford, how to invest, and what sort of workforce they will need in the future. Public data infrastructure fuels growth: It's as essential as steel or energy to corporate decision-makers.

Technology – Especially AI – Will Accelerate These Trends

Chapter 10 described some of the weaknesses and pitfalls of AI as a way to analyze data and generate useful information. And, as I write this in 2024, AI remains capable of all sorts of errors and continues to generate some potentially misleading information.

But I believe that AI will be very similar to other new technologies that have enormous upside potential along with substantial risks: As a society we will become adept at harnessing that potential while mitigating the risks (but not entirely eliminating them). AI will become a powerful tool for data-savvy people and corporations.

While AI's ability to detect deception isn't yet perfect, it is improving extremely rapidly. And AI is not a monolithic technology: The AI tools to summarize text or generate content may evolve completely independently of other tools that are expert at checking content.

The combination of rapid advances in AI and increasingly robust public data infrastructure holds enormous promise. Even now, it's possible to ask tools like ChatGPT questions like, "What are the sources for the information I'm looking at?" For example, I recently saw what purported to be a photo of the Las Vegas Sphere, with its arena-sized digital display, showing an error message as a result of the July 2024 global IT outage. I asked ChatGPT if the image was real. It responded with this[6]:

Searched 3 sites

The photo of the Las Vegas Sphere displaying the Windows "Blue Screen of Death" due to the CrowdStrike outage is fake. Multiple fact-checks confirm that the image is digitally fabricated and not a real projection on the Sphere. Sphere Entertainment and other sources have verified that this image was altered and no credible reports support the claim (wusa9.com) (Check Your Fact).

In the near future, it's likely that researchers and data scientists will be able to ask AI-based tools to check for bias in data sets and assess how new research supports or contradicts previous research. Data disseminators, including media providers, will be able to use AI tools to find some fakery in photos or quotes. And ordinary consumers will become increasingly adept at using AI-enabled assistants from Google, Microsoft, Apple, and many others to investigate sources and claims that they read. Meta's AI is now built into its social media platforms, so users are likely to be able to use it even without leaving social media sites like Instagram, Facebook, and Threads. (By the time you read this, such developments will likely have outpaced what I just described.) And even if AI tools from the large technology companies pose risks of baked-in bias, it is still the case that market efficiency will ultimately favor trustworthy and reliable tools, because they will produce the best outcomes for informing key decisions.

The ability to effortlessly question studies, news, and data is likely to be a game-changer for a fact-forward society. Today, nearly everyone can do a simple web search on their PC or phone. With appropriately accessible tools, it will be just as simple to investigate information and data. Data-savvy individuals will get very adept at asking AI assistants to check things. And on social sites and through email and messaging, they'll help provide a useful perspective to their friends who may have less inclination to scrutinize data carefully.

Smart decisions are valuable, and as a result, consumers are likely to either pay for dependable advice or subscribe to it on ad-supported sites. Commercial services that rate the dependability of data sources may emerge, just as we now have fact-checking sites like Snopes, and PolitiFact and various media bias raters like AllSides and Media Bias/ Fact Check (MBFC). Think of such services as "Consumer Reports for data." A data advisor riding alongside your online presence could keep you from falling victim to false information – or confirmation bias. Perhaps services like the "truth curators" in Stephenson's novel will become available to ordinary folks, but as automated tools, rather than paid human beings.

Technology will also make it easier for educators to raise their students' level of data literacy. Educational curricula like GAISE, the program I described in Chapter 7, should evolve to encompass AI, including the dangers posed by AI-generated fakes and hallucinations, the opportunity to use AI to investigate statistical information, and how to identify the AI tool that will best serve your needs. The goal remains constant: to create an ethos of curiosity around data, incubate and inculcate probabilistic thinking, encourage checking before sharing, and educate students around the appropriate use of the latest tools. Online courses with gamified elements can attract students and boost literacy without requiring teachers. And just as data-savvy parents will help introduce their children to appropriate tools to understand data, the children will also end up exposing their parents to what they learn at school, or on their own, about being data savvy.

Data science, data literacy, and a good public data infrastructure, coupled with technological advances, can also support the rise of equitable opportunities across all parts of society. There are countless and compelling research studies demonstrating that having a skilled workforce that broadly encompasses our population demographics produces better economic outcomes for businesses and society as a whole. There is also a great deal of research documenting the digital divide that exists among different demographic groups (age, race, income).[7] Much of that work focuses on differences in access to computers and the Internet. The digital divide has diminished somewhat over time, largely due to increased internet access through mobile devices. However, as we dig in on the work to increase data literacy, we must ensure that we include all citizens, or the digital divide will not only continue, but likely worsen.

If we are attentive in this regard, there is enormous potential for emerging technology to actually reduce the digital divide and help us to create greater fairness in our society. For example, readily available interactive data visualization tools can put data-based decision-making in reach of people regardless of age, race, or income. Data scientists, enabled by AI, will be able to link different types of data in new ways, which will provide deeper analysis into disparities that exist in our society, including in algorithms that companies and governments use, and offer new insights for how to address them. AI-enabled analytic tools will help reveal – and correct – biases in our data sets. New data collection techniques and methods – and a more data-savvy and better-educated population – will reduce the barriers for all communities and demographic groups to participate in research and ensure their perspectives and behaviors are included in our data sets.

Technology always has antisocial uses. People have used computers to create plausible fake data sets and analyses, and photo editing software to generate convincing fake photos. People have been scammed by imposters using mobile phones or those who stole their identities to take money from their bank accounts. But we would never say that computers, spreadsheets, photo editing software, mobile phones, or online banking are on balance "bad." It's more accurate to say that while they are extremely useful, they can also be abused. In the same way, AI and any other tool used to create, analyze, or authenticate data will be subject to potential abuse. Here is what the solution to such abuse looks like:

- Incorporate data-savvy capabilities in our technology.
- Develop a thoughtful, comprehensive, and consistent regulatory framework that provides guidelines for proper use of the tools and data.
- Create tools to detect those who abuse the technology or the underlying data.
- Pass laws to safeguard the public and punish the bad actors.

Again, it will take a multisector approach to make this happen. The public must demand it, our legislators and government must create the regulatory and legal framework, and private industry must proactively participate (and often lead) in all aspects of it.

Where Will Data-Savvy Leadership Come From?

Training in statistics and data science is still generally regarded as something for only certain types of highly quantitative people. As we have seen from all of the preceding chapters, with data and analysis so central to all of our day-to-day lives, the fundamental concepts and skills for understanding and using data must be seen as essential for all members of society. How do we make this happen?

Research leaders in our society need to band together more cohesively and energetically to promote the idea of sound data and analysis as an antidote to a poorly informed public. Such an effort must not be limited to research institutes like the one I head but should also include school and college educators, government data-generating agencies, philanthropic organizations, media outlets, commercial companies, and highly visible analysts of all stripes. We already have organizations that create standards for public polls and for specific types of research, like medical and psychological studies and government statistics. The goal of this coalition must be broader. It would promote and publicize data literacy and the value of robust, unbiased, transparent data analysis for good decisions. It would highlight stories of how people using solid data make smarter decisions. Every movement needs persuasive, charismatic spokespeople.

We need celebrities and influencers who will proselytize about the importance of developing data-savvy skills. These will need to be people who are both data savvy and media savvy and can use different platforms and approaches to help make data skills fun and appealing. This coalition would act as a counterbalance to those who misuse or abuse data and analysis (and accompanying technology), promoting the data-savvy skills that will allow any of us to find the best possible data to inform our important decisions.

With the mass of questionable content on social media, and its ability to cause outright harm to individuals and to institutions, we might be tempted to throw up our hands in despair. That's not an option. We have the knowledge, tools, and capabilities to ensure that data are consistently a means for improving the well-being of people everywhere. But we need to harness the collective will to bring about this brighter future. Those of us (which means *all* of us) who use data every day – producers, disseminators, and consumers – must work together to bring about this future. It's not enough to be data savvy as individuals. We must view our contributions as part of a larger effort to produce a fact-forward society.

Since reliable and trustworthy data are the foundation for making the smart decisions that underpin so much of human progress, creating a fact-forward society may be the most important thing we ever do.

Notes

About the Cover

1. NORC at the University of Chicago. (2013). NORC insight illuminated: 2013-2014 annual report. NORC at the University of Chicago. https://www.norc.org/content/dam/norc-org/pdfs/NORC%20 2013-14%20AnnualReport_optimized.pdf

Chapter 1

1. Tompson, T., Benz, J., The Associated Press-NORC Center for Public Affairs Research. (July, 2013). The public mood: White malaise but optimism among blacks, hispanics. https://apnorc.org/projects/the-public-mood-white-malaise-but-optimism-among-blacks-hispanics/
2. Colloquially, many people think of data as a singular noun – for example, they might say "This data is useful." But data scientists and researchers think of data as plural; the singular, meaning one piece of information, is "datum." In this book, I'll treat data as plural, so you'll read about "these data" rather than "this data."
3. Much of the story told here comes from Michael Lewis's book, *The Big Short*. Lewis, M. (2011). The big short: Inside the doomsday machine. W.W. Norton.

4. Herndon, T. (2019). Liar's loans, mortgage fraud, and the great recession. Review of Political Economy, 31(4), 479–508. https://doi.org/10.1080/09538259.2020.1747746

5. Among data scientists and statisticians, "data integrity" has a precise definition that focuses on maintaining the quality and consistency of data throughout its lifecycle. We have expanded this definition to refer to a variety of measures of data quality, as explained in more detail in Chapter 4. For the precise definition the industry uses, see Cote, C. (2021, February 4). What is data integrity and why does it matter? Harvard Business School Online's Business Insights Online. https://online.hbs.edu/blog/post/what-is-data-integrity

6. Lewis, M. (2011). The big short. (p. 76).

7. Butler, D. (2013). When Google got flu wrong. Nature, 494(7436), 155–156. https://doi.org/10.1038/494155a

8. Lazer, D. & Kennedy, R. (2015, October 1). What we can learn from the epic failure of Google flu trends. Wired. https://www.wired.com/2015/10/can-learn-epic-failure-google-flu-trends

9. Since the shutdown of Google Flu Trends, Google has made all the data available to researchers who would like to further analyze what was actually happening and to test other potential prediction models.

10. Helft, M. (2008, November 11). Google uses searches to track flu's spread. The New York Times. https://www.nytimes.com/2008/11/12/technology/internet/12flu.html

11. RealClear Polling. (2024). 2016 general election: Trump vs. Clinton. https://www.realclearpolling.com/polls/president/general/2016/trump-vs-clinton

12. Katz, J. (2016, July 19). Who will be President? The New York Times. https://www.nytimes.com/interactive/2016/upshot/presidential-polls-forecast.html

13. Silver, N. (2016, November 8). Who will win the presidency? Five ThirtyEight 2016 Election Forecast. https://projects.fivethirtyeight.com/2016-election-forecast/

14. Kennedy, C., Blumenthal, M., Clement, S., Clinton, J. D., Durand, C., Franklin, C., McGeeney, K., Miringoff, L., Olson, K., Rivers, D., Saad, L., Witt, E. G., & Wlezien, C. (2018). An evaluation of the 2016 election polls in the United States. Public Opinion Quarterly, 82(1), 1–33. https://doi.org/10.1093/poq/nfx047

15. Christian, J. [@Jon_Christian]. (2023, February 21). Chatgpt says I've won various prestigious awards (nope) and taught at columbia (nope) [Post]. X. https://x.com/Jon_Christian/status/1628053956441038849

16. Ortiz, S. (2023, June 9). ChatGPT's hallucination just got OpenAI sued. Here's what happened. ZDNET/Innovation. https://www.zdnet.com/article/chatgpts-hallucination-just-got-openai-sued-heres-what-happened/

17. But there are ways to train AI tools on data collections that are trusted to be accurate. I explain this further in Chapter 10.

18. Reisner, A. (2023, August 19). Revealed: The authors whose pirated books are powering generative AI. *The Atlantic.* https://www.theatlantic.com/technology/archive/2023/08/books3-ai-meta-llama-pirated-books/675063/

19. Blum, D. (2023, January 6). The Mediterranean Diet really is that good for you. Here's why. *The New York Times.* https://www.nytimes.com/2023/01/06/well/eat/mediterranean-diet-health.html

20. Rabin, R. C. (2023, April 4). Moderate drinking has no health benefits, analysis of decades of research finds. *The New York Times.* https://www.nytimes.com/2023/04/04/health/alcohol-health-effects.html

Chapter 2

1. Proctor, R. N. (2012). The history of the discovery of the cigarette–lung cancer link: Evidentiary traditions, corporate denial, global toll. Tobacco Control, 21(2), 87–91. https://doi.org/10.1136/tobaccocontrol-2011-050338

2. (1953, November 30). Medicine: Beyond any doubt. *Time,* 62(22), 60–63. https://content.time.com/time/subscriber/article/0,33009,823156,00.html

3. (1969, April 25). Cigarettes and society: A growing dilemma. *Time,* 93(17), 98–103. https://content.time.com/time/subscriber/article/0,33009,840093-6,00.html.

4. Cappella, J. N., Maloney, E., Ophir, Y., & Brennan, E. (2016, July 1). Interventions to correct misinformation about tobacco products. Tobacco Regulatory Science, 1(2), 186–197. https://pmc.ncbi.nlm.nih.gov/articles/PMC4849128/

5. National Library of Medicine, Profiles in Science. (2019, March). The 1964 report on smoking and health. *Reports of the Surgeon General.* https://profiles.nlm.nih.gov/spotlight/nn/feature/smoking

6. Pierce, J. P., & Gilpin, E. A. (2001). News media coverage of smoking and health is associated with changes in population rates of smoking cessation but not initiation. Tobacco Control, 10(2), 145–153. https://tobaccocontrol.bmj.com/content/10/2/145

7. Durkin, S. J., Biener, L., & Wakefield, M. A. (2009). Effects of different types of antismoking ads on reducing disparities in smoking cessation

among socioeconomic subgroups. American Journal of Public Health, 99(12), 2217–2223. https://doi.org/10.2105/AJPH.2009.161638

8. In IT circles, the term "data democratization" often refers to the principle that any worker in any department should be able to get access to any data anywhere in the company, when it's possible to provide that access without violating privacy concerns. I'd argue that data democratization is a far broader force affecting all consumers, not just corporate data analysts; the corporate version is just one example of how data democratization empowers a far greater number of people to create, analyze, share, and consume data.

9. There's nothing inherently wrong with tools like SurveyMonkey or Qualtrics – we at NORC use these tools in statistically valid ways, as do many other researchers. The point is that just about anybody, regardless of training, can get started with them and generate results of potentially questionable validity.

10. Legg, H. (2021, May 14). Have you heard the news? But who owns what you're hearing and reading? We need to know. USA Today. https://www.usatoday.com/story/opinion/2021/05/14/mainstream-media-ownership-america-needs-news-transparency/5077719001/

11. Ewuru, B. (2022, March 5). Unethical practices in PR: The recent industry accusations against Ronn Torossian, 5WPR, and Everything-PR. Axia Public Relations. https://www.axiapr.com/blog/unethical-practices-in-pr-the-recent-industry-accusations-against-ronn-torossian-5wpr-and-everything-pr

12. NORC at the University of Chicago. (2024). GSS Data Explorer | NORC at the University of Chicago. https://gssdataexplorer.norc.org/trends

13. RFK Human Rights & The Associated Press-NORC Center for Public Affairs Research. (2023). Robert F. Kennedy Human Rights/APNORC Poll. AP NORC. https://apnorc.org/wp-content/uploads/2023/04/RFK_APNORC_PressFreedom_Topline.pdf

14. Masnick, M. (2020, June 23). Hello! You've been referred here because you're wrong about section 230 of the Communications Decency Act. Techdirt. https://www.techdirt.com/2020/06/23/hello-youve-been-referred-here-because-youre-wrong-about-section-230-communications-decency-act/

15. Bradburn, N., Benz, J., Kirchhoff, B., Alvarez, E., Sterrett, D., & Tompson, T. (2016, October). How Americans navigate the modern information environment: A study commemorating the 75th anniversary of NORC at the University of Chicago (p. 21). NORC at the University of Chicago. https://www.norc.org/content/dam/norc-org/pdfs/75th%20Anniversary%20Research%20Project.pdf

16. Media Insight Project. (2019). Journalism values research, Survey 1 and 2. https://apnorc.org/wp-content/uploads/2021/04/topliner_api_s1.utf8_.pdf

17. RFK Human Rights & The Associated Press-NORC Center for Public Affairs Research. (2023). Robert F. Kennedy Human Rights/APNORC Poll. *AP NORC*. https://apnorc.org/wp-content/uploads/2023/04/RFK_ APNORC_PressFreedom_Topline.pdf

18. Sterrett, D., Malato, D., Benz, J., Kantor, L., Tompson, T., Rosenstiel, T., Sonderman, J., & Loker, K. (2019). Who shared it? Deciding what news to trust on social media. Digital Journalism, 7(6), 783–801. https://doi .org/10.1080/21670811.2019.1623702

19. The NORC Data-Savvy Survey of 1,071 adults was conducted in June 2024 online (95%) and by phone (5%), using the NORC's nationally representative, probability-based AmeriSpeak panel. This book is the first publication of findings from this survey.

20. Gladwell, M. (2011, February 6). The order of things. *The New Yorker*. https://www.newyorker.com/magazine/2011/02/14/the-order-of-things

21. Farvid, M. S., Stern, M. C., Norat, T., Sasazuki, S., Vineis, P., Weijenberg, M. P., Wolk, A., Wu, K., Stewart, B. W., & Cho, E. (2018). Consumption of red and processed meat and breast cancer incidence: A systematic review and meta-analysis of prospective studies. International Journal of Cancer, 143(11), 2787–2799. https://doi.org/10.1002/ijc.31848

22. Bakalar, N. (2018, October 3). Eating processed meats tied to breast cancer risk. *The New York Times*. https://www.nytimes.com/2018/10/03/well/ eat/eating-processed-meats-tied-to-breast-cancer-risk.html

23. Picheta, R. (2018, October 3). Processed meats linked to breast cancer, says study. *CNN*. https://www.cnn.com/2018/10/03/health/processed-meat-breast-cancer-study-intl/index.html

24. Mazziotta, J. (2018, October 3). Eating processed meats linked to a greater risk of breast cancer. *People*. https://people.com/health/processed-meats-greater-risk-breast-cancer/

25. Whiteman, H. (2018, January 5). Just two sausages per week may raise breast cancer risk. MedicalNews Today. https://www.medicalnewstoday .com/articles/320535

26. American Cancer Society. (2024, January 17). Key statistics for breast cancer. How common is breast cancer? https://www.cancer.org/cancer/ types/breast-cancer/about/how-common-is-breast-cancer.html

27. Sumner, P., et al., (2014). The association between exaggeration in health related science news and academic press releases: retrospective observational study. BMJ. 349, g7015. https://doi.org/10.1136/bmj.g7015.

28. Kinsey, A. C., Pomeroy, W. B., & Martin, C. E. (1998). *Sexual behavior in the human male*. Indiana University Press. p. 656.

29. Wickware, F. S. (1948, August 2). Report on Kinsey. *Life*, *25*(5), 87–98. https://books.google.com/books?id=10cEAAAAMBAJ&pg=PA87#v=o nepage&q&f=false
30. Branch, J. A. (2014, May 21). Alfred Kinsey: A brief summary and critique. ERLC. https://erlc.com/research/alfred-kinsey-a-brief-summary-and-critique/
31. Flores, A. R., & Conron, K. J. (2023). Adult LGBT population in the United States. UCLA School of Law Williams Institute. https://williamsinstitute.law.ucla.edu/wp-content/uploads/LGBT-Adult-US-Pop-Dec-2023.pdf
32. McCarthy, J. (2019, June 27). Americans still greatly overestimate U.S. gay population. Gallup. https://news.gallup.com/poll/259571/americans-greatly-overestimate-gay-population.aspx

Chapter 3

1. This reflects the employment situation for October 2023. See U. S. Bureau of Labor Statistics. (2023, November 3). *Employment situation news release*. https://www.bls.gov/news.release/archives/empsit_11032023.htm
2. Concepts and definitions (CPS). US Bureau of Labor Statistics. Retrieved July 16, 2024, from https://www.bls.gov/cps/definitions.htm. For more information on the different ways the government reports unemployment statistics, see also https://www.bls.gov/web/empsit/ces_cps_trends.htm
3. Cox, J. (2023, November 3). U.S. payrolls increased by 150,000 in October, less than expected. *CNBC*. https://www.cnbc.com/2023/11/03/jobs-report-october-2023-us-payrolls-increased-by-150000-in-october-less-than-expected.html
4. Laborde, S. (2024, May 27). 50 Key daily data creation statistics (staggering 2023 numbers). Techreport. https://techreport.com/statistics/software-web/daily-data-creation-statistics/
5. SurveyMonkey. (retrieved 2024). About us. https://www.surveymonkey.com/about/
6. Hipes, P. (2021, August 5). Nielsen says it will try portable people meter wearables on for size. *Deadline*. https://deadline.com/2021/08/nielsen-portable-people-meter-wearables-launch-ratings-1234809472/
7. Carroll, J. (2005, March 29). American public opinion about sports. Gallup. https://news.gallup.com/poll/15421/Sports.aspx

8. The Associated Press-NORC Center for Public Affairs Research at the University of Chicago. (2022, March 15). Evaluating progress for racial equality [Survey]. https://apnorc.org/projects/evaluating-progress-for-racial-equality/

9. U.S. Fish & Wildlife Service. (2023). 2022 National survey of fishing, hunting, and wildlife-associated recreation (p. 86). https://www.fws.gov/media/2022-national-survey-fishing-hunting-and-wildlife-associated-recreation

10. U.S. Census Bureau and U.S. Department of Housing and Urban Development. (2024, May 23). Median sales price of houses sold for the United States. Federal Reserve Bank of St. Louis. https://fred.stlouisfed.org/series/MSPUS

11. Frank, R. (2023, October 19). Billionaires are driving South Florida home prices to new records. *CNBC*. https://www.cnbc.com/2023/10/19/billionaires-are-driving-south-florida-home-prices-to-new-records-.html

12. U. S. Bureau of Labor Statistics. Usual weekly earnings of wage and salary workers news release - 2022 Q05 Results. Bureau of Labor Statistics. Retrieved July 16, 2024, from https://www.bls.gov/news.release/archives/wkyeng_01192023.htm

13. Omeokwe, A. (2023, November 12). The low-wage pay surge is over, threatening the consumer boom. *Wall Street Journal*. https://www.wsj.com/economy/jobs/the-low-wage-pay-surge-is-over-threatening-the-consumer-boom-6924fdac

14. Wadden, T. A., Bailey, T. S., Billings, L. K., Davies, M., Frias, J. P., Koroleva, A., Lingvay, I., O'Neil, P. M., Rubino, D. M., Skovgaard, D., Wallenstein, S. O. R., Garvey, W. T., & STEP 3 Investigators. (2021). Effect of subcutaneous semaglutide vs placebo as an adjunct to intensive behavioral therapy on body weight in adults with overweight or obesity: The STEP 3 randomized clinical trial. JAMA, 325(14), 1403–1413. https://doi.org/10.1001/jama.2021.1831

15. Jaschik, S. (2014) Virtually no difference: Large study finds nearly identical academic performance by students who submitted and didn't submit SAT or ACT scores at test-optional colleges. Inside Higher Ed. https://www.insidehighered.com/news/2014/02/19/study-finds-little-difference-academic-success-students-who-do-and-dont-submit-sat

16. Lee, D. H., Rezende, L. F. M., Joh, H.-K., Keum, N., Ferrari, G., Rey-Lopez, J. P., Rimm, E. B., Tabung, F. K., & Giovannucci, E. L. (2022). Long-term leisure-time physical activity intensity and all-cause and cause-specific mortality: A prospective cohort of US adults. Circulation, 146(7), 523–534. https://doi.org/10.1161/CIRCULATIONAHA.121.058162

17. Messerli, F. H. (2012). Chocolate consumption, cognitive function, and Nobel laureates. New England Journal of Medicine, 367(16), 1562–1564. https://doi.org/10.1056/NEJMon1211064

18. NORC at the University of Chicago. (2024). GSS Data Explorer. https://gssdataexplorer.norc.org/trends

19. Case, A., & Deaton, A. (2021). Life expectancy in adulthood is falling for those without a BA degree, but as educational gaps have widened, racial gaps have narrowed. Proceedings of the National Academy of Sciences, 118(11), e2024777118. https://doi.org/10.1073/pnas.2024777118

20. Levy, D. T., Nikolayev, L., Mumford, E., & Compton, C. (2005). The Healthy People 2010 smoking prevalence and tobacco control objectives: Results from the SimSmoke tobacco control policy simulation model (United States). Cancer Causes & Control, 16(4), 359–371. https://doi.org/10.1007/s10552-004-7841-4

21. Centers for Disease Control. (2011, September 9). Vital signs: Current cigarette smoking among adults aged ≥18 Years—United States, 2005—2010. Morbidity and Mortality Weekly Report (MMWR), 60(35), 1207–1212. https://www.cdc.gov/mmwr/preview/mmwrhtml/mm6035a5.htm

22. Cornelius, M. E. (2023). Tobacco product use among adults – United States, 2021. Morbidity and Mortality Weekly Report (MMWR), 72(18), 475–483. https://doi.org/10.15585/mmwr.mm7218a1

23. Parrish, S. (2017, June 21). All models are wrong. FS Blog. https://fs.blog/all-models-are-wrong/

24. von Lieshout, R. (2022, May 24). Predictive engine maintenance: Harnessing the power of data. Aviation Maintenance Magazine. https://www.avm-mag.com/predictive-engine-maintenance-harnessing-the-power-of-data

25. Newman, R. (2015, June 30). How we scaled data science to all sides of Airbnb over 5 years of hypergrowth. VentureBeat. https://venturebeat.com/dev/how-we-scaled-data-science-to-all-sides-of-airbnb-over-5-years-of-hypergrowth/

26. NORC at the University of Chicago. (2020). Hamilton plans tour with data [Case study]. https://www.norc.org/content/dam/norc-org/pdfs/Case%20Study_Hamilton.pdf

27. Kannan, P. V., & Bernoff, J. (2019). The age of intent: Using artificial intelligence to deliver a superior customer experience. Mascot Books.

Chapter 4

1. Hamblin, J. (2018, May 11). The scientific case for two spaces after a period. *The Atlantic*. https://www.theatlantic.com/science/archive/2018/05/two-spaces-after-a-period/559304/

2. Johnson, R. L., Bui, B., & Schmitt, L. L. (2018). Are two spaces better than one? The effect of spacing following periods and commas during reading. Attention, Perception, & Psychophysics, 80(6), 1504–1511. https://doi.org/10.3758/s13414-018-1527-6

3. Schwab, K. (2018, October 2). How Gillette designed a razor for men who can't shave themselves. *Fast Company*. https://www.fastcompany.com/90232951/how-gillette-designed-a-razor-for-men-who-cant-shave-themselves

4. Smith, S. (2013, January 21). Market research example: How Coke lost millions with this mistake. *Qualtrics*. https://www.qualtrics.com/blog/coca-cola-market-research/

5. Cobb, J. C. (2015, July 10). What Coca-Cola's marketing blunder can teach us about America. *TIME*. https://time.com/3950205/new-coke-history-america/

6. Gladwell, M. (2005). *Blink: The power of thinking without thinking*. Little, Brown. (p. 159).

7. Ludwig, D. (2016, October 5). Doctor: Low-fat diets stuffed with misconceptions (Opinion). *CNN*. https://www.cnn.com/2016/10/05/opinions/debate-low-fat-diet-ludwig/index.html

8. Lissner, L., & Heitmann, B. L. (1995). Dietary fat and obesity: Evidence from epidemiology. European Journal of Clinical Nutrition, 49(2), 79–90.

9. Clemente-Suárez, V. J., Mielgo-Ayuso, J., Martín-Rodríguez, A., Ramos-Campo, D. J., Redondo-Flórez, L., & Tornero-Aguilera, J. F. (2022). The burden of carbohydrates in health and disease. Nutrients, 14(18), 3809. https://doi.org/10.3390/nu14183809

10. Cleveland Clinic. (2019, October 1) Why people diet, lose weight and gain it all back. https://health.clevelandclinic.org/why-people-diet-lose-weight-and-gain-it-all-back

11. Mahmood, S. S., Levy, D., Vasan, R. S., & Wang, T. J. (2014). The Framingham Heart Study and the epidemiology of cardiovascular disease: A historical perspective. Lancet (London, England), 383(9921), 999–1008. https://doi.org/10.1016/S0140-6736(13)61752-3

12. The Associated Press-NORC Center for Public Affairs Research at the University of Chicago. (2023). Evaluating progress for racial equality [Survey]. https://apnorc.org/projects/evaluating-progress-for-racial-equality/

13. Wakefield, A. J., Murch, S. H., Anthony, A., Linnell, J., Casson, D. M., Malik, M., Berelowitz, M., Dhillon, A. P., Thomson, M. A., Harvey, P., Valentine, A., Davies, S. E., & Walker-Smith, J. A. (1999). Retracted: Ileal-lymphoid-nodular hyperplasia, non-specific colitis, and pervasive developmental disorder in children. Lancet (London, England), 351(9103), 637–641. https://doi.org/10.1016/s0140-6736(97)11096-0

14. Children's Hospital of Philadelphia. (2014, November 5). Vaccines and autism [Text]. The Children's Hospital of Philadelphia. https://www.chop.edu/centers-programs/vaccine-education-center/vaccines-and-other-conditions/vaccines-autism

15. Taylor, B., Miller, E., Farrington, C. P., Petropoulos, M. C., Favot-Mayaud, I., Li, J., & Waight, P. A. (1999). Autism and measles, mumps, and rubella vaccine: No epidemiological evidence for a causal association. Lancet (London, England), 353(9169), 2026–2029. https://doi.org/10.1016/s0140-6736(99)01239-8

16. Tanne, J. H. (2002). MMR vaccine is not linked with autism, says Danish study. British Medical Journal, 325(7373), 1134. https://www.ncbi.nlm.nih.gov/pmc/articles/PMC1124634/

17. Leppink, J., Winston, K., & O'Sullivan, P. (2016). Statistical significance does not imply a real effect. Perspectives on Medical Education, 5(2), 122–124. https://doi.org/10.1007/s40037-016-0256-6

18. Combs, J. G. (2010). Big samples and small effects: Let's not trade relevance and rigor for power. Academy of Management Journal, 53(1). https://doi.org/10.5465/amj.2010.48036305

19. Sullivan, G. M., & Feinn, R. (2012). Using effect size—or why the P value is not enough. Journal of Graduate Medical Education, 4(3), 279–282. https://doi.org/10.4300/JGME-D-12-00156.1

20. U. S. Census Bureau. U.S. Census Bureau QuickFacts: Missouri, Population estimates, 07-01-2023, Age and Sex, Persons 65 years and over. Retrieved July 16, 2024, from https://www.census.gov/quickfacts/fact/table/MO/PST045222

21. AP-NORC Center for Public Affairs Research. (2022). Immigration attitudes and conspiratorial thinkers: A study issued on the 10th anniversary of the Associated Press-NORC Center for Public Affairs Research [Issue brief]. (p. 32). AP NORC. https://apnorc.org/wp-content/uploads/2022/05/Immigration-Report_V15.pdf

22. Brisimi, T. S., Cassandras, C. G., Osgood, C., Paschalidis, I. Ch., & Zhang, Y. (2016). Sensing and classifying roadway obstacles in smart cities: the street bump system. IEEE Access, 4, 1301–1312. https://doi.org/10.1109/ACCESS.2016.2529562

23. Crawford, K. (2013, April 1). The hidden biases in big data. *Harvard Business Review*. https://hbr.org/2013/04/the-hidden-biases-in-big-data

24. Stampfer, M. J., Colditz, G. A., Willett, W. C., Manson, J. E., Rosner, B., Speizer, F. E., & Hennekens, C. H. (1991). Postmenopausal estrogen therapy and cardiovascular disease: Ten-year follow-up from the Nurses' Health Study. New England Journal of Medicine, 325(11), 756–762. https://doi.org/10.1056/NEJM199109123251102

25. Prentice, R. L., Langer, R., Stefanick, M. L., Howard, B. V., Pettinger, M., Anderson, G., Barad, D., Curb, J. D., Kotchen, J., Kuller, L., Limacher, M., & Wactawski-Wende, J. (2005). Combined postmenopausal hormone therapy and cardiovascular disease: Toward resolving the discrepancy between observational studies and the Women's Health Initiative clinical trial. American Journal of Epidemiology, 162(5), 404–414. https://doi.org/10.1093/aje/kwi223

26. Obermeyer, Z., Powers, B., Vogeli, C., & Mullainathan, S. (2019). Dissecting racial bias in an algorithm used to manage the health of populations. Science, 366(6464), 447–453. https://doi.org/10.1126/science.aax2342

27. Dastin, J. (2018, October 10). Insight—Amazon scraps secret AI recruiting tool that showed bias against women. *Reuters*. https://www.reuters.com/article/world/insight-amazon-scraps-secret-ai-recruiting-tool-that-showed-bias-against-women-idUSKCN1MK0AG/

28. Chouldechova, A., Benavides-Prado, D., Fialko, O., & Vaithianathan, R. (2018). A case study of algorithm-assisted decision making in child maltreatment hotline screening decisions. *Proceedings of the 1st Conference on Fairness, Accountability and Transparency*. PMLR (81), 134–148. https://proceedings.mlr.press/v81/chouldechova18a.html

Chapter 5

1. Cadwalladr, C., & Graham-Harrison, E. (2018, March 17). Revealed: 50 Million Facebook profiles harvested for Cambridge Analytica in major data breach. *The Guardian*. https://www.theguardian.com/news/2018/mar/17/cambridge-analytica-facebook-influence-us-election

2. Davies, H. (2015, December 11). Ted Cruz using firm that harvested data on millions of unwitting Facebook users. *The Guardian*. https://www.theguardian.com/us-news/2015/dec/11/senator-ted-cruz-president-campaign-facebook-user-data

3. Rosenberg, M., Confessore, N., & Cadwalladr, C. (2018, March 17). How Trump consultants exploited the Facebook data of millions. *The New York Times*. https://www.nytimes.com/2018/03/17/us/politics/cambridge-analytica-trump-campaign.html

4. Lewis, P., & Hilder, P. (2018, March 23). Leaked: Cambridge Analytica's blueprint for Trump victory. *The Guardian.* https://www.theguardian.com/uk-news/2018/mar/23/leaked-cambridge-analyticas-blueprint-for-trump-victory

5. AP-NORC. (2018, April 24). Americans' views of privacy and data security in the digital age. https://apnorc.org/projects/americans-views-of-privacy-and-data-security-in-the-digital-age/

6. Neate, R. (2018, July 26). Over $119bn wiped off Facebook's market cap after growth shock. *The Guardian.* https://www.theguardian.com/technology/2018/jul/26/facebook-market-cap-falls-109bn-dollars-after-growth-shock

7. Leswing, K. (2018, March 25) Mark Zuckerberg takes out full-page newspaper ads to say "sorry." *Business Insider.* https://www.businessinsider.com/mark-zuckerberg-newspaper-ads-apologize-for-cambridge-analytica-scandal-2018-3

8. Raymond, N., & Raymond, N. (2022, December 23). Facebook parent Meta to settle Cambridge Analytica scandal case for $725 million. *Reuters.* https://www.reuters.com/legal/facebook-parent-meta-pay-725-mln-settle-lawsuit-relating-cambridge-analytica-2022-12-23/

9. Kupferschmidt, K. (2023, July 27). Does social media polarize voters? Unprecedented experiments on Facebook users reveal surprises. https://www.science.org/content/article/does-social-media-polarize-voters-unprecedented-experiments-facebook-users-reveal

10. González-Bailón, S., Lazer, D., Barberá, P., Zhang, M., Allcott, H., Brown, T., Crespo-Tenorio, A., Freelon, D., Gentzkow, M., Guess, A. M., Iyengar, S., Kim, Y. M., Malhotra, N., Moehler, D., Nyhan, B., Pan, J., Rivera, C. V., Settle, J., Thorson, E., . . . Tucker, J. A. (2023). Asymmetric ideological segregation in exposure to political news on Facebook. Science, 381(6656), 392–398. https://doi.org/10.1126/science.ade7138

11. Ward, I. (2023, December 7). Disinformation researchers adjust to restrictions from platforms. Bloomberg.com. https://www.bloomberg.com/news/articles/2023-12-07/social-media-researchers-struggle-to-track-disinformation-on-x-meta

12. AP-NORC. (2018, April 24). Americans' views of privacy and data security in the digital age. https://apnorc.org/projects/americans-views-of-privacy-and-data-security-in-the-digital-age/

13. Hill, K. (2024, March 11). Automakers are sharing consumers' driving behavior with insurance companies. *The New York Times.* https://www.nytimes.com/2024/03/11/technology/carmakers-driver-tracking-insurance.html

14. Center for Open Science. TOP Guidelines. COS. https://www.cos.io/initiatives/top-guidelines

15. Williamson, E. (2022, May 23). After 10 years, 'many labs' comes to an end – but its success is replicable. *UVA Today*. https://news.virginia.edu/content/after-10-years-many-labs-comes-end-its-success-replicable

16. Center for Open Science. Reproducibility Project: Cancer Biology. Retrieved July 17, 2024, from https://www.cos.io/rpcb

17. Stern, J. (2023, August 2). An unsettling hint at how much fraud could exist in science. *The Atlantic*. https://www.theatlantic.com/science/archive/2023/08/gino-ariely-data-fraud-allegations/674891/

18. Uri, Joe, & Leif. (2021, August 17). [98] Evidence of fraud in an influential field experiment about dishonesty. Data Colada. https://datacolada.org/98

19. (2005). Timeline of a controversy. *Nature*, news051219-3. https://doi.org/10.1038/news051219-3

20. The retraction watch leaderboard. *Retraction Watch*. https://retractionwatch.com/the-retraction-watch-leaderboard/

21. Dilanian, K. (2023, December 16). Most people think the U.S. crime rate is rising. They're wrong. https://www.nbcnews.com/news/us-news/people-think-crime-rate-up-actually-down-rcna129585

22. Federal Bureau of Investigation. Federal Bureau of Investigation Crime Data Explorer. https://cde.ucr.cjis.gov/LATEST/webapp/#/pages/explorer/crime/crime-trend

23. Ibid.

24. Morgan, R. E., & Smith, E. L. (2023, December). The National Crime Victimization Survey and National Incident-Based Reporting System: A complementary picture of crime in 2022. US Department of Justice, Bureau of Justice Statistics. https://bjs.ojp.gov/library/publications/national-crime-victimization-survey-and-national-incident-based-reporting-0

25. Thompson, A., Tapp, S. N., Harrell, E., & Mueller, S. (2022). Criminal victimization, 2022 [NCJ 307089]. (NCJ 307089; p. 33). U. S. Department of Justice, Office Programs, Bureau of Justice Statistics. https://bjs.ojp.gov/library/publications/criminal-victimization-2022

26. Morgan, R. E., & Smith, E. L. (2023, December). The National Crime Victimization Survey and National Incident-Based Reporting System: A complementary picture of crime in 2022. US Department of Justice, Bureau of Justice Statistics. https://bjs.ojp.gov/library/publications/national-crime-victimization-survey-and-national-incident-based-reporting-0

27. Li, W., & Lartey, J. (2024, June 27). Crime rates and the 2024 election: What you need to know. *The Marshall Project.* https://www.themarshall project.org/2024/06/27/trump-and-biden-spar-over-crime-rates-ahead-of-their-debate-what-do-we-really-know

28. Asher, J. (2024, April 8). The UCR vs NCVS conundrum [Substack newsletter]. *Jeff-Alytics.* https://jasher.substack.com/p/the-ucr-vs-ncvs-conundrum

29. Dai, W. (Daisy), & Luca, M. (2019). Digitizing disclosure: The case of restaurant hygiene scores [Working paper 18-088]. (18–088; pp. 1–32). Harvard Business School. https://www.hbs.edu/ris/Publication%20 Files/18-088_7781070c-6910-4e26-aafd-9150b93a2d93.pdf

30. Cheesman, H. (2018, March 8). Study: Low hygiene scores on Yelp lead to decrease in consumer purchase intent. *Yelp -Official Blog.* https:// blog.yelp.com/news/study-low-hygiene-scores-yelp-lead-decrease-consumer-purchase-intent/

31. Hulett, S. (2015, September 29). High lead levels in Michigan kids after city switches water source. Michigan Public Radio. https://www.npr .org/2015/09/29/444497051/high-lead-levels-in-michigan-kids-after-city-switches-water-source

32. Langkjær-Bain, R. (2017). The murky tale of Flint's deceptive water data. Significance, 14(2), 16–21. https://doi.org/10.1111/j.1740-9713 .2017.01016.x

33. Del Toral, M. A. (2015). High lead levels in Flint, Michigan-Interim Report [Memorandum] (WG-15 J; pp. 1–5). United States Environmental Protection Agency. https://mediad.publicbroadcasting.net/p/michigan/ files/201602/Miguels-Memo.pdf

34. Langkjær-Bain, R. (2017). The murky tale of Flint's deceptive water data. Significance, 14(2), 16–21. https://doi.org/10.1111/j.1740-9713 .2017.01016.x

35. Ibid.

36. Hanna-Attisha, M. (2018). *What the eyes don't see: A story of crisis, resistance, and hope in an American city.* (Illustrated edition). One World. (p. 285.)

37. Davis, M. M., Kolb, C., Reynolds, L., Rothstein, E., & Sikkema, K. (2016). Flint Water Advisory Task Force Final Report (p. 28). https://www .michigan.gov/-/media/Project/Websites/formergovernors/Folder6/ FWATF_FINAL_REPORT_21March2016.pdf?rev=284b9e42c7c84001 9109eb73aaeedb68

38. AAPOR. (2022, November 3). Transparency initiative. https://aapor.org/standards-and-ethics/transparency-initiative/

39. My organization, NORC, is a charter member of the AAPOR's Transparency Initiative and a strong supporter of these principles.

40. Tobin, J. M. (2024, June 19). Generally accepted accounting principles (GAAP). Accounting.com. https://www.accounting.com/resources/gaap/

41. Boostrom, R. (2011). Tyco International: Leadership crisis. Auburn University, Center for Ethical Organizational Cultures. https://harbert.auburn.edu/binaries/documents/center-for-ethical-organizational-cultures/cases/tyco.pdf

42. Herold, T. What was the Tyco International scandal? *Herold Financial Dictionary*. https://www.financial-dictionary.info/terms/tyco-international-scandal/

43. Segal, T. (2024, June 3). Enron scandal and accounting fraud: What happened? *Investopedia*. https://www.investopedia.com/updates/enron-scandal-summary/

44. Cornell Law School Legal Information Institute. (2021, April). Sarbanes-Oxley Act. LII/Legal Information Institute. https://www.law.cornell.edu/wex/sarbanes-oxley_act

45. Atiyeh, C. (2019, December 4). Everything you need to know about the VW diesel-emissions scandal. *Car and Driver*. https://www.caranddriver.com/news/a15339250/everything-you-need-to-know-about-the-vw-diesel-emissions-scandal/

46. Rathee, S., Banker, S., Mishra, A., & Mishra, H. (2023). Algorithms propagate gender bias in the marketplace—With consumers' cooperation. Journal of Consumer Psychology, 33(4), 621–631. https://doi.org/10.1002/jcpy.1351

47. Sweeney, L. Discrimination in online ad delivery. Social Science Research Network, Rochester, NY. January 28, 2013. https://papers.ssrn.com/abstract=2208240

48. Bussmann, N., Giudici, P., Marinelli, D., & Papenbrock, J. (2020). Explainable machine learning in credit risk management. Computational Economics, 57(1), 203–216. https://doi.org/10.1007/s10614-020-10042-0

49. Hosanagar, K., & R155 Jair, V. (2018, July 23). We need transparency in algorithms, but too much can backfire. *Harvard Business Review*. https://hbr.org/2018/07/we-need-transparency-in-algorithms-but-too-much-can-backfire

50. Philosophy & Technology. (2022). Transparency as manipulation? Uncovering the disciplinary power of algorithmic transparency. 35(69). https://link.springer.com/article/10.1007/s13347-022-00564-w

51. Domagala, N. (2021, November 29). What is our new Algorithmic Transparency Standard? *Data in government.* https://dataingovernment .blog.gov.uk/2021/11/29/what-is-our-new-algorithmic-transparency-standard/

52. Regulation (EU) 2016/679 (GDPR), Article 22. Automated individual decision-making, including profiling. European Parliament and Council. https://gdpr-text.com/read/article-22/

53. Information Commissioner's Office & The Alan Turing Institute. (2022, October 17). Explaining decisions made with AI. Information Commissioner's Office; ICO. https://ico.org.uk/for-organisations/uk-gdpr-guidance-and-resources/artificial-intelligence/explaining-decisions-made-with-artificial-intelligence/

54. Observatory of Public Sector Innovation. (2022, November 9). Algorithmic Transparency Recording Standard. Observatory of Public Sector Innovation. https://oecd-opsi.org/innovations/algorithmic-transparency-standard/

Chapter 6

1. Office of the Press Secretary. (2003, March 19). President Bush addresses the nation. Operation Iraqi Freedom. https://georgewbush-whitehouse .archives.gov/infocus/iraq/news/20030319-17.html

2. Coelho, C. (2013, March 14). Iraq War: 190,000 lives, $2.2 trillion. Brown University. https://news.brown.edu/articles/2013/03/warcosts

3. Bush, G. W. (2011). *Decision points* (Reprint edition). Crown. (ebook p. 133).

4. Riedel, B. (2021, September 17). 9/11 and Iraq: The making of a tragedy. Brookings. https://www.brookings.edu/articles/9-11-and-iraq-the-making-of-a-tragedy/

5. Phythian, M. (2006). The perfect intelligence failure? U.S. pre-war intelligence on Iraqi weapons of mass destruction. Politics & Policy, 34(2), 400–424. 10.1111/j.1747-1346.2006.00019.x

6. Ensor, D. (2003, March 14). Fake Iraq documents "embarrassing" for U.S. CNN. https://www.leadingtowar.com/PDFsources_claims_yellow cake/2003_03_14_CNN.pdf

7. Commission on Intelligence Capabilities. (2005, March 31). Commission on the Intelligence Capabilities of the United States Regarding Weapons of Mass Destruction. https://www.govinfo.gov/content/pkg/GPO-WMD/pdf/GPO-WMD.pdf

8. CBS Interactive. (2004, January 29). Kay: "We were almost all wrong." *CBS News.* https://www.cbsnews.com/news/kay-we-were-almost-all-wrong/

9. Associated Press-NORC Center for Public Affairs Research. (2023). Assessing the news media: Trust, coverage, and threats to a free press. https://apnorc.org/wp-content/uploads/2023/04/APNORC_RFK_Report_2023.pdf

10. Feynman, R. P. (with Gates, B.). (2018). *"Surely You're Joking, Mr. Feynman!": Adventures of a Curious Character* (R. Leighton, Ed.; Reissue edition). W. W. Norton & Company. (p. 343).

11. Zeller, S. (2008, September 17). Cherry-picking the record. PolitiFact. https://www.politifact.com/factchecks/2008/sep/17/barack-obama/cherry-picking-the-record/

12. Bank, J. (2008, September 11). School funding misleads. FactCheck.org. https://www.factcheck.org/2008/09/school-funding-misleads/

13. Walter, N., Cohen, J., Holbert, R. L., & Morag, Y. (2019). Fact-checking: A meta-analysis of what works and for whom. Political Communication, 37(3), 350–375. 10.1080/10584609.2019.1668894

14. Jacobson, L. (2018, February 5). The age of cherry-picking. PolitiFact. https://www.politifact.com/article/2018/feb/05/age-cherry-picking/

15. Di Liberto, T. (2024, January 9). What's in a number? The meaning of the 1.5-C climate threshold. Climate.gov. http://www.climate.gov/news-features/features/whats-number-meaning-15-c-climate-threshold

16. Petersen, A. M., Vincent, E. M., & Westerling, A. L. (2019). Discrepancy in scientific authority and media visibility of climate change scientists and contrarians. Nature Communications, 10(1), 3502. 10.1038/s41467-019-09959-4

17. Sharp, M. R. (2024, August 13). Pickleball injuries are on this rise. Here are 10 tips to avoid them while playing. UC Davis Health. https://health.ucdavis.edu/welcome/news/headlines/pickleball-injuries-are-on-this-rise-here-are-tips-to-avoid-them-while-playing/2024/08

18. Weber, L. (2022). Both sides now. Northwestern School of Education and Social Policy Magazine, 23(1), 14–16. https://sesp.northwestern.edu/magazine/summer-2022/the-perils-of-bothsidesism.html

19. Pariser, E. (2012). *The filter bubble: How the new personalized web is changing what we read and how we think* (Reprint edition). Penguin Books.

20. Krugman, P. (2023, July 14). Wonking out: In economics, a game of teams. *The New York Times.* https://www.nytimes.com/2023/07/14/opinion/inflation-economists-soft-landing.html
21. Simmons, J. P., Nelson, L. D., & Simonsohn, U. (2011). False-positive psychology: Undisclosed flexibility in data collection and analysis allows presenting anything as significant. Psychological Science, 22(11), 1359–1366. https://doi.org/10.1177/0956797611417632
22. Fanelli, D. (2012). Negative results are disappearing from most disciplines and countries. Scientometrics, 90, 891–904. https://doi.org/10.1007/s11192-011-0494-7
23. Carroll, H. A., Toumpakari, Z., Johnson, L., & Betts, J. A. (2017). The perceived feasibility of methods to reduce publication bias. PLoS ONE, 12(10), e0186472. https://doi.org/10.1371/journal.pone.0186472
24. Tatsioni, A., Bonitsis, N. G., & Ioannidis, J. P. A. (2007). Persistence of contradicted claims in the literature. JAMA, 298(21), 2517-2526. https://doi.org/10.1001/jama.298.21.2517
25. Gill, D. (2021, February 24). New study disavows marshmallow test's predictive powers. *UCLA Anderson Review.* https://anderson-review.ucla.edu/new-study-disavows-marshmallow-tests-predictive-powers/
26. Ibid.
27. Watts, T. W., Duncan, G. J., & Quan, H. (2018). Revisiting the marshmallow test: a conceptual replication investigating links between early delay of gratification and later outcomes. Psychological Science, 29(7), 1159–1177. https://doi.org/10.1177/0956797618761661
28. Flier, J. S. (2022). The problem of irreproducible bioscience research. Perspectives in Biology and Medicine, 65(3), 373–395. https://doi.org/10.1353/pbm.2022.0032
29. Ibid.
30. Ibid.
31. AP-NORC. (2023, June 15). Major declines in the public's confidence in science in the wake of the pandemic. *AP-NORC.* https://apnorc.org/projects/major-declines-in-the-publics-confidence-in-science-in-the-wake-of-the-pandemic/
32. Gaylin, D. S., Held, P. J., Port, F. K., Hunsicker, L. G., Wolfe, R. A., Kahan, B. D., Jones, C. A., & Agodoa, L. Y. C. (1993). The impact of comorbid and sociodemographic factors on access to renal transplantation. JAMA, 269(5), 603–608. https://doi.org/10.1001/jama.1993.03500050081030

33. Ryan, C. D., Schaul, A. J., Butner, R., & Swarthout, J. T. (2020). Monetizing disinformation in the attention economy: The case of genetically modified organisms (GMOs). European Management Journal, 38(1), 7–18. https://doi.org/10.1016/j.emj.2019.11.002

34. Lynch, D., & Vogel, D. (2001). The regulation of GMOs in Europe and the United States. Council on Foreign Relations. https://www.cfr.org/report/regulation-gmos-europe-and-united-states

35. Tagliabue G. (2017). The EU legislation on "GMOs" between nonsense and protectionism: An ongoing Schumpeterian chain of public choices. GM Crops & Food, 8(1):57-73. https://doi.org/10.1080/21645698.2016.1270488.

36. Sturge, G. (2022, November 7). From migration to railways, how bad data infiltrated British politics. The Guardian. https://www.theguardian.com/commentisfree/2022/nov/07/migration-railways-bad-data-british-politics-inaccurate-incomplete

37. Arthur, C., & Inman, P. (2013, April 18). The error that could subvert George Osborne's austerity programme. The Guardian. https://www.theguardian.com/politics/2013/apr/18/uncovered-error-george-osborne-austerity

38. U.S. Department of Commerce. Economic indicators. U.S. Department of Commerce. Retrieved on July 16, 2024. https://www.commerce.gov/data-and-reports/economic-indicators

39. Aragão, R., & Linsi, L. (2020). Many shades of wrong: what governments do when they manipulate statistics. Review of International Political Economy, 29(1), 88–113. 10.1080/09692290.2020.1769704

40. Hernandez, A. (2023, October 31). Politicians love to cite crime data. It's often wrong. Virginia Mercury. https://virginiamercury.com/2023/10/31/politicians-love-to-cite-crime-data-its-often-wrong/

41. Li, W., & Lartey, J. (2024, June 27). Crime rates and the 2024 election: What you need to know. The Marshall Project. https://www.themarshallproject.org/2024/06/27/trump-and-biden-spar-over-crime-rates-ahead-of-their-debate-what-do-we-really-know

42. Chambers, C., & Munafo, M. (2013, June 5). Trust in science would be improved by study pre-registration. The Guardian. https://www.theguardian.com/science/blog/2013/jun/05/trust-in-science-study-pre-registration

43. Weintraub, P. G. (2016). The importance of publishing negative results. Journal of Insect Science, 16(1), 1–2. https://doi.org/10.1093/jisesa/iew092

Chapter 7

1. Greene, S. Tracking California's water supplies: How much water does the state have stored? *Los Angeles Times.* https://www.latimes.com/projects/california-drought-status-maps-water-usage/
2. You may wonder how this information about water supplies in the Los Angeles area relates to the wildfires that devastated Los Angeles in the winter of 2025. The data journalists at the *LA Times* were attempting to address a yearslong ongoing information problem about regional water supplies and drought, rather than the acute availability of water in specific locations to put out fires. The *LA Times* extensively covered the problem of lack of water for localized firefighting in a separate series of articles.
3. The Stanford Daily. (2021, March). Alumni spotlight: Andrea Fuller '09. *Stanford Alumni.* https://alumni.stanforddaily.com/alumni-spotlight-andrea-fuller-09/
4. Fischer-Baum, R., & Mehta, D. (2017, January 18). How America's thinking changed under Obama. *FiveThirtyEight.* https://projects.fivethirtyeight.com/obama-polling-trends/
5. Financial Times. (2023, November 27). How China is tearing down Islam. *Financial Times.* https://ig.ft.com/china-mosques/
6. Our World in Data. (2024). Life expectancy vs. health expenditure [Graph]. Our World in Data. https://ourworldindata.org/grapher/life-expectancy-vs-health-expenditure?time=1970..2022
7. Got, J. (2020, October 23). Why data literacy is imperative for every journalist. *Journalism in the Time of Crisis.* https://medium.com/journalism-in-the-time-of-crisis/why-data-literacy-is-imperative-for-every-journalist-5dc1743e49da
8. Wihbey, J. P. (2019). *The social fact: News and knowledge in a networked world.* The MIT Press.
9. Wihbey, J. P. (2019, May 1). Prescription for journalists from journalists: Less time studying Twitter, more time studying math. *The Conversation.* http://theconversation.com/prescription-for-journalists-from-journalists-less-time-studying-twitter-more-time-studying-math-113248
10. Wihbey, J., & Coddington, M. (2017). Knowing the numbers: Assessing attitudes among journalists and educators about using and interpreting data, statistics, and research. International Symposium on Online Journalism Journal, 7(1), 5–24. https://isoj.org/research/knowing-the-numbers-assessing-attitudes-among-journalists-and-educators-about-using-and-interpreting-data-statistics-and-research/

11. From a video interview conducted with Alberto Cairo, April 1, 2024.
12. Brookings Institution. (2024). Urban-Brookings Tax Policy Center. *Brookings*. https://www.brookings.edu/centers/urban-brookings-tax-policy-center/
13. Dykes, B. (2017, March 10). Why companies must close the data literacy divide. *Forbes*. https://www.forbes.com/sites/brentdykes/2017/03/09/why-companies-must-close-the-data-literacy-divide/
14. Gartner. (2024). Software market insights: Business intelligence (BI) and data analytics. *Gartner*. https://www.gartner.com/en/digital-markets/insights/software-market-insights-business-intelligence-and-data-analytics
15. Forrester Consulting. (2022). Building data literacy: The key to better decisions, greater productivity, and data-driven organizations. https://www.tableau.com/sites/default/files/2022-03/Forrester_Building_Data_Literacy_Tableau_Mar2022.pdf
16. Australian Public Service Commission. (2022, December 19). APS Data Literacy Foundational Pathway. https://www.apsc.gov.au/initiatives-and-programs/aps-professional-streams/aps-data-profession/data-literacy
17. Crozier, R. (2022, October 10). Singapore government sets new data literacy baseline. *iTnews Asia*. https://www.itnews.asia/news/singapore-government-sets-new-data-literacy-baseline-586234
18. U.S. Department of Education, National Center for Education Statistics, Integrated Postsecondary Education Data System (IPEDS), Completions component, Fall 2022 (provisional data). Unpublished NORC analysis.
19. High School Transcript Study (HSTS) and Postsecondary Education Transcript Study (PETS) Beginning Postsecondary Students Longitudinal Study. Unpublished NORC analysis.
20. U.S. Department of Education, National Center for Education Statistics, National Assessment of Educational Progress (NAEP), 2009 and 2019. Unpublished NORC analysis.
21. Ziv, S. (2022, October 6). Should high schools teach financial literacy? More states say yes. *Forbes*. https://www.forbes.com/sites/shaharziv/2022/10/06/should-high-schools-teach-financial-literacy-more-states-say-yes/
22. American Statistical Association. (2005). Guidelines for assessment and instruction in statistics education: college report. https://www.amstat.org/docs/default-source/amstat-documents/2005gaisecollege_full.pdf
23. Schield, M. (2022). Statistical literacy: Seven simple questions for policymakers. Statistical Journal of the IAOS, 38(2), 471–475. 10.3233/SJI-220957

24. Levitt, S. D. (Host). (2021, August 27). America's math curriculum doesn't add up (No. 42) [Audio podcast episode]. In Freakonomics. Renbud Radio. https://freakonomics.com/podcast/americas-math-curriculum-doesnt-add-up/

25. Data Science 4 Everyone. (2024). About our coalition. Data Science 4 Everyone. https://www.datascience4everyone.org/about

Chapter 8

1. International Energy Agency. (2020). World air passenger traffic evolution,1980–2020. IEA. https://www.iea.org/data-and-statistics/charts/world-air-passenger-traffic-evolution-1980–2020

2. National Air and Space Museum. (2021, December 17). Airline deregulation: When everything changed. National Air and Space Museum. https://airandspace.si.edu/stories/editorial/airline-deregulation-when-everything-changed

3. I'm indebted to travel industry expert Henry Harteveldt of Atmosphere Research who shared much of this history of standards and infrastructure in the air travel business.

4. From a video interview conducted with Henry Harteveldt, April 3, 2024.

5. The Options Clearing Corporation. (2024). Historical volume statistics. The Options Clearing Corporation. https://www.theocc.com/market-data/market-data-reports/volume-and-open-interest/historical-volume-statistics

6. Annear, S. (2014, October 23). MBTA rolls out "phase one" of real-time Green Line tracking. *Boston Magazine.* https://www.bostonmagazine.com/news/2014/10/23/mbta-green-line-tracking-real-time-mobile-app/

7. Groves, R. M., Mesenbourg, T., & Siri, M. (Eds.). (2023). Toward a 21st Century National Data Infrastructure: Mobilizing Information for the Common Good. National Academies Press. https://doi.org/10.17226/26688 (p. 56).

8. Orvis, K. (2024, March 28). OMB publishes revisions to statistical policy directive no. 15: Standards for maintaining, collecting, and presenting federal data on race and ethnicity. The White House. https://www.whitehouse.gov/omb/briefing-room/2024/03/28/omb-publishes-revisions-to-statistical-policy-directive-no-15-standards-for-maintaining-collecting-and-presenting-federal-data-on-race-and-ethnicity/

9. Santos, R. L. (2024, April 8). Meeting our future: Improving race/ethnicity data with updated federal standards. *United States Census Bureau, Director's Blog.* https://www.census.gov/newsroom/blogs/director/2024/04/improving-race-ethnicity-data.html

10. Groves, R. M., Mesenbourg, T., & Siri, M. (Eds.). (2023). Toward a 21st Century National Data Infrastructure: Mobilizing Information for the Common Good. National Academies Press. https://doi.org/10.17226/26688

11. Tanenbaum, A. S. (1989). *Computer networks* (2nd). Prentice Hall International. (p. 254).

12. Groves, R. M., Mesenbourg, T., & Siri, M. (Eds.). (2023). Toward a 21st Century National Data Infrastructure: Mobilizing Information for the Common Good. National Academies Press. https://doi.org/10.17226/26688 (p. 72).

13. The Associated Press-NORC Center for Public Affairs Research. (2021). AP-NORC/MeriTalk: Public Sentiment Survey 2021. https://apnorc.org/wp-content/uploads/2021/08/MeriTalk-Omnibus-2021_Topline_FINAL.pdf

14. Assistant Secretary for Technology Policy & Office of the National Coordinator for Health IT. (2018, September 6). How HIPAA supports data sharing. HealthIT.gov. https://www.healthit.gov/topic/interoperability/how-hipaa-supports-data-sharing

15. Niles, S. (2024, April 19). What others are saying: The American Privacy Rights Act. U.S. Senate Committee on Commerce, Science, & Transportation. https://www.commerce.senate.gov/2024/4/what-others-are-saying

16. Vigdor, N. (2019, November 10). Apple Card investigated after gender discrimination complaints. *The New York Times*. https://www.nytimes.com/2019/11/10/business/Apple-credit-card-investigation.html

17. Hulsey, L. (2024, February 23). 2023 will go down for record-setting number of data breaches. *Governing*. https://www.governing.com/management-and-administration/2023-will-go-down-for-record-setting-number-of-data-breaches

18. From a conversation with Len Burman, director emeritus of the Tax Policy Center.

19. Reiter, J. P., & Park, J. (Eds.). (2024). Toward a 21st Century National Data Infrastructure: Managing Privacy and Confidentiality Risks with Blended Data. National Academies Press. https://doi.org/10.17226/27335

20. Ibid. (p. 9).

21. Ibid. (p. 3).

22. Ibid. (p. 5).

23. Ibid. (p. 6).

24. Ibid. (p. 26).

25. Institute of Electrical and Electronics Engineers (IEEE). (2024). Homomorphic encryption use cases. *IEEE Digital Privacy*. https://digitalprivacy.ieee.org/publications/topics/homomorphic-encryption-use-cases

26. Amar, A., & McAuley, E. (2024). Privacy-preserving record linkage. Booz Allen Hamilton. https://www.boozallen.com/insights/ai/privacy-preserving-record-linkage.html
27. Reiter, J. P., & Park, J. (Eds.). (2024). (pp. 31–32).

Chapter 9

1. You can easily generate these charts and many others at https://gssdataexplorer.norc.org/trends
2. Manyika, J., Chui, M., Farrell, D., Van Kuiken, S., Groves, P., & Doshi, E. A. (2013, October 1). Open data: Unlocking innovation and performance with liquid information. McKinsey Global Institute. https://www.ckinsey.com/capabilities/mckinsey-digital/our-insights/open-data-unlocking-innovation-and-performance-with-liquid-information
3. Gurin, J. (2014). *Open data now: The secret to hot startups, smart investing, savvy marketing, and fast innovation*. McGraw Hill.
4. Statistics Canada. About us. Statistics Canada. https://www.statcan.gc.ca/en/about/about
5. Statistics Canada. Subjects. Statistics Canada. https://www150.statcan.gc.ca/n1/en/subjects
6. Statistics Canada. (2022, April 21). New motor vehicle registration data visualization tool. Statistics Canada. https://www150.statcan.gc.ca/n1/pub/71-607-x/71-607-x2019028-eng.htm
7. Statistics Canada. (2022, March 23). Canadian international merchandise trade web application - Exports. Statistics Canada. https://www150.statcan.gc.ca/n1/pub/71-607-x/2021004/exp-eng.htm
8. Statistics Canada. (2023, February 28). Public Use Microdata File collection. Statistics Canada. https://www.statcan.gc.ca/en/microdata/pumf
9. Statistics Canada. (2023, September 8). Transparency and accountability. Statistics Canada. https://www.statcan.gc.ca/en/transparency-accountability
10. OECD Directorate for Public Governance. (2023). 2023 OECD Open, Useful and Re-usable data (OURdata) Index. https://www.oecd.org/en/publications/2023/12/2023-oecd-open-useful-and-re-usable-data-ourdata-index_cc9e8a9e.html
11. "The OECD Survey on Open Government Data 5.0, which ran from May to December 2022, collected evidence in 36 OECD member countries and 4 accession countries. Data from Hungary and the United States is not available as these countries did not complete the survey." See https://www.oecd.org/publications/2023-oecd-open-useful-and-re-usable-data-ourdata-index-a37f51c3-en.htm, p. 26.

12. AirNow. (2024). Partners. *AirNow.* https://www.airnow.gov/partners/

13. AirNow. (2021). How is the NowCast algorithm used to report current air quality? AirNow. https://usepa.servicenowservices.com/airnow/en/how-is-the-nowcast-algorithm-used-to-report-current-air-quality?id=kb_article&sys_id=bb8b65ef1b06bc10028420eae54bcb98

14. General Services Administration. (2024). DataCatalog. Data.gov. https://catalog.data.gov/dataset?q=&sort=views_recent+desc

15. USA Spending. (2024). Government Spending Explorer. USASpending.gov. https://usaspending.gov/explorer

16. General Services Administration. (2024). U.S. social indicators. Performance.gov. https://www.performance.gov/explore/social-indicators/

17. USAFacts. (2023, December 14). Which groups have experienced an increase in hate crimes? *USAFacts* https://usafacts.org/articles/which-groups-have-experienced-an-increase-in-hate-crimes/

18. NORC at the University of Chicago. (2024). Implementing Data Infrastructure to Reduce Firearms Violence. NORC at the University of Chicago. https://www.norc.org/research/projects/firearms-data-infrastructure.html

19. NORC at the University of Chicago. (2020). The state of firearms data in 2019. NORC at the University of Chicago. https://www.norc.org/content/dam/norc-org/pdfs/State%20of%20Firearms%20Research%202019.pdf

20. Roman, J. K. (2020). A blueprint for a U.S. firearms data infrastructure. NORC at the University of Chicago. https://www.norc.org/content/dam/norc-org/pdfs/A%20Blueprint%20for%20a%20U.S.%20Firearms%20Data%20Infrastructure_NORC%20Expert%20Panel%20Final%20Report_October%202020.pdf

21. Lohr, S. L., Weinberg, D. H., & Marton, K. (Eds.). (2023). Toward a 21st Century National Data Infrastructure: Enhancing Survey Programs by Using Multiple Data Sources. National Academies Press. https://doi.org/10.17226/26804

22. The Associated Press-NORC Center for Public Affairs Research. (2021). AP-NORC/MeriTalk: Public Sentiment Survey 2021. https://apnorc.org/wp-content/uploads/2021/08/MeriTalk-Omnibus-2021_Topline_FINAL.pdf

23. The White House. (2013). Open Government Initiative. The White House. https://obamawhitehouse.archives.gov/open

24. Commission on Evidence-Based Policymaking. (2017). The promise of evidence-based policymaking: Report of the Commission on Evidence-Based Policymaking. https://www2.census.gov/adrm/fesac/2017-12-15/Abraham-CEP-final-report.pdf

25. An Act to Amend Titles 5 and 44, United States Code, to Require Federal Evaluation Activities, Improve Federal Data Management, and for Other Purposes, H.R. 4174, 115th Cong. (2019). https://www.congress.gov/bill/115th-congress/house-bill/4174

26. America's DataHub Consortium. (2024). Accelerating data and statistical innovation. *America's DataHub Consortium.* https://www.americasdatahub.org/

27. America's DataHub Consortium. (2022, September 25). America's DataHub Consortium announces Innovation Challenge winners [Press release]. https://www.americasdatahub.org/wp-content/uploads/2022/10/20220925_InnovationChallengeWinners.pdf

28. America's DataHub Consortium. (2023, October 31). National Science Foundation's National Center for Science and Engineering statistics funds over $7.5 million in National Secure Data Service Demonstration Projects [Press release]. https://www.prnewswire.com/news-releases/national-science-foundations-national-center-for-science-and-engineering-statistics-funds-over-7-5-million-in-national-secure-data-service-demonstration-projects-301973279.html

29. Hart, N., & Saul, J. (2023, September 28). Evidence 2.0: The next era of evidence-based policymaking. *Stanford Social Innovation Review.* https://ssir.org/articles/entry/the_next_era_of_evidence_based_policymaking

30. ICSP Private Data Steering Group. (2023, January 6). The use of private datasets by federal statistical programs: Extent, challenges, and lessons learned. https://www.statspolicy.gov/assets/docs/ICSP-The%20Use%20of%20Private%20Datasets%20by%20Federal%20Statistical%20Programs-1-6-2023.pdf

31. Groves, R. M., Mesenbourg, T., & Siri, M. (Eds.). (2023). Toward a 21st century national data infrastructure: Mobilizing information for the common good. National Academies Press. (p. 30) https://doi.org/10.17226/26688

32. Ibid. (p. 40)

Chapter 10

1. This is an unedited transcript of a dialogue with ChatGPT-4o, conducted on June 28, 2024. The original prompt was as follows: "Here's what you need to know about me. My name is Dan Gaylin. I am the CEO of NORC, a nonprofit research organization. You can read my biography here: https://www.norc.org/about/experts/dan-gaylin.html I will be asking you questions about AI. It is very important that you answer these

questions in paragraphs, not bullets or numbered lists. And each answer must be no more than 70 words long. Got it?" In what follows, both the questions and the responses have been reproduced verbatim.

2. The direct quotes in this chapter come from video interviews conducted for this book with Richard Coffin, chief research officer of USAFacts; Michael Franklin, professor of computer science at the University of Chicago; PV Kannan, CEO of [24]7.ai; Bo Li, associate professor of computer science at both the University of Illinois and the University of Chicago; Charlene Li and Katia Walsh, coauthors of *Winning with Generative AI*; Maribel Lopez, founder of Lopez Research; and Cynthia Rudin, computer science professor at Duke University.

3. Moore, J., & Acharya, A. (2023, November 9). The Future of music: How Generative AI is transforming the music industry. Andreessen Horowitz.https://a16z.com/the-future-of-music-how-generative-ai-is-transforming-the-music-industry/

4. Toys"R"Us. (2024, June 21). *The Origin of Toys"R"Us: Brand Film Teaser | Toys"R"Us* [Video]. *YouTube*. https://www.youtube.com/watch?v=F_WflzYGlg4

5. Holloway, E. (2023, June 7). Say what? AI doesn't understand anything. *Mind Matters*. https://mindmatters.ai/2023/06/say-what-ai-doesnt-understand-anything/

6. Ladden-Hall, D. (2024, May 31). Google explains why its AI overviews told users to eat rocks and glue pizzas. *Daily Beast*. https://www.thedailybeast.com/google-explains-why-its-ai-overviews-told-users-to-eat-rocks-and-glue-pizzas

7. Acunzo, J. (2024, May). *AI has read the internet. It has not read the room* [Post]. *LinkedIn*. https://www.linkedin.com/posts/jayacunzo_ai-has-read-the-internet-it-has-not-read-activity-7200192491751383041-KCnF

8. From a video interview conducted with Richard Coffin, May 21, 2024.

9. Lång, K., Josefsson, V., Larsson, A.-M., Larsson, S., Högberg, C., Sartor, H., Hofvind, S., Andersson, I., & Rosso, A. (2023). Artificial intelligence-supported screen reading versus standard double reading in the mammography screening with artificial intelligence trial (MASAI): A clinical safety analysis of a randomised, controlled, non-inferiority, single-blinded, screening accuracy study. The Lancet Oncology, 24(8), 936–944. 10.1016/S1470-2045(23)00298-X

10. Barnett, A. J., Schwartz, F. R., Tao, C., Chen, C., Ren, Y., Lo, J. Y., & Rudin, C. (2021). A case-based interpretable deep learning model for classification of mass lesions in digital mammography. Nature Machine Intelligence, 3(12), 1061–1070. https://doi.org/10.1038/s42256-021-00423-x

11. Donnelly, J., Moffett, L., Barnett, A. J., Trivedi, H., Schwartz, F., Lo, J., & Rudin, C. (2024). AsymMirai: Interpretable mammography-based deep learning model for 1–5-year breast cancer risk prediction. Radiology, 310(3), e232780. https://doi.org/10.1148/radiol.232780

12. Li, C. (2024). Books. Charlene Li. https://charleneli.com/books/

13. From a video interview conducted with Charlene Li, March 8, 2024.

14. From a video interview conducted with Katia Walsh, March 15, 2024.

15. From a video interview conducted with Michael Franklin, May 31, 2024.

16. Liu, C., Russo, M., Cafarella, M., Cao, L., Chen, P. B., Chen, Z., Franklin, M., Kraska, T., Madden, S., & Vitagliano, G. (2024). A declarative system for optimizing AI workloads. arXiv. https://doi.org/10.48550/arXiv.2405.14696

17. From a video interview conducted with Maribel Lopez, March 11, 2024.

18. From a video interview conducted with PV Kannan, March 11, 2024.

19. Barrabi, T. (2024, February 21). "Absurdly woke": Google's AI chatbot spits out "diverse" images of founding fathers, popes, Vikings. New York Post. https://nypost.com/2024/02/21/business/googles-ai-chatbot-gemini-makes-diverse-images-of-founding-fathers-popes-and-vikings-so-woke-its-unusable/

20. Brewster, T. (2021, October 14). Fraudsters cloned company director's voice in $35 million heist, police find. Forbes. https://www.forbes.com/sites/thomasbrewster/2021/10/14/huge-bank-fraud-uses-deep-fake-voice-tech-to-steal-millions/

21. Puig, A. (2023, March 20). Scammers use AI to enhance their family emergency schemes. Federal Trade Commission Consumer Advice. https://consumer.ftc.gov/consumer-alerts/2023/03/scammers-use-ai-enhance-their-family-emergency-schemes

22. Swenson, A., & Chan, K. (2024, March 14). Election disinformation takes a big leap with AI being used to deceive worldwide. AP News. https://apnews.com/article/artificial-intelligence-elections-disinformation-chatgpt-bc283e7426402f0b4baa7df280a4c3fd

23. Jingnan, H. (2024, April 5). Using AI to detect AI-generated deepfakes can work for audio—But not always. NPR. https://www.npr.org/2024/04/05/1241446778/deepfake-audio-detection

24. Bond, S., & Parks, M. (2024, February 16). Tech giants pledge action against deceptive AI in elections. NPR. https://www.npr.org/2024/02/16/1232001889/ai-deepfakes-election-tech-accord

25. Graham, M. H. (2024, June 26). Deepfakes: Federal and state regulation aims to curb a growing threat. Thomson Reuters Institute. https://www.thomsonreuters.com/en-us/posts/government/deepfakes-federal-state-regulation/

26. Wang, B., Chen, W., Pei, H., Xie, C., Kang, M., Zhang, C., Xu, C., Xiong, Z., Dutta, R., Schaeffer, R., Truong, S. T., Arora, S., Mazeika, M., Hendrycks, D., Lin, Z., Cheng, Y., Koyejo, S., Song, D., & Li, B. (2024). DecodingTrust: a comprehensive assessment of trustworthiness in GPT models [Working Paper arXiv:2306.11698v5]. *arXiv*. https://doi.org/10.48550/arXiv.2306.11698

27. Yuan, Z., Xiong, Z., Zeng, Y., Yu, N., Jia, R., Song, D., & Li, B. (2024). RigorLLM: Resilient guardrails for large language models against undesired content. *arXiv*. https://doi.org/10.48550/arXiv.2403.13031

28. Mortman, H. (2022, August 30). #RIP GORBACHEV: REAGAN: 'Trust, but verify." GORBACHEV: "You repeat that at every meeting." 1987 [Video]. *YouTube*. https://www.youtube.com/watch?v=qwh2w7osIp4

29. Schmelzer, R., & Walch, K. (2024, August 22). *How do Big Data and AI work together?* TechTarget. https://www.techtarget.com/searchenterpriseai/tip/How-do-big-data-and-AI-work-together

30. Steinrueecken, C., Smith, E., Janz, D., Lloyd, J., & Ghahramani, Z. (2019). The automatic statistician. In F. Hutter, L. Kotthoff, & J. Vanschoren (Eds.), *Automated Machine Learning: Methods, Systems, Challenges*. Springer International Publishing. https://doi.org/10.1007/978-3-030-05318-5_9

31. Pannett, R. (2024, June 20). Can AI police itself? Experts say chatbots can detect each other's gaffes. *Washington Post*. https://www.washingtonpost.com/technology/2024/06/20/ai-chatbots-hallucinations-study/

32. Hartshorne, D. (2024, April 30). The best AI content detectors in 2024. *Zapier*. https://zapier.com/blog/ai-content-detector/

33. Fu, A. (2024, June 27). Fact-checkers urge collaboration, caution in using artificial intelligence tools. *Poynter*. https://www.poynter.org/ifcn/2024/how-fact-checkers-journalists-use-ai/

34. Johnson, C. K. (2024, January 28). Science sleuths are using technology to find fakery and plagiarism in published research. *AP News*. https://apnews.com/article/danafarber-cancer-scandal-harvard-sleuth-science-389dc2464f25bca736183607bc57415c

35. The PubPeer Online Journal Club. (2024). PubPeer—Search publications and join the conversation. *PubPeer*. https://pubpeer.com/static/about

36. Retraction Watch. Retrieved July 30, 2024, from https://retractionwatch.com/

37. Tugend, A. (2023, December 6). Experts on A.I. agree that it needs regulation. That's the easy part. *The New York Times*. https://www.nytimes.com/2023/12/06/business/dealbook/artificial-intelligence-regulation.html

38. Ruschemeier, H. (2023). AI as a challenge for legal regulation – the scope of application of the artificial intelligence act proposal. ERA Forum, 23(3), 361–376. https://doi.org/10.1007/s12027-022-00725-6

39. Bernoff, J. (2024, May 17). AI tools write with an "accent." Here's how to detect it. *Josh Bernoff.* https://bernoff.com/blog/ai-tools-write-with-an-accent-heres-how-to-detect-it

40. Gartner. (2024). Gartner Hype Cycle research methodology. *Gartner Insights.* https://www.gartner.com/en/research/methodologies/gartner-hype-cycle

41. (2024). Gartner hype cycle. In *Wikipedia.* https://en.wikipedia.org/w/index.php?title=Gartner_hype_cycle&oldid=1242563152

Chapter 11

1. I am grateful to members of NORC's executive committee and board of trustees who accepted my invitation to participate in an online video discussion in July 2024 of the possible directions for a data-savvy future. The participants included Katherine Baicker, Provost of the University of Chicago; Kerwin Charles, Dean of the Yale School of Management; Robert Gertner, Professor of Strategy and Finance at the University of Chicago Booth School of Business and Chairman of NORC's Board of Trustees; Raynard Kington, Head of School at Phillips Academy in Andover, Mass.; Raina Merchant, Vice President and Chief Transformation Officer for Penn Medicine; and Susan Paddock, Executive Vice President and Chief Scientist of NORC. While the participants suggested many fascinating ideas, I remain fully responsible for the content of this chapter.

2. Duke, A. (2018). *Thinking in bets: Making smarter decisions when you don't have all the facts.* Portfolio/Penguin.

3. There are several sources that report similar statistics on the number of US adults participating in fantasy sports. They are based on opt-in web surveys that are reweighted to reflect the US population, but still may not be fully representative of the US adult population. Accordingly, this statistic should be considered approximate.

4. See, for example, research about how people navigate the news ecosystem depending on the topic they need to research. See AP, NORC at the University of Chicago, & American Press Institute. (2014). *The Personal News Cycle* (The Media Insight Project, p. 34). AP NORC Center. https://apnorc.org/projects/the-personal-news-cycle/

5. People are more trusting of the sources they rely on for information, which tend to be more traditional news sources. See AP, NORC at the University of Chicago, & American Press Institute. (2017). "My" media versus "the" media: Trust in news depends on which news media you mean (The Media Insight Project, p. 18). AP NORC Center. https://apnorc.org/projects/my-media-versus-the-media-trust-in-news-depends-on-which-news-media-you-mean/

6. I posed this query to ChatGPT-4o on July 20, 2024: "A photo of the Las Vegas sphere appeared yesterday with the Windows 'Blue Screen of Death' on it, as a result of the CrowdStrike IT outage. Was the photo real or fake?" In the response, ChatGPT linked to two sites with these URLs: https://www.wusa9.com/article/news/verify/national-verify/las-vegas-sphere-blue-screen-of-death-image-is-fake/536-dd009fe6-8ac7-4044-9c3a-ec114107f6e3andhttps://checkyourfact.com/2023/07/13/fact-check-las-vegas-sphere-windows-error/

7. Vogels, E. A. (2021). Digital divide persists even as Americans with lower incomes make gains in tech adoption [Survey]. Pew Research Center. https://www.pewresearch.org/short-reads/2021/06/22/digital-divide-persists-even-as-americans-with-lower-incomes-make-gains-in-tech-adoption/

Acknowledgments

I AM DEEPLY grateful to my family and close friends who encouraged me to write *Fact Forward*. I would also like to express my deep appreciation of my colleagues at NORC, who practice, daily, the principles described in this book and whose work inspired me to start writing and speaking on the topics of data democratization, data literacy, and a data-savvy society. Zachary Schisgal, executive editor at Wiley, originally approached me with the idea of creating a book on these topics and his knowledge and support throughout were invaluable.

I would also like to acknowledge the talented and dedicated researchers, mentors, and colleagues with whom I have worked throughout my career and who have been instrumental in shaping my understanding of the value of reliable and trustworthy research and data. Two NORC colleagues deserve special mention: Greg Lanier, whose enthusiasm and strategic advice over the past decade have been fundamental in developing and refining the concepts discussed in this book, and Jenny Benz, whose keen intellect and insightful contributions throughout the manuscript were absolutely essential.

Additionally, thanks are due to the many experts who offered their knowledge and insights via interviews and correspondence, including NORC's Board of Trustees, who offered both expertise and support throughout the project. I would also like to gratefully acknowledge the direct contributions and support of many others who made this book a reality:

Core Editorial Team
Eric Young, Project Manager
Josh Bernoff
Alison Gross
Anna-Leigh Ong
Sarah Roti
Mark Sheehy

Design and Graphics
Mu-Hsien Lee, Creative Lead
TJ Fulfer

Research Support
Mike Dennis and the AmeriSpeak team
Karen Grigorian
Jordan Hinkle
Tom Hoffer
Carla Owens
Ashley Rayner
Steve Schacht

Reviewers and Advisors
Jeff Telgarsky, Lead Reviewer
Lisa Blumerman
Mike Davern
David Dutwin
Felicia LeClere
Susan Paddock
John Roman
Kirk Wolter

Steadfast Writing and Coffee Break Companions
Daisy the dog
Reuben the cat

About the Author

DAN GAYLIN IS a leading authority on how data affect all facets of our lives. He has more than three decades of experience as a senior researcher and business leader in organizations that provide data and analysis to government, the private sector, and the public. *Fact Forward: The Perils of Bad Information and the Promise of a Data-Savvy Society* is his first book.

Dan is president and CEO of NORC at the University of Chicago, a highly respected global research institute that uses data and analysis to study all aspects of the human experience. At NORC, Dan has guided multiple data innovations, including AmeriSpeak, a nationally representative data system of the American people that has set the standard for transparency and accuracy; the AP-NORC Center for Public Affairs Research, a survey journalism partnership with the Associated Press; and VizStudio, a data visualization solution that turns complex data into clear and compelling visual stories.

Dan is also an astute observer of how data are gathered, analyzed, and reported – sometimes sloppily or deceptively – and how those dynamics affect personal and organizational decision-making. As a frequent speaker both nationally and internationally, Dan addresses the democratization of data, data transparency, and data literacy.

261

He is a leading advocate for the idea that the United States and other nations must invest in a comprehensive public data infrastructure to create data-savvy citizens and a fact-forward society. His presentations and publications emphasize data quality, transparency, and accessibility, as well as ways to address the needs of people, communities, and civil society in data collection and analysis within the rapidly evolving digital landscape.

Dan's expertise is grounded in his extensive previous work as a healthcare researcher. He has led many long-term multimillion-dollar projects that integrate primary data collection, secondary data analysis, and qualitative research methods. Notably, he spearheaded the development of the congressionally mandated evaluation of the Children's Health Insurance Program (CHIP) and directed major patient care demonstration evaluations for the Centers for Medicare & Medicaid Services (CMS). Dan's work has been published in leading peer-reviewed journals, including the *New England Journal of Medicine*, *JAMA*, and *Health Affairs*, contributing valuable insights to the field of data science, access to healthcare, and quality of care.

Prior to NORC, Dan served as senior advisor at the US Department of Health and Human Services (HHS), where he was director of research and strategic planning for the Office of Health Policy. In this role, he managed a portfolio of cross-department research projects to inform high-level policy initiatives and chaired HHS-wide research workgroups reporting to the Secretary and the White House on critical topics such as data and research policy, prescription drug policy, and children's health insurance. He has also held senior positions at the Lewin Group, a private healthcare consultancy, and the Urban Institute, a public policy think tank.

Index